Expedition to Borneo

Expedition to Borneo

The search for Proboscis monkeys and other creatures

David Macdonald

Line drawings by Priscilla Barrett

J. M. Dent & Sons Ltd
London   Melbourne   Toronto

First published 1982
© 1982 David Macdonald

This book is set in 12 on 13pt Itek Times by
Keystroke Ltd, Godalming
Printed and made in Great Britain by
Richard Clay (The Chaucer Press) Ltd, Bungay

J. M. Dent & Sons Ltd
Aldine House   33 Welbeck Street   London W1M 8LX

British Library Cataloguing in Publication Data

Macdonald, David
    Expedition to Borneo.
    1.   Scientific expeditions—Borneo
    I.   Title
    915.98′3   Q115

    ISBN 0-460-04517-2

Contents

Colour photographs

by David Macdonald and Mark Collins

Between pp. 54-5

Our home at Kampong Menunggol
Female Proboscis monkey picking mangrove leaves
Flowering tree trunks: the phenomenon of 'cauliflory'
Fruit bats hanging in the shade of a banana leaf
A mangrove denuded of leaves stands above a carpet of Nipa palm fronds
A fragile fungus of the forest floor

Between pp. 118-9

The conspicuous warning coloration of a caterpillar of the moth *Thusea*
A lantern bug
A tarsier, photographed by R. Hanbury Tenison in Mulu
The Punan woman near Long Sukang
A view from within the caves at Niah
Flying frog with its parasol-like feet
The Malay civet radio-tagged at Mulu

He who binds to himself a joy
Doth the winged life destroy.
He who kisses the joy as it flies
Lives in eternity's sunrise.

Blake

Author's Foreword

In 1972 I travelled to Borneo for the first time, in the company of two friends, Mark Collins and Andrew Neighbour. We comprised an expedition approved by both the Royal Geographical Society and Oxford University, whence I had graduated a few weeks earlier. The expedition was financed by various sponsors, principally the Berbinder and Poulton Trusts, and by the fruits of my filming during the trip for the BBC's Natural History Unit; I am overwhelmingly grateful to these, and all the other people who helped us, both in Britain and in Borneo, particularly the Director and staff of the Brunei Museum and the Commanding Officer and other members of the Royal Brunei Malay Regiment.

I must warn the reader of what lies in store. This is not a book by an expert; it is not an authoritative treatise on Borneo or her peoples, nor a definitive account of the Proboscis monkey – the creature around which our activities revolved. Rather, this is the story of our exploration of many worlds, each of them as different from the other as from the ones we had left behind in Britain. It is the story of encounters with hospitable people, extraordinary animals and intransigent outboard motors, the story of our naïveté and our enchantment, our blisters and disappointments, and, above all, the story of a wonderful place whose charm I want in some small measure to pass on to the reader who has not shared my good fortune in being able to travel there. Travel has been my fondest teacher, and her tutelage has been kindly. 'The world is like a looking glass,' wrote Thackeray in *Vanity Fair*, 'smile at it, and it smiles back.' Borneo certainly smiled on us.

I am greatly in debt to those of my family and friends who have read and criticized this book, ferreting out inconsistencies and errors. In addition, among those who are truly expert in things South East Asian, the Earl of Cranbrook, Rodney Needham and Tim Whitmore have taken great pains to correct my blunders in their respective fields.

There is one final point. The tropical forests of the world, particularly of South East Asia, are dwindling fast and with them will go their faunas and, even faster, their peoples. I am mindful of the trees from other wild places to which I owe the paper on which this book is printed, and I hope that the story helps to convince the reader that such places, even though he may never visit them, are truly precious.

1

To Singapore, En Route

Through the bobbing mass of heads and milling bodies wafted a comforting smell of roasting peanuts, while in the glow shed by the peanut vendor's fire there danced faces, each assuming a momentary identity. Glimpsed expressions jostled back to the anonymity of the night. The bright colours of festival clothes rippled in and out of the light cast by a street lamp. Hundreds of tiny starlings roosting in a nearby tree disconsolately trilled their unrest, disturbed by the noise, smoke and light.

From the shadows a white-clad figure appeared. He moved stealthily, then froze in mid stride, shoulder drawn back, hand raised high. Threatening moments passed. A fiendish shriek – and his hand seared a path down through the air as his bare foot crashed to the boards below. Again he froze. The crowd was stilled; every eye turned to the platform on which he stood. Another white-garbed form appeared, stalking slowly from the darkness, poising in mid pace, only to stalk again, a measured step. The hand was raised, a shriek, a crash. Stalking, freezing, the combatants edged around each other. Their savage blows and thrusts passed within inches of the other's body. Their tortured shrieks became more maniacal, and the crashing of bare feet upon wooden boards fell into a synchrony with which the murmurings of the crowd were soon in tune.

The crescendo passed; the combatants edged apart and slipped from the platform into the darkness whence they had come. So ended the stylized karate dance performed on the central green of Brunei's capital city, Bandar Seri Begawan, in honour of the Sultan's twenty-sixth birthday.

Soon the white-clad figures were replaced on the rostrum by traditional Brunei singers. Elsewhere across the green other stands rose above the crowd – more karate dancers, groups of actors in national dress, and singers, each haloed by pools of light.

So, on this my first night in Brunei, I found myself among score upon score of people whose language I did not understand, whose facial expressions were alien to me and whose thoughts, as they realized that their immediate neighbour in the crowd was a stranger, I could only guess.

Shying from so much novelty my thoughts drifted back through the past couple of weeks, and the days that had brought me to Brunei. I had arrived via Singapore with two companions, Mark Collins and Andrew

Neighbour. Our main brief had been to complete our equipment and then to find the cheapest and quickest way of transporting it and ourselves from Singapore to the tiny Sultanate of Brunei, then a British protectorate, on the north-west coast of Borneo. From Brunei's capital we would start on the real purpose of our expedition – to observe some of the strange and exotic animals that inhabit Borneo and, especially, to search for the Proboscis monkey.

The excitement of arriving in a distant land is intense. Every unfamiliar detail takes on a vital significance. So it was for us when we emerged from a battery of customs, health and immigration checks, and ventured out of Singapore's International Airport. It was already the small hours of the morning as we set out, in a rather battered Morris Oxford, in search of a hotel. The driver fired questions at us about the purpose of our visit and stared inquiringly into the rear of the cab while zig-zagging skilfully across the traffic signals, apparently oblivious of red lights. We struck common ground when he learnt that his car was named after the town we hailed from. On discovering this affinity he promptly changed route to take us to a cheaper, and better, hotel.

The days that followed were largely a slog from one travel agent to the next, one shipping company to the next – visits which were, for the most part, fruitless. In the evenings we explored the city and started to discover just what an extraordinary mixture of ideas and customs are to be found on this island state.

Singapore was supposedly named by Sang Nilautama, a seafaring descendant of Alexander the Great, who was driven there by a storm. As he scrambled ashore he was greeted by an animal with a bright red body, white breast and black head. With doubtful zoological expertise he diagnosed this apparition as a lion and christened the spot on which it stood, Singapura – lion city. Centuries later Sir Stamford Raffles created the essence of modern Singapore when, in 1819, he came to an agreement with the East India Company which allowed it to build a trading post at the mouth of the Singapore river. Full sovereignty was conceded to the island in 1824.

Recently things have moved fast. On 16 September 1963 Singapore joined the Federation of Malaysia, along with Sarawak and Sabah. Two years later, on 9 August 1965, Singapore became independent of Malaysia as a sovereign republic. Now over two million people, of whom a staggering 60 per cent are under twenty-five years old, throng the island. Over three-quarters of them are Chinese, but the variety of other races crammed into this 584 square kilometre island produces a satisfactorily diverse atmosphere, not to mention making Singapore a successful centre of world trade. The hotch-potch of peoples – Malays, Chinese, Indians, against a background of British colonialism – that make up Singapore give the island a unique flavour, with at least a superficially happy marriage between the unlikely partners of intensive capitalism and Eastern ideologies. One of the first things to catch our attention were the posters instructing shopkeepers and bus conductors to serve men with long hair last whenever queues built up. Lest there be any confusion as to what constituted long hair, billboards were on display showing rear views of long and normal (verging on crew-cut) hair styles. The island's constitution opens with a denunciation of any form of discrimination.

Our nightly wanderings took us either up Mount Faber, from whence the panorama of Singapore's lights could be seen shimmering below, or deeper and deeper into the old part of the city, through Chinatown towards the complex lanes that inexorably led to the one dramatically and sinisterly named Death Street. Within earshot of modern three-lane roads with their continual hum of traffic we found a network of tiny alleyways, lined on either side by three- or four-storey houses. Each window had its own verandah draped with Chinese garments – billowing trousers and coolee hats. Inscrutable old ladies perched on the verandahs like dilapidated hawks, heads cocked as they scanned the struggling crowd below.

These narrow streets were crammed with tightly packed stalls, thronged by colourfully clad Chinese and Malays in a cacophony of barter. The mountains of fresh food seemed to us to be exotic, sometimes barbarous – metre-long Monitor lizards, some mercifully dead, others occasionally doused in water to sustain them as they lay strapped on long poles at the edge of a butcher's stall, and trays full of turtles, some a species with shells so soft that they were pliable to the touch. These were animals which we were later to meet in more fitting surroundings. From slatted wooden cages beneath the stalls civets peered out mournfully at prospective owners – small ones for a child's pet, larger ones for the cooking pot. These cat-like animals have a particularly unnerving rear end in that the males appear at first sight to have four prominent testes; actually the second pair constitutes an enormous scent gland. For centuries this gland has attracted the attention of perfumiers who scraped the inner cavities of the civet's nether region for a gooey material with which, when suitably concocted into expensive perfume, ladies anoint themselves. In *As You Like It* Shakespeare mused that 'Civet is of a baser birth than tar, the very uncleanly flux of a cat'; but these urine-drenched specimens staring glumly back at me as I peered into their dingy prisons were unmoved by their literary notoriety or by the fact that the key component of their secretion, Civetone, made chemical history in 1926 when it was found to be made of molecular rings containing more carbon atoms linked in each

ring than previously thought possible for any compound.

On down the street, past fruit shops stacked with the exotic fruits of the Malay Peninsula – sweet rambutans and evil-smelling durians, fruits that were to become part of our staple diet over the ensuing months – but for now we were swept along in a torrent of novelty from which only fleeting details were snatched. The kaleidoscope of colour around us jarred to a halt in front of dingy pet stalls. They were prolific and heart rending. Wicker cages were crammed full of finches, some of them badly mutilated after being caught in nets and roughly removed, others with sticky traces of lime matting their feathers, captured when they landed on sticks daubed with the treacherous glue from which they had been unable to escape.

We paused for a drink at a stall with several buckets of different coloured juices, some lime flavour, some coconut, and each dispensed in dented metal mugs. The vendor dipped his ladle into one bucket and handed us our portions; the tastes were new. As we drank we watched a nearby stallholder cutting off fish heads. He placed the knife over the fish and then struck the back of the blade with a cow's horn held in his other hand. We moved on. The stalls became more widely spaced; the burble of Chinese music and shouting voices quietened and the caterwauling children disappeared: we were in Death Street. . . . Outside the tall houses were low benches and tables. Stretched out on the benches or sitting in little groups were old, old Chinese people – ancient impressions of men and women, indistinguishable from each other in their sexless oriental suits, they were grey and bald with features traced on taut skin. Some sent by their families, others with no family to send them, they accumulated in Death Street to reflect on their lives, to think and to die.

We had first heard of Death Street, together with so many of the other things we saw in Singapore, from the Elliotts. Tom Elliott, a professor of pharmacology and a long-standing expatriate with whom Andrew had some tenuous contact, had more or less adopted us the morning after our arrival in Singapore. We had appeared, unannounced, at his spacious home at the summit of one of the hills near the coast, and sombrely watched as our luggage spewed forth from the waiting taxi to form an intimidating pile outside the Elliotts' residence. As the taxi vanished down the drive a slight man appeared at the edge of the verandah, squinting at us. We inquired whether Professor Elliott was at home. The man hedged around the issue of his own identity, obviously sensing the folly of committing himself. Moments of mumbled conversation about the pleasant view and reasonable weather had stammered past before this sardonic character admitted that he was Tom Elliott. We launched into an account of how we were an Oxford University expedition, en route to Borneo, and how a friend's friend had advised us to contact him. Tom's home had been an expatriate's staging post for long enough for him to have heard it all before. He cut short our explanation, pointed critically towards our luggage and murmured, 'Well, you'd better bring that in too if you are staying, I suppose'. We lived with the Elliotts for the next two weeks.

That first afternoon at Tom's was spent over Tiger Beer, discussing Singapore's history, in which, as a friend of Chao En-lai, he had played an active role. Mark and I tried to adjudicate while Andrew and Tom expressed strong and opposite views on trades unions. In the early afternoon we were joined by a huge man, twice Tom's size in every dimension. Clothed only in a towel, he flopped extravagantly into a chair as we were introduced, and promptly fell asleep. This was Tom's son, Alan. Next to arrive was Tom's wife Annie, a lilting Hamilton accent betraying her Scottish background. She was closely followed by Carol, their daughter, but Chinese. Before the evening was out two more daughters had arrived, one Malay and one Indian. We were rapidly coming to the conclusion that a combination of Tom's winking eyes and his multi-coloured family added up to a very tolerant wife and a delightfully dissipated youth; in fact the Elliots had adopted their own Commonwealth.

Mrs Hong, one of Tom's innumerable contacts, helped us to book the cheapest fare on the cheapest boat leaving Singapore for Brunei. Since the boat was not due to sail for several days, we had plenty of time to explore.

One morning we set out by taxi from the Elliotts' home, directing the cabby to the British Army base at Nee Soon with the idea of gleaning some advice on jungle crafts. The driver's only redeeming feature was a talent for juggling the top set of his false teeth on the tip of his tongue; intermittently he would throw his head back, the teeth plopping elegantly into position. This trick required him to lay his head flat on the back of his seat. We rudely tried to draw his attention to the road, but soon abandoned this back-seat driving as our comments were apparently misinterpreted when the driver handed us his teeth for inspection!

At the army camp, then occupied by the Royal Highland Fusiliers, we were put in the care of a young lieutenant who advised us to visit Arab Street, a complete street of stalls overlooking a fetid river and given over to the sale of 'surplus' British Army goods. A private was summoned to drive us into town and to guide us to the best stalls, making sure that we were not cheated. The soldier hailed from Edinburgh. As we walked from stall to stall up this crowded, rather dirty procession of canvas shops fingering shirts, feeling blades on the edge of jungle knives called goloks and trying on different sized uniforms, this private conversed with the various stallholders in a fluent Scottish brogue. It was a novel experience to be offered a 'wee hoochie cover', or alternatively a 'gae guid mossie net' by an Indian stallholder. But we managed to buy three complete sets of jungle gear at a ridiculously cheap price.

Singapore is a jungle of notorious streets: Arab Street, Death Street, Bugis Street. Bugis Street is a haunt of the night people, who move amid the tantalizing shadows where one suspects everything and knows nothing. We arrived quite early on a balmy night. The street was lined with cafés and bars. Tables were scattered here and there. We sat at a light blue, circular table and a surprisingly white-coated waiter plied us with fresh lime soda. A quarter of an hour or so passed before a woman wearing a sequinned silver cocktail dress sauntered past our table, jarringly conspicuous in the crowd of tattered shorts and coolee hats. A blonde approximation to Venus strolled by in hotpants, paused to chat, then cruised languorously on. Within an hour the street was vibrating with sultry voices and stiletto heels – women of every colour, but mostly one creed. But were they women? Bugis Street is the centre for people wanting the 'operation'. I had been warned that we might have trouble telling the genuine from the ersatz. True, there was an occasional Adam's apple to be seen, or a less than swinging hip. A lovely girl in an elegant evening dress sat down at our table. As she sat down her dress fell open, across unquestionably female thighs; she leant forward asking if we'd like to see a photograph of her when she was younger. The picture showed a young private in soldier's uniform. I went home mightily confused.

By day we visited the University grounds which were pleasingly spacious. A vivid bird bigger than a blackbird hopped on the branches nearby; the yellow of its body was offset by black wings and tail, and a jet black band encircled the nape of its head. Speedy recourse to our 'bird book' diagnosed this flashy character as a Black-naped Oriole. At the University we sought advice from the local zoologists on various animals we hoped to find in Brunei. Hearing that our first destination in search of Proboscis monkeys would be a coastal swamp the staff cautioned us on the danger of unwarily standing on cone shells. From their dramatic account there seemed to be good reason for caution. Cone shells are molluscs, housed in beautiful cone-shaped shells (a specimen of one species, the Glory of the Sea, was auctioned for £1000 in 1964). But they are carnivorous, poisoning their prey. The scraping tongue, or radula, which garden snails use to rasp up their vegetable food, is modified into a harpoon and connected to a long thin secretory tube with a muscular pumping apparatus at its base, wherein lies a poison gland. Hence these curious snails are called by a generic name admirably suited to a village gossip – Toxiglossidae – poisoned tongues. Passing fish are actually harpooned by these poison-bearing projectiles. The poison affects the fish's nerves and acts with equal facility on human nerves too, sometimes with fatal consequences.

The eventual departure of our boat for Brunei was delayed twice as a result of a surfeit of alcohol among the crew members. At last the daily phone call to the dockyard brought a positive reply: we were to embark that afternoon. The sight of our derelict 'ship' inspired from Alan Elliott the sort of heartfelt grunt expected from a horse with colic. Our 'cabin', being the cheapest, was a cubicle lying immediately adjacent to and opening into the engine room. A few minutes of exploration revealed that the porthole was completely detachable from its socket and that the bolt connecting the bunks to the wall had perished, permitting them to rock restfully with the action of the waves. With more courage than conviction we made our way to the deck to wave farewell to Alan, who was practising his hobby – karate, smashing bricks on the quayside – our last sight of Singapore. As the engine revved and the ship slowly edged out of the harbour our cabin began to fill with an oily vapour emanating from the engines. Soon forced to evacuate it, we explored the deck amidst cans of cat food, Land Rovers and a hotch-potch of other passengers.

That four-day boat trip to Brunei was a miserable joy. It was unquestionably miserable: no more stalwart euphemism could fairly describe the foul and scorching cabin. The only other European aboard, a Yorkshireman, was Captain of the craft and he suffered a mania that necessitated him taking every opportunity to scream abuse at us through the loud hailer from the bridge. Otherwise he refused to talk to us at all, even when we knocked on the door of his cabin: he promptly locked it.

On the evening of the first day we were confronted with the deceptively encouraging choice of whether we wanted Chinese or Malay food; heartened, even in the absence of criteria on which to make our decision, we selected Chinese while the people next to us opted for Malay cuisine. An identical bowl of tepid water in which floated a boiled cabbage leaf was served to both parties and it was on this, together with cold stale rice, that we lived for the next four days. And yet, in spite of this diesel-drenched discomfort we were filled with excitement and expectation. The four-day voyage passed contentedly: the wind was cooler, the frigate birds more beautiful, the flying fish more fascinating than we could ever have hoped.

The first day out of harbour I was staring vacantly out to sea when my attention was caught by slivers of light which seemed to run alongside us. At first I thought they were reflections – light, air and water interwoven by the thrashing propellers – but it seemed that some of these silvery shafts actually broke the surface. Suddenly it dawned on me that they were flying fish. Like silver bullets they sped alongside in small shoals, their bodies cutting through the water as they taxied over the surface beating the waves with their tails. The large pectoral fins of these fish can be spread like wings, carrying their owners along, looking rather vertigo-stricken, at over fifty kilometres per hour. Some flights last well over ten seconds.

Very probably this flying behaviour is a way of escaping from underwater predators, but as we saw these fish time and time again one might soon come to believe that they were being perpetually pursued. Perhaps the boat was alarming them, triggering the anti-predator escape response which can, on occasion, carry them nine metres into the air. These fish are

really more gliders than flyers, although in South America there is a freshwater fish *(Gasteropelecidae)* which makes true flapping movements with its 'wings' and has correspondingly enormous 'shoulder' muscles to do this.

The aerial exploits of fish slipped into a more humble perspective as we revelled in the mechanical precision of Brown Boobies (a relative of European gannets), plunging headlong to spear fish. These birds hunt in flocks, hovering and swooping at tremendous speeds to hit the waves with a shuddering thwack. The wonder of flight is the hallmark of South East Asian animals and in particular of the island of Borneo to which we were heading. Not only do birds and fish fly in Borneo, but so do snakes, lizards, frogs and a so-called flying lemur (which is not a lemur at all). The flying frog is amazing – it drops from the branches of trees, spreads its toes to reveal enlarged webs and floats on air. This striking amphibian was 'discovered' by the nineteenth-century naturalist, Alfred Russel Wallace, when a Chinese workman presented him with a specimen. Wallace thought it 'a most curious and interesting reptile' but was unfairly sceptical of the workman who claimed to have seen the frog float down from the trees in a gentle glide. The toes of the flying frog are very long and

each one is fully webbed to make a miniature parasol when extended.
These frogs are about ten centimetres long with the back and limbs a deep
green and their spectacular webs are black rayed with yellow. Wallace
discussed the importance of this remarkable beast to evolutionary theory,
at a time when Darwin's ideas were very new. He speculated that the frog
had been preadapted for its aerobatics by the webbed toes and suckered
feet which had originally been fashioned for swimming. In fact,
throughout his book, *Malay Archipelago,* Wallace refers again and again
to Darwin's ideas, although many historians believe they were almost as
much Wallace's own. Wallace even dedicated his book 'To Charles
Darwin, author of the *Origin of Species*, ... not only as a token of
personal esteem and friendship but also to express my deep admiration
for his genius and his works.'

Behind these generous words lie the roots of a story which gave rise to
what may be the most important idea any Western thinker has ever
produced – the theory of natural selection – important because it has
forced an entire civilization to rethink its place in the natural world. The
same interest in natural selection lay behind our own expedition, since we
were ultimately interested in the evolution of Proboscis monkey societies.
Evolution is a familiar idea today; 'survival of the fittest' is a catch-phrase
and it is widely accepted that our own ancestors shared common roots
with other present-day apes (and if one goes back through enough millennia, the common roots of all the other animals too). It is easy to forget
how recently these ideas gained credence through the mammoth works of
men like Darwin and Wallace. Previous ideas had been very different. In
the seventeenth century a Cambridge don, John Lightfoot, was seriously
engaged in calculating the date of the creation as 23 October 4004 BC; in
1830 Baron Georges Cuvier published his catastrophe theory, which
suggested a succession of catastrophes after each of which God restocked
the earth with more up-to-date creatures. Debate raged thereafter over
how many catastrophes there had been (most people seemed to go for two
or three dozen, with Noah's flood being the most recent). Carl von Linné,
the famous eighteenth-century biologist whose system of classification of
the animal kingdom is still largely followed today, was the first person to
place man 'officially' among the primates, and yet during the same period
he had seriously to review all the evidence which maintained that certain
plants fruited as lambs in order to refute the idea. For that matter, it is not
so long ago that Pliny argued that insects were engendered by dust and
filth transformed by the rays of the sun.

Alfred Russel Wallace spent eight years in the Malay archipelago,
where he collected 125,000 specimens, and it was while sailing 14,000
miles among the very islands to which we were heading that he had the

idea which was to lay to rest all these earlier beliefs. The problem was that Darwin was simultaneously thinking along the same lines. Almost every idea has its origins in somebody else's thoughts, and in this case it happens that both Darwin and Wallace had read Malthus' work on population. Malthus argued that populations should increase geometrically, that is to say, if a pair of animals have four offspring, and each of these mate and have four offspring in turn, and so on, the population will increase from generation to generation from two to four to eight to sixteen, and so forth. But such rapid increases were not seen, so Malthus concluded that the excess production must be dying off. What Darwin and Wallace both realized was that there was thus a potential for selective death; if circumstances changed in a way that favoured some individuals of a species more than others, then these individuals would prosper. They would leave more surviving offspring than others who were less well adapted to their circumstances, and so their features would spread and the species would evolve. Darwin probably had the idea first, but he was slow to publish it until, in 1858, Wallace wrote to him explaining his own, identical, theory. This dilemma over the paternity of the idea was resolved by the two of them reading a joint paper to the Linnean Society in London!

So, as Wallace had watched the animals we were watching now, he had formulated ideas that heralded an ideological revolution – he had realized that the ancestors of flying fish had been fish with conventional fins. Some of their progeny had slightly enlarged pectoral fins, and perhaps they had the curious habit of breaking the surface when pursued. These individuals had survived to breed where their brothers had perished and so, generation by generation, the feature had spread and become elaborated. Similarly, the webbed feet that had served the flying frog's ancestors so well for swimming preadapted it for transmutation into an ar-boreal parachutist. As our boat bumped its way across the South China Sea, we were heading towards an island whose fauna was not only exotic, but had also helped to stimulate the very dearest ideas on which biology is built.

After one night inhaling the production of the engine room, we slept out on the deck – and yet as I lay half awake on the hard, wet, wooden boards of our rolling ship and gazed at an ever more tropical sky, I realized that I was there not because I had been forced out by the fumes but because I was in love with every particle of my new surroundings, sur-roundings which were the fruits of a year of copious plans and a gauntlet of fund raising.

The days were split between azure skies and turquoise seas. In July the South China Sea is gentle and hot – calm between the tumult of raging monsoons. The monsoon (from the Arabic word for seasons – *mausim*) shuttles back and forth to the equator as land and sea warm and cool with the seasons. Where the land warms up, hot air rises (eventually to circle to the poles) and creates low pressure areas. More air is sucked into these vacuums and its passage is felt as wind. In the northern summer the air above the scorched lands of Asia rises and pulls winds northwards, across the ocean and loaded with rain. But in autumn the main heat of the sun travels south, and with it the low pressure system which drags the monsoon winds in a southerly direction. The rains are heralded by a type of cuckoo, the Koel, known by Malay people as the harbinger of storms, which travels south from the Asian continent to the Malay archipelago just as the winds switch from south-west to north-east.

At the end of the second day, having waded through my bowl of cabbage leaf soup, I staggered to the top deck in the wake of an ever rougher sea to find Mark deep in conversation with a gnomish figure who was introduced as Ang. Ang was one of the ship's officers and, because he spoke some English, he appointed himself as our adviser, to prepare us for what he clearly saw as the ordeal ahead in Brunei. As I joined the conversation Ang was expounding his views on Vietnam, where he had been the previous year. At that time Vietnam was still torn by the American war effort. 'Bloody good. Bloody place, man,' asserted Ang as I arrived. I inquired 'Where?', to which he answered 'Bloody Vietnam, man' to our surprise. Ang claimed in his broken American that he wanted to get back to Vietnam at the earliest opportunity. The lure of this strife-torn land turned out to be 'Bloody shipload bloody woman, man', a theme which Ang developed on subsequent nights as he took enormous delight in warning us of the hazards that lay in store for young European males venturing into the Malay countryside. He recounted elaborate examples of foresters, traders and the like who had been ensnared by the charms of aged Malay women in the course of travelling in Borneo. He described, with an enchanting sense of the indelicate, how these crones mix irresistible juices with rice before feeding it to their unsuspecting victims who, having eaten, had no more will than a rabbit fixed by the gaze of a weasel. The evidence was irrefutable said Ang, clasping his flask of whisky to his chest, and he was soon tearfully beseeching us to return to 'Bloody Vietnam' with him instead.

As our friendship with Ang flourished he introduced Ming, the radio operator, and soon the two of them were furtively trundling off down the deck to raid slices of bread from the Captain's kitchen to supplement our meagre diet.

We woke as dawn broke on the fourth day of our voyage. Mist hung in tangled filaments along the glowing horizon, to drift away as the sun rose.

New colours appeared: gone was the endless opalescent blue which had travelled with us for these long days, now a green ribbon threaded through the thinning mist. As the steamer slowly chugged up the estuary leading to Brunei's harbour, we stretched over the deck rail, binoculars pressed to our eyes, straining for glimpses of the gateway to a land whose name had symbolized adventure during the past year of planning.

Even the bureaucratic paraphernalia of the immigration officials could not dampen our enthusiasm. The final stage of entry, the health examination, was conducted in Ming's cabin where we found Ming and the doctor hunched over not so hard-boiled eggs. Shifting his concentration between us and his egg, and making it clear which he found more attractive, the doctor inquired if we felt well and waved us through. So, freed into Brunei, we set forth.

Thus it was, one day later, that we found ourselves among the hoards of people massing for the dusk celebrations of the Sultan's birthday. My attention was drawn back to the present as a further instalment of the karate dance stalked dramatically onto the rostrum. This over, we slowly pushed our way through the crowd towards another of the stadia; although I did not know the jostling people, or understand their languages, I began to feel more at home with every passing minute and to sense the first stirrings of a glowing happiness, symptomatic of an addiction for Borneo and her people which has stayed with me ever since.

As a traveller one passes through various stages. The first is utter uncertainty – the fleeting and unpleasant state of being a complete stranger as you launch forth into a place and a people whose daily life is completely alien. Almost at once this passes as you come to recognize street names, or trees – things to serve as coat hangers from which to drape a sense of familiarity. Although you still understand very little of your surroundings you come to expect the unexpected, to be familiar with your own uncertainty and to revel in them both. As dusk drew in around the Sultan's birthday celebrations we were filled with the sense of excitement to come. In the trees above us thousands of starlings flew in to roost, while below them people roasted peanuts over scorching wood until the air felt warm and red.

2

Of Mangroves, Monkeys and Mud

When we came to Borneo our goal was to find and to observe two primates, each unusual in very different ways. These were the Proboscis monkey and the tarsier. As the first part of our journey, and of this book, will be concerned with our adventures in search of Proboscis monkeys, I shall explain first why this strange beast fascinated us so much.

Monkeys fall into two major groups – those from the Old and those from the New World. These two categories are distinguished from each other on the basis of differences in the structure of the nose and skull, and other features, such as prehensile tails – an additional 'limb' with which only monkeys in the New World are equipped. Our quest was among Old World monkeys, which include baboons, macaques, langurs and Colobus monkeys. These monkeys also fall into two major categories, distinguished by their food and, consequently, the anatomy of their intestines and their lifestyles. The first category contains the 'generalists', the omnivorous baboons and macaques, whereas the second comprises herbivorous leaf-eating monkeys, such as the Colobus monkeys of Africa and the langurs of Asia. These vegetarian monkeys have a complex forestomach for processing their leafy diet, a task which the trees, understandably, make as difficult as possible. The Proboscis monkey, which is confined to Borneo, is one of these herbivorous monkeys. It is known to be unusual in very many ways, not least because of its remarkable appearance, of which more later, and is fascinating in spite of, and perhaps partly because of, being almost unknown to science.

For many years now biologists have been accustomed to looking at the shapes and forms of animals in an effort to understand why they have evolved in the way they have. An apparently small difference in the shape and structure of a bird's bill, for instance, can make it easier for that species to crack a particular sort of grain. Similarly, animal colouration can be adapted to the habitat in which a species is found. Think, for instance, of camouflage among the birds, such as the Bittern and the Treecreeper, that blend perfectly with their surroundings. Animals and their structures are adapted to function in a given habitat under given circumstances. Their bodies are fashioned for the jobs they perform; they are precisely adapted. Biology is about adaptation. Well established though this notion is, it is only in more recent decades that similar ideas have begun to be focused on animal societies. Just as a bird may have a beak especially adapted to allow the best use of certain food and colours that help it escape detection, it will also have behaviour which enables it to thrive in its habitat. Furthermore, where there is no structure, a behaviour may solve a problem: vultures drop large rocks on eggs which are too robust to be opened by their beaks alone, while a mongoose tackles the same dilemma by grasping the egg in its front paws and propelling it rapidly between its back legs to smash against a boulder. Similarly, a tiny finch on the Galapagos Islands and chimpanzees in East Africa have both solved the problem of extracting grubs from nooks and crannies by using a probe made of thorn.

If an animal's behaviour towards food is adapted to its surroundings, then so too may be its entire lifestyle, its family ties and society. If species are compared, even those which are similar in appearance and closely related, they show marked differences in social organization. Some primates, for instance, live in huge troops with many males, females and offspring, moving as a group through their range. Other species are more solitary and perhaps live in pairs, while still others form groups where there is only one or just a few males together with many females and juveniles. In some species the wanderings of neighbouring troops will overlap. In others the social units may partition the land into strictly defined territories whose boundaries are maintained by squabbles between neighbours.

Such differences in the features of social organization are not unique to the monkeys, but rather reflect an underlying principle, stamped on the whole animal kingdom as a hallmark of the laws of evolution. Think how viciously a robin chases intruders from his range, but how gregarious the rook is. Viewing just this sort of difference in social organization between species of many different sorts of animals, ranging from apes to insects, zoologists have noted a correspondence between the nature of societies (e.g. group living or solitary) and the lifestyle and habitat of the species (e.g. fruit eaters have different societies from their carnivorous cousins, and life on the open plains poses different problems for family life than does a treetop dwelling). A pioneer study which empasized how societies are adapted to circumstances was made by John Cook who investigated the lifestyle of African weaver birds, of which there are some eighty species. He found that different species from the same habitat often had similar societies; insect-eating forest-dwelling species, for instance, were rather solitary, whereas grain eaters of the open country foraged in flocks. Other differences were tuned to the fine structure of each habitat: grain-eating species of weaver birds inhabiting savannas were colonial, nesting under one roof in communal nests built among the branches of isolated thorn trees. Other seed eaters nesting in tall grasses also lived in flocks, but each male defended a breeding territory within which the separate nests of his individual mates were scattered. So, among weaver birds, species which eat grain seem to prosper by living in flocks, while their insect-eating relatives live solitary lives. On a finer scale differences in nesting behaviour among the grain eaters may depend on whether their nest sites are susceptible to predation in the open grassland or are protected by the welcoming thorn of an acacia tree. Scattering the nests may be advantageous for grass dwellers relying on inconspicuousness, on the principle of not putting all the eggs in one basket. This broad association between habitat type and social organization shows how societies are adapted to their ecological circumstances.

Observations of this type have given rise to the belief that social behaviours are adapted in subtle and diverse ways to the species' ecology, in exactly the same way as we are accustomed to think of anatomy. As more studies are completed, the social lives of many animals are seen to be staggeringly complex, and the challenge is to find why each society has its particular features, and what is their adaptive significance. The more successful an adaptation, the more offspring the animal exhibiting it will contribute to the next generation, and hence the greater the proportion of individuals with that trait there will be. The 'survival of the fittest' in Darwin's terms means the survival of those best adapted to their environment.

It was this sort of interest in social behaviour that had brought us to Borneo. The particular allure of the Proboscis monkey was that it lived in a strange and extreme habitat, the mangrove swamp of the Bornean coast. How, we wondered, would its social behaviour and lifestyle fit into the general mosaic of what was already being discovered about monkey society?

Obviously societies of monkeys differed in broad terms from one species to another: baboons may live in herds of more than a hundred animals, omnivorously gleaning the African savannas, while only a handful of Howler monkeys form a social group, subsisting on leaves in the tropical forests of America. Differences in societies can be seen at a much more subtle level too. Take, for instance, the two related species of leaf-eating monkey, the Black and White Colobus and the Red Colobus, both of which inhabit the forests of East Africa. Tim Clutton-Brock had studied the biology of both these species in the same forest: they live in the same areas and are both vegetarians, yet Clutton-Brock had found very marked differences in their social organization and behaviour. The Red Colobus lives in groups of up to forty individuals, which include several adult males. In contrast the Black and White Colobus lives in groups of only five to ten animals, normally with only one mature male. Both species

follow different patterns in their ranging behaviour: the Red Colobus has
an extensive range, perhaps one square kilometre in size, while the troops
of Black and White Colobus defend territories sometimes under a fifth of a
square kilometre. After two years of study these contrasts could be understood in the light of the different feeding behaviour of the two species.
The Black and White Colobus gets nearly all its food as mature leaves
from only two different species of tree. In contrast, the Red Colobus rarely
eats mature leaves, preferring fruits, buds and flowers of a large variety of
different tree species. To find sufficient of these delicacies, the Red
Colobus has to forage over an enormous range to ensure that somewhere
within it there are always enough trees coming into flower or fruit, but
once such a tree is found there is plenty of food to go round. Because of the
way fruiting trees are dotted about the forest, the smallest range which will
support a single Red Colobus can equally well support a large troop. Of
course, if their food supply permits the formation of big troops, the
monkeys can capitalize on other benefits such as an increase in corporate
alertness to danger, resulting from more pairs of wary eyes on the lookout.
The question was, where did Proboscis monkey societies fit into this way
of thinking?

Much of the coast of Brunei is surrounded by a band of mangrove
swamp, and it was there that our search for Proboscis monkeys began.
Through the Museum at Bandar Seri Begawan we had made arrange-
ments to pick up a boat at 7 am; we set out immediately with a guide to
search for a study area and base for the duration of our stay. Our guide,
Rahim, the staff zoologist from the Brunei Museum, was a quiet kindly
man, whose command of English was sufficient to answer most of our
questions. We were filled with high hopes for the day's success in finding
Proboscis monkeys. This racing start to our quest was possible only
through the aid of Pengiran Shariffuddin, the Director of the Museum. He
had greeted us by saying 'I like to make people happy', and proceeded to
do everything in his power to do just that for us. He had arranged for us to
borrow the boat, to be guided by Rahim, and had steered us through the
maze of official documents, permits and cholera checks that followed in
our wake. As we navigated the corridors of officialdom in search of an
opening to the swamps we were painfully aware that there were many
more roads to failure than to success for our expedition; we could hardly
forget the chilling, and probably unfair, sentiments echoed in the official
report of E. Banks, then Curator of the Sarawak Museum, following the
1932 Oxford Expedition to Borneo: 'Every bit as important as selecting
technical ability is the rejecting of men lacking normal manners, uncouth
in appearance, or unpleasant in personality . . . doing much to antagonize
both European and native against the expedition's better interest.' We

wished no such epitaph to follow us through the swamps. When Rahim loaded us and a boatman into the Museum's boat it seemed that at least we had made it to the starting point.

As we chugged slowly through the estuarine forests, scanning the surrounding trees through binoculars, we pressed Rahim for answers to impossible questions begat by our excessive enthusiasm. How likely was it that we would find monkeys? Rahim smiled, shaking his head in the way that only those from the East can shake their heads: a sort of gyroscopic waggle about a point on the centre of the skull. Perhaps this shake meant 'no'. 'You do not think we will find any monkeys today?' I persisted. Rahim's head began another orbit. 'Oh, you do think that we will find monkeys today?' Our guide's head shook, or did it nod? We would have to wait to see the monkeys for ourselves.

These coastal swamps are tidal and we had set out at high tide. As the day drew on without a sight of a monkey, the tide began to fall, exposing the roots of the mangrove trees sunk into the thick grey mud of the swamp and now, as we navigated small channels between swamp islets in the estuary of Sungai (River) Brunei, it became a substantial problem to prevent the boat from grounding in ever more shallow water. In these little rivulets I really felt that I had arrived in a new and strange world. The tall canopy of mangrove leaves cut out all but a piebald dappling of light from the scorching sun overhead. Trees rose from huge buttress root systems. A twisting mesh of root and limb spread out from the trunks of the mangrove trees. Some fell in cascades, like fountains mysteriously solidified in mid air, others, like turned metal with intricate patterns drawn on their surface, draped in convoluted loops from high above the water's surface down into the mud. Between the mangroves grew a thick matrix of a palm known as Nipa palm, *Nipa fruticans*, from which hung long razor-sharp fronds whose incessant rustling seems to be the very breath of the swamp.

We passed from shadow into glaring shafts of sunlight and back to dappled shadow; as the boat drifted on, water and mud merged alike in pastel brown beneath this patchwork archway. I squinted to see first in the darkness and then in the agonizing brightness. The novelty was overwhelming; I could see only a fraction of that which I looked at, my eyes frustratingly inept in this new world. Rahim pointed. 'There!' We heard a loud plop but nothing remained save a growing circle on the disturbed water where some beast had disappeared before I could even glimpse it. 'Monitor,' Rahim said: a Monitor lizard, a large carnivorous semi-aquatic lizard looking not unlike a baby crocodile. How frustrating it was again and again to hear those plops and how we squinted between dark and bright, determined to spot the next one before it dived into the water.

In places we had to get out of the boat in order to cross a particularly shallow area, and on one such jaunt I became acquainted with the maiming qualities of the Nipa palm. Reaching out for a handhold while we waded forwards in the water, I instinctively grabbed hold of the palm frond for balance, only to find a large cut straddling my hand. Rahim looked away; I felt embarrassed at my ignorance and perhaps he did too. There was indeed a lot to learn, and I took solace in a remark made by the late Tom Harrisson (subsequently to be the Curator of the Sarawak Museum and most famous of Borneo's admirers) who, having been parachuted into Borneo in 1945 to lead the Kelabit Highlanders into war against the Japanese, remarked all too literally that he landed in Borneo 'on the bones of my arse and knowing nil'.

We drifted around a bend and the boatman, Abdullah, tapped me on the shoulder and pointed with his gaze. All I could see on the bank was a maze of roots and stumps, draped in the muddy skeletons of Nipa fronds. But there, on a vaulted mangrove root, lay a miniature dragon – a Monitor lizard. In the dim light it seemed, like everything else, to be coloured in shades of mud. The Monitor was long and slender, over a metre from head to tail. Its skin was wrinkled and ill-fitting, but taut over its flat bony head. We drifted closer with the gentle current. Its forked tongue whipped in and out of the remarkably snake-like head. People once believed that Monitor lizards were ancestors of snakes (in North Africa the Desert Monitor is still called the King of Snakes), and the Earless Monitor of Borneo may be related closely to snakes. The Monitor turned its head to look at us, its tongue slipping in and out more frequently – reaching like a hand to grasp particles of our scent, molecules of odour ensnared on the mucus of the forked tongue and swept back to be sensed in the smelling organ at the back of the throat. Suddenly, with head up and scrabbling claws, the lizard dropped to the mud below and was gone.

We paddled to the spot where the lizard had disappeared. Huge gashes sliced the smooth surface of the mud where it had been rent by five long talons at each stroke. Monitors are predacious, swallowing prey whole, or tearing off large chunks of flesh. They are also carrion eaters. Indeed, their brains are especially boxed within a reinforced bony sheath to protect them from the passage of large lumps of food which can be squeezed into the cavernous jaws whose gape is all the more spacious as their bones are movable. There are some twenty-five species of Monitor (or Varanid) lizard, of which the most famous is the Komodo Dragon, which can reach three metres in length and weigh seventy-five kilos (about the same as a large sheep).

As we pushed under a particularly low hanging palm frond and slipped from the narrow tributary out, once again, into one of the larger rivers, there was a loud squawk to my left and a beating of wings. Out across the water's surface, casting irritable looks behind it, went one of the most curious birds I have ever seen. One might believe that the committee which built this so-called snake bird, or darter, came up with the design after a trip to a rather fanciful Disney cartoon. As it sped away from us the snake bird's heavy duck-sized body was propelled by maniacal flappings of short stumpy wings, while its head made a reconnaissance of the air far in advance and at the end of a ludicrously long and spindly neck. This fish-eating bird is unusual because of its method of catching its prey by spearing them with the beak, ending up with an arrangement like a kebab.

It was well after midday and we had still seen no signs of Proboscis monkeys. Sensing our faltering spirits, Rahim suggested we try a different location – an uninhabited island called Pulau Chermin. He told us that a small population of Proboscis monkeys was reported to be stranded there. Pulau Chermin was apparently a small island in Brunei bay and Rahim thought that we could easily travel around its coastline, scanning for the monkeys. It seemed that if the monkeys were in residence, there was a good chance that we would see them.

The boat took us far out in a wide sweep along the coast, across the clear shallow sea and over the Sunda Shelf. This underwater shelf is a relic of the days when, as recently as the Ice Ages, the various islands now forming the western half of the Malay archipelago were joined together by land (now submerged and forming the shelf). In fact islands such as Sumatra, Java and Borneo that are now bordered by these shallow seas were once part of a massive oriental continent called Sundaland. They were united with Malaya and Thailand until the end of the last Ice Age, in the Pleistocene, about fifteen thousand years ago, when the sea level rose to sever the land links and isolate the islands from the surviving continent. During the periods when the land bridges were intact, some of the mainland flora and fauna were able to invade and inhabit the areas that are islands today. Further to the east, in contrast, there has been a deep strait for much longer which formed an effective barrier to invading species. Differences in the fauna and flora on either side of this strait, the Strait of Lombok, were first noticed by Alfred Russel Wallace, and so the zoological line that can be drawn between Borneo and the islands to the south-east is called Wallace's Line. A similar shelf, the Sahul Shelf, stretches north-west from Australia surrounding the islands up to and including New Guinea and again forming a border which marks the extremes of migration of ancient Australian creatures.

The consequences of these games of geological musical chairs on the distribution of animals in South East Asia can still be seen clearly today. For instance, nearly ninety species of frog live in a variety of different habitats, in Borneo, but only fifteen of them are found on the Philippine

island of Palawan, lying to the north-west of Borneo, and only seven reach
Luzon, the next island of the chain. Even the land links between these
islands were selective, for not only are there fewer species of frog on the
more distant islands, but those species that are there have been heavily
selected. A species of frog which was very aquatic in its habits, for
example, would require a continuous supply of fresh water if its members
were to travel. This was obviously not available on Luzon or Palawan,
where most frogs are rather terrestrial in their habits and aquatic species
are barely represented.

Our trip took us through another wide river, Sungai Limbang, at the
mouth of which was an old deserted kampong, or Malay village. The
kampong houses had once stood on stilts, but after years of neglect and
desertion most of the framework had decayed and dwindled into the lapping water below. All that remained were the stilts made of almost indestructible 'iron wood' or belian, a wood so hard that it would barely be
grazed by a stroke from the sharpest parang (Malay jungle knife). Out at
sea we came upon these struts standing high and eerily above the water's

surface, casting glistening shadows among the waves, and on which
perched our one zoological triumph of the day – the snake bird.

We motored further out to sea. Every so often, although apparently a
long distance from land, we would run aground on a raised spit of sand
and have to redistribute our weight to dislodge the boat.

Pulau Chermin presented a rather rocky coastline around which the
water was becoming progressively more choppy. Rahim had some doubts
as to whether or not we could land without damaging the boat. We circled

the island, twice being slapped by harsh bursts of driving rain which leapt unexpectedly out of the greying horizon. We moved the buffeted boat nervously into a small cove and ran aground some twenty to thirty metres out to sea. Here we disembarked and pushed the boat ashore, where Rahim cautioned that if the weather deteriorated further we would have to run for home, lest the monsoon catch us with a vindictive flick of its tail before finally departing to the north.

The island was so quiet and dank that we found ourselves tiptoeing up the bank and speaking in whispers. Rahim explained that nobody visited Pulau Chermin nowadays although in the course of time many must have landed upon her shores. The island was bordered by the inevitable mangrove and Nipa palm but, once through this curtain, we were immediately into a thick jungle of trees draped in vines and creepers. Through them ran a network of overgrown paths that had, perhaps, originally been trodden by people. Rahim said that pirates had once used the island as a base. Although the paths were distinguishable, as we ducked and dodged along them, they had not been used recently and were overgrown with lianas, spiny rattans and bamboos; each branch brushed aside shed a cloud of dust around us, while the spikes pulled and tore at our clothing and hair. We seemed to be trespassing in a long disused Hollywood film set. So thick was the vegetation overhead and so dusty were the creepers around us that everything appeared to be drenched in shades of grey. Even where a shaft of sunlight pierced this monochromatic world and burnt a spot of brightness on the ground, the colours were bleached impressions of greens and browns.

We moved carefully on down the elusive path, every footstep accompanied by a series of cracks as thorns snapped in their dry death below. Everything on Pulau Chermin was armed and hostile; the shrubs and bushes growing around us all brandished long evilly barbed spines. The lianas and rattans hanging from the high storey above us were similarly armed and made fiendish adversaries. They whirled and curled to ensnare your clothing and then lulled you into a false sense of security as you walked on, taking up the slack in their curls before suddenly jerking taut and wrenching you backwards, torn and impaled.

Mark and I walked ahead of Rahim and Andrew. The way was blocked by a clump of thick bamboo through which the path had obviously once penetrated with some determination, but now only a chink remained between the upright stems. We pushed through this to be greeted by a cacophony of clattering noises, jitterings and cheepings, and all around us small black bodies shot right, left and centre, nearly colliding with us, swerving off, chirping irritably, and then just as unexpectedly silence reigned again. We had been stalking slowly forward before these

miniature demons had exploded in our path; we were completely un-
prepared for them and so quick was the explosion and so complete the
ensuing silence that we hardly knew what had happened. Our hearts beating audibly, we looked blankly at each other and moved on a few more
paces before another shower of black sparks erupted in our path. One
sped straight towards my face; I ducked and it swerved away. Dozens and
dozens of bats, probably undisturbed in their island sanctuary for many
years, displayed obvious irritation that this privacy had been so rudely invaded; from every clump of vegetation we came to they erupted forth,
chittering and chattering in their indignation.

It took no more than twenty minutes to walk from one end of the
island to the other. As we reached the far end and the vegetation on the
side of the path began to clear, out of the ground grew a sheer face of rock.
This seemed so out of character with the rest of the island that it
demanded further exploration. Climbing the face we came to a ridge that
ran like a small sheep track up the side of the rock to its summit, just taller
than the tallest tree on the island. It would give us a chance to see if we
could locate Proboscis monkeys in the treetops, monkeys which we had
almost forgotten under the influence of bats and thorns.

The ridge was thin and crumbly, the only holds being the occasional
tropical fern growing out of cracks in the rock. As we clambered up –
although not a great distance from the ground – and as each successive
handhold disappeared in a crumble of sand and earth, I began to wonder
how we were going to get down again. Once we reached the top we could
indeed see over the crowns of most of the island's trees. However, other
than the occasional bat still twittering its parting shot at us, there was little
sound of activity. The descent was as bruising as I had feared!

We left the big rock and cut across the island in a diagonal to the boat,
still without a sign of a Proboscis monkey. We did come across a nest of
termites, however, creatures which look like ants, although they are not
related to them. The nest was made of mud and hung beneath a rock.
These were *Hospitalitermes,* a species which, as their name suggests, are
'hospitable', sharing their nests with other species of termite. There is even
one account of them sharing their nests with a colony of bees! Stretching
out from the nest in several thin bands were columns of black termites.
Each column was only half a dozen termites wide, but a cordon of individuals with a racier build and pointed mouth parts scurried up and
down the edge of the ranks. They were the soldiers, guarding the workers
as they foraged for food. Mark was intrigued by these creatures, so much
so that in later years he has devoted much of his working life to their study.
In one project he found that a nest such as this one might comprise some
500,000 foraging individuals, which works out at a foraging population of

as many as 180 per metre! Some of the workers were carrying little balls in their jaws, and Mark subsequently discovered that these balls were made up of foods, such as fungi, algae and mosses. *Hospitalitermes* can peel a layer of flesh only one cell thick from fungi. By capturing termites and weighing the bundles of plant fragments they were carrying, Mark found that the colony gathered just over twelve grams of dry vegetable matter each day – perhaps the weight of a big feather, not much for the labours of half a million workers! He also found that the food balls were of two types: light ones containing wood, algae and fungi, and dark ones containing dark lichen. The termites went on longer trips to gather their dark balls and Mark believes that they were specifically searching for lichen containing important amino acids. It is easy to make such glib summaries, but think of the incredible organization whereby the colony makes up its collective 'mind' that a particular column will search for lichens! No one even begins to understand how these complex behaviour patterns are controlled, even if one can well understand how their consequences are important to the survival of the animals involved – in this case the acquisition of an important nutrient.

The termite with which *Hospitalitermes* cohabits and so earns its name is called *Termes*. In fact they live in different parts of the same nest and it seems they most probably benefit from the other's presence because of the different armaments of their soldiers' jaws. The *Hospitalitermes* soldiers defend wide passageways by producing noxious secretions which overcome invaders. The soldiers of *Termes,* in contrast, defend very narrow passageways where one could easily believe there was not room for *Hospitalitermes* to manoeuvre. Together they make an effective team, each soldier equipped for chemical warfare, squirting any intruder with noxious fluids.

Picking our way between the columns of foraging termites we continued back towards the boat. As we neared the beach we came upon a large tree that clearly had fallen some years before, its roots rent from the soil. Now as it lay at an angle to the ground, forming an alcove with its colossal trunk, a metre or more above the ground, it was veiled in mosses, lichens and creepers. Beneath it, covered in green moss and algae, we found an old stone, the surface of which was pitted and eaten by the weather. Scraping the vegetation from the stone's surface, we could see that it had been engraved with an intricate floral pattern among which were the remains of what might have been Arabic script: a gravestone. On many nights in the subsequent months when I lay looking out to the mangrove swamps and across the silhouetted tops of moonlit trees I wondered what sort of life, what sort of death, had led this person to be buried in such isolation.

The sun was sinking on the horizon as our little craft bobbed slowly back across the waters of the Sunda Shelf. As we steered through the deserted kampong, now, at high tide, standing even more alone, the rays of the sun were shattered and split by the tops of the mangroves and cast piercing shadows through these poignant relics of a village. Thoughts of the shadowy dead village and the old weathered gravestone on Pulau Chermin were moulded together with the gentle rocking of the boat as we meandered through the mangrove islands; the evening was peaceful and timeless. It was only when we were back in Bandar Seri Begawan that it struck me that the day had passed with no sight of a Proboscis monkey and no clue as to where we should search next.

At 6 o'clock the next morning we set out in the boat with Rahim again. We followed much the same route as the day before, and although there was pleasure in being more familiar with our surroundings, we were subdued after our overblown optimism of the day before. Perhaps we would not find these monkeys quite so easily; perhaps we would not find them at all.

Rahim and Abdullah, the boatman, decided that we should try a new approach: at every opportunity we were to cut our engine and drift with the current of the outgoing tide. We did this, at the same time scanning the trees through our binoculars. Leaf after leaf whirled across my lenses in a giddy chase as the current pulled us through the swamps. After no more than an hour we found ourselves drifting downstream past a small coastal kampong. On the opposite bank I glimpsed a movement which was followed by a resounding crash as a heavy body fell to the Nipa palm that formed a carpet below the crowns of the mangrove trees. Triumphant, Rahim turned to us and confirmed that we had prompted the hurried departure of a Proboscis monkey. I had not even had time to focus my binoculars! We had heard a Proboscis monkey, though we could barely claim to have seen one. But our spirits shot sky high and we drifted on, still scanning every leaf and every twig for another sign of a monkey. None was forthcoming, however, and my thoughts began to turn to the cautionary tales of friends who were professional monkey watchers. I remembered their woeful warnings that, even after years of experience, the most common view of the animal whose family life one strives to unveil is nothing more than a glimpse of a tail, a flash of fur, or a movement of branches as the quarry sidles from view into dense foliage. Were we to spend the next three months in the same tantalizing way, I wondered, seeing only the violent movements of branches and hearing accompanying crashes as monkeys plummeted through the undergrowth — as keen to avoid us as we were to meet them? Would we ever really watch Proboscis monkeys?

We had reached the coast and Rahim suggested that the best policy would be to head back upriver to Brunei and then to start the drifting operation again. An hour later we were drifting down the section of the river where we had seen, or rather heard, the monkey earlier. Suddenly, through the thick foliage of a particularly large mangrove tree, I saw a flash of red. Through our binoculars we glimpsed a large red monkey, flitting in and out of view between the leaves of the trees as we drifted past, but we were unable to hold our position against the current in any one vantage point. We craned and stretched to see its face and the phenomenal nose which had captured our imagination sufficiently to bring us 10,000 miles. At last the red monkey turned towards us. There was no huge snout, only a Pinocchio-like snub nose – it was a female. The female Proboscis monkey is blessed with a nose which would be considered ample by many people's standards, but it pales into insignificance when compared with the immense appendage for which the males of the species are famed. Nevertheless, we had seen her and seen her for more than a couple of seconds.

The monkey glared at us, apparently displeased by this intrusion and slowly, hand over fist as a fireman might go down a pole, she descended the mangrove trunk. I was struck by the human way that she climbed. As she looked menacingly down the shafts of my binoculars, I realized that she was not alone; clinging to her bulbous belly was a tiny golden infant. A few seconds more and it was all over; she had disappeared into the thick matrix of Nipa palm. We cast about for sight of other monkeys, but could see none.

Elated at our first real view of a Proboscis monkey, we drifted on for several hours but with no further success. Determined to press forward and capitalize on the advantage, we arranged with Rahim that he would drop us at the kampong immediately opposite where we had made the sightings of the monkey and her infant. We would make our camp there.

As a matter of principle (and economics) we had brought nothing but the bare essentials with us to Brunei. So, equipped with little more than our hammocks and 'mossie' nets, acquired from Arab Street, and weighed down with cameras and notebooks, we were left by Rahim on the decrepit wooden jetty which jutted out below this fishing hamlet. Much as we wanted to meet the villagers, we were preoccupied with not arriving like bulls in a proverbial china shop, and so, rather than intrude on kampong life, we found a clearing a hundred metres outside the village and there we unloaded our goods. The jungle was fairly thin around the clearing. Most of the trees were tall, but spindly, no more than half a metre in girth. The ground was littered with leaves among which peeped sprigs of greenery and fragile fern. We piled our luggage beside a tree, noting the enthusiasm

with which a party of ants inspected the box containing our stores. Creepers hung from the trees, the ground was dry, and butterflies drifted by; it seemed a good place to stay. In the next few weeks I often saw these butterflies congregate around places where buffalo had urinated but on that first day we simply took their presence as an indication of the tranquillity of the site.

Once established in our 'camp', we set off to explore the immediate vicinity. A closer look at the mangrove trees themselves proved intriguing for amid the clusters of dry broad green leaves hung structures that looked like runner bean pods; at first sight this is more or less what we took them to be: pods waiting to dry, dehisce and explode forth their seeds. This is far from the truth, however, for the mangrove, thriving in the inhospitable swamp habitat, has adapted its reproductive behaviour to combat the rigorous conditions. The mangrove flower, once fertilized, does indeed form a fruit, but instead of this being dispersed from the adult plant to germinate and grow in some new location, the mangrove retains a hold upon its offspring which develop as they hang from the adult tree. The pods that I had seen were in fact the seedling trees hanging from the parent. The seedlings grow until they are about twenty-five centimetres long and the buds of leaves are already appearing at the top. At the bottom end of the infant tree is a daggerlike point. When they are weaned from the parent tree these seedlings drop off and are so designed that they fall through the air like a dart, and on landing, if it is low tide, pierce the mud and remain standing upright as if they had been growing there since germinating. Ideally the seedlings fall when it is low tide and so they will have got a grip in their terrestrial home before the tide rises again. In this way the mangrove avoids its seeds being swept away before they can get a chance to put down roots in the ever-changing habitat of the mangrove swamp. Of course the mechanism does not always work and the seedling will drop when the tide is not at its lowest ebb. In this case the young plant is swept away; perhaps it still has some chance to implant itself elsewhere as the tide recedes from the mud. However, a good proportion of the seedlings fall when the mud is fully exposed and within a matter of days their root systems develop and their leaves flourish to give the impression that they have been firmly established for months.

The elegance of the mangrove's adaptations does not end there, however. Spending its life partly submerged in saline waters, the mangrove tree has a serious problem of getting sufficient oxygen to its root system so that it may breathe. To overcome this, the roots of certain species develop appendages known as pneumatophores. These grow up from the root and emerge through the mud and shallower water to reach the air, appearing as little pinnacles growing out from the mud like a pin cushion. Anyone who walks barefoot on the mud will have discovered that however great the advantage of these 'external lungs' to the trees, they are equally to the disadvantage of the traveller: not content with their own fiendishly pointed shape which readily penetrates the soles of one's feet, they enter into a conspiracy with the thousands of barnacles that coat them and whose shells each have a razor sharp lip. Each barnacle is so small that one hardly knows they are there until one touches them with a foot or hand and finds it lacerated and infected with the often far from clean waters of the swamp. The subtler members of the pneumatophore clan are inclined to hide just below the surface of the mud so that the unsuspecting victim stands on an apparently innocent piece of soft squidgy mud to sink deep, his foot irretrievably plunging upon the sharp spike.

I spent a few moments beachcombing below the mangroves. A large lump of root lay rotting at my feet and I swung at it with my golok. Inside it was like a sponge – a labyrinth of tubular passageways with neatly polished walls. Some of the passageways contained worms, three or four centimetres long and wriggling at this rude incision into their homes. These were no ordinary worms; in fact they were not worms at all but molluscs, cousins of the mussels familiar on European shores and in French restaurants. The creatures were a type of shipworm: in the course of time their ancestors traded their protective but cumbersome shells for an ability to burrow through wood almost with the ease that an earthworm tunnels through soil. The shipworm's shells have become reduced to a pair of tiny rasping blades around its head. By rocking these two blades a dozen times a minute a shipworm can drill through nineteen millimetres of wood a day. It was humbling to think that a relative of the slithering strand of life that lay in my palm could have influenced the course of world history: when the Spanish Armada sailed against the British navy in 1558, it had already spent several months in harbour in an age when ships were bedevilled by shipworm infestation, and one theory holds that this time in dock would have been sufficient for these wood-boring demons to honey-comb every hull. Perhaps Elizabeth I owed as much to these living awls as to Francis Drake's seamanship!

As evening approached we set about slinging our hammocks, clearing the undergrowth with our jungle knives. Three pairs of trees that seemed suitable bedposts were found and the hammocks and mosquito nets suspended between them. As darkness closed in we lit our primus stove and gathered around to cook the dehydrated fish we had bought from Brunei market. Dried shrimps, whitebait and rice: inexperienced as chefs, we were far from able to cope with this dehydrated fare. We simply boiled it in our billy cans and were left with a soggy mass of gritty material, reminiscent of sodden blotting paper. This ordeal over, we retired to our various hammocks and stared up through the mosquito nets to the leaves of the towering forest and on to the darkening sky above.

To anyone who has not heard them, the sounds of the jungle at night are truly unbelievable. A cacophony of whines and whirls, of cheeps and squeaks gradually mounts in volume to reach a synchronous crescendo before dying away, only to mount again to a new and ever more shattering pitch. It soon becomes apparent that there is an astounding quantity of life around. I tried desperately to locate each individual sound – an ever-increasing proportion of the orchestra seemed to be playing within my mosquito net. Among the chirps of the numerous insects and through the whizzing of wings and the droning hums came crackles and scratchings; leaves rustled underfoot. Something was climbing the bark of one of the trees from which my hammock was slung. It became hard to believe that the lumbering thing below could be anything other than an enraged Malayan sun bear trying to chew through the hammock ropes. Quietly I tried to ease cramped legs to a different position in the hammock – if only I could get my left leg out and on top of my right knee – but the whole hammock swung and only violent gymnastics prevented it from overturning, producing enough noise to attract all the sun bears in Christendom and elsewhere. At that point I was distracted by the silhouette of a scorpion making its way across the top of my mosquito net. A quarter of an hour of breathless manoeuvring revealed that it was a leaf. It was rather a cheap net and there were some holes in it; whatever else found these entrances, mosquitoes certainly did – swat at one and tip yourself out of the hammock, and in the process let in the demonic hoard that danced outside in anticipation. But soon the irrational fantasies of this first night in the jungle dwindled to insignificance, swamped by the beauty of the noises of the darkness.

Long before dawn I awoke to an almost deafening trilling nearby. Creeping from the hammock I stalked towards the noise, a torch shrouded in my sock to dull the beam. The trilling seemed to originate from the bark of a large tree. My light fell on the beast just as it flew, churring, away. It was a large green cicada – one of the 15,000 species of which, to judge by the sounds around me, many lived near our camp. The song of these bugs is produced by the vibrations of a pair of shell-like drums at the base of the abdomen. Males produce these songs, probably in an attempt to advertise their presence to females, or perhaps to other males. The songs of some species can be monotonous, but since some spend years below ground as larvae (one species takes seventeen years to grow up) before emerging for one brief singing season, they can hardly be blamed for making the most of it. In the torchlight I caught sight of another chorister, a bright green frog sitting on a tree trunk not far from the spot where the cicada had been. Again my curiosity was unwelcome and the frog leapt nimbly away from its vertical perch into the darkness. Tree frogs can move easily on vertical surfaces as they have specially adapted suckers, well supplied with mucus at the end of each digit. What is more, each digit has an extra bone (as if our fingers had four elements rather than three), and this allows the frogs to swivel their limbs through wider arcs without dislodging their suction pads from precipitous surfaces. The green tree frog is reputed to leap into the darkness to snap at any insect that passes nearby, and to do so with no regard to likely landing places; instead, as it falls, the frog depends on catching onto a passing leaf with its wonderfully adhesive feet. Having inspected two members of the resident orchestra I crept back to the hammock.

When I awoke again day was dawning and I was thrilled by memories of the Bornean night. A few stalwart insects still chirped, and increasing numbers of birds took up the refrain. How warm and friendly everything seemed! Nevertheless, I still wondered what had caused all those rustling noises. I was interrupted in my musings by an animal scampering along a

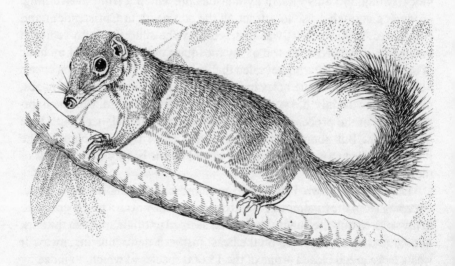

bough above me. At first sight it seemed to be a squirrel. Indeed the Malay name for squirrels and for tree-shrews, as this really was, is the same: tupai. The tree-shrew has brown fur with an almost greenish tinge, arched rounded ears, a sharp snout and its eyes seem to be encircled by a thin rim of hairless skin, giving it a rather unmade-up look. A battle has raged in zoological circles over this little animal, the debate revolving around the fine distinction of whether tree-shrews are primitive insectivores or primates, resembling the early ancestors of monkeys, apes and ourselves. The evidence mainly concerns their skeleton but some discussion has centred on the primate-like tendency of tree-shrews to have only small litters of young. Their small families were explained by biologist R.D. Martin who studied their maternal behaviour. In one species Martin found that female tree-shrews give birth to their twin babies in a different nest to that in which they customarily sleep, at least in captivity. The mother then leaves the babies alone, swaddled in dry leaves, visiting them only briefly every two days to suckle. When the babies are disturbed they kick their legs, creating an alarming commotion in their leafy nest and presumably deterring further investigation by inquisitive predators. Perhaps the mother tree-shrew only rarely visits her babies to avoid drawing predatory attention to them. This could explain why tree-shrews have such small litters (irrespective of any primate affinity), for the mothers have to produce a lot of milk for each two-day feed and it is hard to believe that they could manage this for a large brood.

The tree-shrew scuttled sleekly through the branches, its tail twirling extravagantly as it balanced from precipitous bough to spindly twig. Every few seconds it paused momentarily, pressing its hindquarters close to the branch then sprinting on, as if anxious to leave far behind the droplets of scent it was undoubtedly distributing. Suddenly this frantic creature froze, its nose held high. Its stillness seemed quite out of character! The moment snapped past and the tree-shrew sped forward, chirping, to launch into combat with an unseen opponent. The two tree-shrews disappeared, lost from view in squeaking rivalry.

Not far from our hammocks we found some coconuts, brown and hairy, just as they appear when hanging from bird tables in English gardens. We picked up some of these and took them back to our little camp. Unwittingly, in our naïveté, we were committing theft. The next problem was how to get at the juice within. We set to with our ex-army jungle knives, hacking and splintering the coconuts, eventually cracking them in half and spilling most of the milk. During the course of this operation our boatman, Abdullah, appeared on the scene. He nodded a polite greeting and squatted down in the Malay fashion to watch as we proceeded with our onslaught, a look of mounting wonder crossing his features. Moments passed, chips of coconut flew here and there, but we had little success. Abdullah began to smile, then to grin. He chuckled and then he laughed aloud. Not entirely sure what we were doing that was so very funny, we sat back and laughed heartily as well, giving further swipes at the offending coconut in the meantime. We guessed he must be entertained by the blunt edge of our unwieldy knife in comparison to the scimitar-like parang which hung at his own side.

Beside himself with mirth, Abdullah stumbled off to the kampong, shouting. He soon reappeared with two other men, whom we had not seen before. They all squatted there, splitting their sides with merriment, patting each other on the back and pointing at our coconut; we laughed back. This went on for some time before we eventually broke into one of the coconuts and offered them some of it, only to prompt a fresh wave of hilarity. The dùll knife explanation was becoming less credible but, undaunted, we began to eat the coconut. At this point the men dashed off and soon came back with another couple of men, each with two women. The women peered round the trees and looked at us; everyone was having a thoroughly entertaining time. Anyway our breakfast of perfectly tasty coconut passed and the crowd began to disperse. It was not until several days later that we were to understand the reason for their mirth.

Once our audience had gone, and while awaiting Rahim's arrival at an already appointed midday venue, we set about making plans for the day. Exhausted in the mounting heat by this mental effort and our onslaught on the nut, we all stretched out for a while in the shade of a tree. We were contentedly listening to the birdsong when I happened to glance at Mark's feet, safely encased in a pair of jungle boots. An incredible beast with a bright green head had appeared over his toe. I glanced quickly at Mark. He was soundly asleep. I held my breath as more head and then some neck edged into view, followed by one foot and then another, so that the head and shoulders and two arms of this amazing creature were perched on Mark's toe. From this vantage point it perused him at its leisure.

From its slender line and reptilian eyes I had thought at first that it must be a snake, but the appearance of the shoulders and arms obviously dashed this theory. Now, as I saw it in more detail, I thought it seemed to be some kind of frog; its whole body appeared to be bright green. However, if it were a frog, it was surely the frog of all frogs, a racehorse among amphibia, since it was slender and athletic in appearance. A hop and it landed squarely on Mark's foot, its back legs tucked up beneath it, poised to spring again should it be threatened. It was then that Mark's foot twitched in his sleep, at which point our horrified visitor nearly overbalanced in his excitement, and I caught sight of a long thin tail stretching perhaps twenty centimetres away down the side of Mark's boot. This was no frog in spite of its deceptive stance.

Mark's slumbers were obviously taking him back to the rigours of the previous night. He began to twitch feverishly. As his foot moved back and forward, our visitor swayed, desperately trying to maintain his balance. Losing his nerve, he leapt to the nearest tree, in one bound covering a distance that must have been over three metres and landing a good two metres up the trunk. Then, in squirrel fashion, he scuttled around the trunk for a final glimpse of his slumbering host and was lost from sight. Andrew, positioned on the other side of Mark, had also seen the pair of eyes appearing over the boot and we discussed what type of lizard it could be. Mark was loath to accept our account of his visitor, especially as he denied strenuously that he had been asleep in the first place. Nevertheless, Andrew and I persisted, and on Rahim's arrival we described the animal to him in great detail. Rahim told us that it was probably a Belinkasa, or Green Calotes. These lizards are also referred to, most unjustly, as

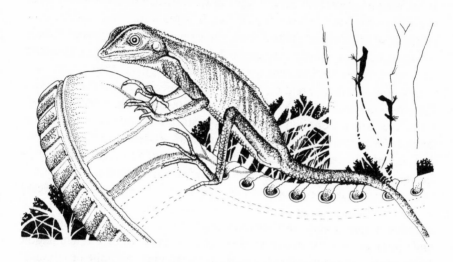

'bloodsuckers', but they certainly do nothing so lurid. However, their wizardry does extend to dramatic changes of colour from green to brown if they are frightened.

The rest of that day and the greater part of the next were spent in the boat with Rahim in further search of Proboscis monkeys. We did catch a glimpse of one or two, but they were as fleeting as before – just a second or so and then they disappeared and we still failed to see the enlarged nose of the male which earns the Proboscis monkey its name. Rahim could not continue to devote all his time to us, so from then on we were on our own. Before leaving, Rahim went to tell Abdullah that he would call back in a week to find out if we were still determined to live in the swamp, which he clearly doubted! Rahim returned with the good news that Abdullah's brother, who had recently moved house, was prepared to let us live in his old home. Rahim pointed to a wooden house standing in the water at the front of the jetty where our boat was moored. This building became our home for the coming months.

According to Abdullah the house was just about on its last legs, hence his brother's move. It stood out in the swamp on its stilts: at high tide the waves lapped a few centimetres below the floor, at low tide it stood a good two metres above the mud. A wooden staircase ran from the floor of the house down into the swamp, where one could moor a boat, and three floating tree trunks were roped together leading to the bank. These floated further or nearer to each other depending on the tide: crossing them at high tide demanded considerable co-ordination. The struts of the roof and walls were of split bamboo, as was the floor which bounced welcomingly as we walked across it. The roof was thatched with Nipa palm leaves while the walls were made of banana tree bark. The main stilts, six of them, were all made of 'iron' wood. Through the floor the swamp waters were clearly in view; the gaps between the bamboos were narrow enough to cradle a dropped roll of film, but pens and coins were swiftly gulped by the mud below. The house was really only one room, but a small partition divided it. A verandah at the end of the house was stacked with rolled-up fishing traps, and was big enough for one man to stretch out on. True, there were a few holes in the walls where the banana bark had rotted or been pushed out, but these were soon patched up. It seemed that our ambition to become part of the local community was off to a good start.

By the time our removal from the clearing to the house was completed it was high tide again, and bobbing at the steps of our new house we found a small dugout canoe just large enough to hold two men. This vessel seemed to go with the house so Mark and I untied it and, taking a paddle each, set out to explore the neighbouring waterways. In spite of spending so much time rowing boats up and down the Thames at Oxford, neither of us had the sense of balance necessary to keep this tiny craft going for very long. We wobbled timidly out across the tide, in a way which has been described to me subsequently, and rather sternly, as 'insanely incautious'. Finding ourselves gradually being swept downstream towards the sea, we tried to turn in order to paddle upstream again. Our circle of turn was too tight and, in a flurry of paddles, we capsized. Grabbing onto the drifting vessel, we could not right it, try as we might. We drifted slowly down past the house, shouting to Andrew to get out the motor boat and come to rescue us. Andrew stood on the verandah of our house, seemingly unable to comprehend the seriousness with which we were making our request, and laughed as we drifted miserably down river. Between screeching abuse at Andrew, we comforted ourselves by cracking jokes about crocodiles, poisonous sea snakes and river fever. Eventually, to our relief, we saw Andrew clamber into the boat and start to pull the cord to start the engine. However, nothing but pathetic phuts came forth as we drifted on towards the coast. We had no intention of abandoning the upturned boat, but holding on to it thwarted our attempts to swim across the current.

The mouth of the river and the sea beyond were soon clearly in sight and, as the banks began to widen and we entered the estuary, Andrew was gradually lost to sight. As we rounded the bend we heard with relief the bursting stutter of the motor starting. Some ten minutes later Andrew hove into view. It appeared that the propeller had become entangled with vegetation and the petrol valve had been dislodged in the resulting affray. He chugged along beside us and finally pulled the canoe onto dry land. Once righted, Mark managed to paddle it successfully back to the house, but we had lost one of the duckboards during the course of the escapade.

We had imagined ourselves in at least some danger as we drifted towards the coast. Little did I imagine then that in the months to come we would be swimming in the same river every day, racing the Malay boys in the hundred metre stretch to the other side of the swamp and back.

Back at the house we wrung out our garments. Mark had received a specimen lighter from a tobacco company to take with him as a publicity stunt. The idea had been to show how tough the lighter was, but it never lit anything from that day on.

No sooner were we semi-dry than the fisherman who had been the previous occupant of the house arrived with his wife and small baby. They sat cross-legged in a line on the verandah. New to the local code of tea party etiquette, we lit the primus and started to boil a billy can of tea, pointing hopefully at it and grinning inanely. The fisherman looked at his wife and son, who was only a few months old, and back at us again. Assuming this to be a positive response we continued to brew the tea. The tea, perhaps because of our nervousness, was far from good; in fact it was almost undrinkable. Andrew decanted it into the motley collection of empty cans and battered cups which comprised our crockery. The three of us sat cross-legged in a row facing the family, none of us understanding a word of the other's language, each occasionally looking up and grinning hopefully in a wan gesture of friendliness.

We felt very unsure of our position; we did not even know whether we should be paying rent or how we should express our gratitude for the use of this man's house. The silence of the tea party was broken only by the regular slurping of the baby as he suckled from his mother's breast. The tea finished and three biscuits shared between us, the fisherman's family got up and without a backward glance walked slowly away across the treacherous logs. We had not the remotest clue if we had behaved properly or broken every law of decorum, nor could we judge from their actions what they thought of us or whether they intended to come back again. We did not know what we should do next or whether we should return the visit. Feeling that, try though we might, we had not made too good a start with our neighbours, I wandered off for a walk behind the kampong. As I meandered along the trail I shuddered with embarrassment at our ignorance. We were living in this man's house, had stupidly lost a duckboard of his canoe and did not know how to express gratitude or apology. We must have seemed very insensitive to our host, though in fact we were struggling to behave properly. I had tried to learn some Malay before the trip, but my tortured mispronunciation had thwarted even that gesture of respect. It was small consolation to rationalize that everyone has to start somewhere.

I had not gone far along a muddy trail when some chirping noises above me caught my attention and I saw a small troop of silvery-coloured monkeys. These were Silver Leaf monkeys, one of the three species of Leaf monkey found in Borneo. There were about seven animals in the troop; a youngster clambered among them, quite a different colour from the adults, for whom he seemed to be the centre of attention. The little band moved off, travelling as a unit as they leapt and scampered from tree to tree with great agility, and I soon lost sight of them.

These dainty Leaf monkeys are relatives of the Proboscis monkey, lumped together under the title of Langur monkeys. As vegetarians the langurs are relatives of the Colobus monkeys of Africa (but distinguished by having retained a thumb on their hands which Colobus monkeys have lost). Not much is known about the comparative sociology of the various species of langur in Borneo, but one study of two species from Sri Lanka, which may be rather similar, emphasized how monkey communities were adapted to their food supply. These two species, studied by C.M. Hladik, share the same general habitat in Sri Lanka, and the differences in their social organization reinforce the idea that animal societies are adapted to the finest details of ecological circumstances. The Hanuman langur is buff-coloured with a creamy head and black face; the inauspiciously named Purple-faced langur is dark grey with a black face and lighter cheek whiskers. In the deciduous forests where Hladik compared these two species he found that most of the Purple-faced monkeys' food was leaves, while the Hanuman langur ate almost as much fruit as leaves; the Hanumans were much more 'choosy' in their diet. The two species may have been able to coexist simply because they ate different foods. The interesting point is that these two species lived at about the same population density (about two animals per hectare) but while the Hanuman langurs lived in large groups covering big home ranges, the Purple-faced monkeys, in contrast, lived in tiny ranges with only a small troop in each. The membership of these groups also differed, with only one male in each of the small Purple-faced langur groups and several in each Hanuman langur group. Each of these differences seemed to stem from one critical factor, the distribution of food trees: for the fruit-nibbling Hanumans it might be a long way from one fig tree to the next and consequently they needed large ranges to embrace plenty of trees. How did the lifestyle of the monkeys that I could still hear in the trees ahead of me compare with that of their cousins the Proboscis monkeys in the nearby, but quite different, swampy habitat? I hurried back to the house and we set out in the boat to search once more for Proboscis monkeys.

Again we were almost successful. As we drifted into a small rivulet we were greeted by a succession of a dozen or more crashes as red-brown bodies hurled themselves in alarm from the tops of the mangrove trees to the Nipa palm beneath, and then dashed in a frenzy through the Nipa forest clattering their way noisily along a route which we could not hope to follow.

3

Novices in the Swamp

For hours that day we had chugged along under the scorching sun, up and down the estuaries around Kampong Menunggol, where we were now firmly based. We had headed further afield, out into the northern limb of Sarawak, known as Limbang, before turning far out to sea for another circuit of Pulau Chermin and then back along the main Brunei river. There had been neither sight nor sound of a Proboscis monkey to reward our efforts. We had spent some time chasing a darter further and further through its territory in the hope of photographing it close to. Every time we came within range the bird took off and moved another hundred metres until finally we reached the end of its territory, whereupon the performance was repeated in reverse down to the far end. An hour of zig-zagging up and down had passed without a single frame being exposed. We cursed the instinct which informs birds of the maximum distance at which lenses are effective and, abandoning attempts at photography, we settled down to watch as the darter began to fish. After a few minutes it emerged and sat on a sunny log, its wings spread and glistening in the sun. These birds are unusual in that they do not coat their feathers in waterproof oils as do many diving birds. Consequently, they do actually get wet under water and so have to dry in the sun after a bout of fishing. Presumably the advantage to the bird is that without waterproofing, the air trapped in its plumage is quickly expelled during the dive and perhaps makes it more streamlined and less buoyant underwater. While loss of buoyancy may give greater manoeuvrability underwater, getting wet is certainly dangerous and is avoided by most water birds – contrast the proverbial water off a duck's back. Another rather intriguing explanation has been proposed for the behaviour of all those cormorant-like birds that apparently dry their wings by stretching them in the sunshine – namely that they are actually sending signals about bountiful fishing sites! The idea developed from a theory about bird roosts which suggested that birds living in roosts benefited from an exchange of information about the whereabouts of good feeding areas. Then it was noticed that at least one cormorant – the Reed cormorant – did not always 'sun' its wings even when it was soaking wet, and yet it almost always did so when its fishing trips had been successful. So the idea developed that the successful fisherman was signalling the presence of a good fishing area to his companions.

Hot and weary, we began to head for home. We had almost given up hope of seeing monkeys but as we eased up river towards the kampong and turned the last bend before our home, we suddenly heard that familiar crashing sound – Proboscis monkeys on the run. Cutting the engine and drifting on round the bend we spotted the stragglers of the fast vanishing troop. The palm tops swayed dangerously as the monkeys rained onto them from the mangrove trees, then all was quiet again.

A brief glimpse of the fleeing animals was typical of our sightings of Proboscis monkeys to date. As we moodily commiserated with one another we suddenly realized that we were being scrutinized by a colossal male Proboscis monkey less than ten metres away. He was sitting in full view among the low branches of a small mangrove, continuing to eat, apparently unconcerned by us. We were gripped by the irony of having spent hour after hour trying to slip close to one of these elusive beasts, only to be so close to one now that it must inevitably be spooked and flee.

The current slowly swirled our small boat to within five metres of the monkey, who continued to eat complacently. As we drifted nearer I could even hear him chewing and then, staring straight at us, he produced a Rabelaisian burp! He sat in an indolently human posture, his bottom supported by a branch and his legs dangling below. This huge old man was gorging his way happily through seedling after seedling that hung from the mangrove trees. He appeared to be skinning the seedlings, chewing some soft pith from within while discarding long ribbons of greenish external flesh. Holding both ends of a twenty centimetre long sapling plucked from its parental bough, in a way reminiscent of a man eating corn-on-the-cob, the monkey ran his teeth along the whole length of the plant before continuing his purposeful chewing. The seedling finished, he looked round as only one can look who realizes that all whom he observes are in his power. He pulled his great bulk up, swivelled around on his bottom to face away from us and slipped silently out of sight into the bushy mangrove.

The monkey had been magnificent; our proximity to him had provided a breathtaking opportunity to get the full measure of his stout and powerful physique with the added bonus of observing how he tackled the mangrove seedlings. Away from the aura of his magnificence, however, we could hardly refrain from viewing him in a slightly less respectful light, for if any beast can be said to be humorous, then it is the Proboscis monkey. Big, heavily built and pot-bellied, their size, shape and posture all combine to give them an undeniably decadent air. They sit aloft in the mangrove trees, one leg dangling below, the other bent at the knee and resting on the branch, that knee supporting the bent elbow on which the animal's chin rests while chewing his way through life and apparently pondering the misdeeds of the universe. All told, a deeply philosophical guise whose

Aristotelian air is marred only by the tight grey pants and thick woolly red coat which combine to give an impression not very different from that of a rather butch motorcyclist. The old male had sported a pendulous fleshy nose which, distended beyond all good taste, dangled flaccidly across his mouth. While the nose is splendid in its own right, it really only gains its full significance in the context of the remainder of the beast's peculiar anatomy: the enormous pot-belly, the deep chestnut crewcut, the flaming red muscle-bound shoulders — all these somehow focus attention on the astonishing nose — and it is when the Proboscis monkey starts to eat that the full glory of this organ can be seen. As the monkey chews through a leaf, the grinding motion of its jaws provokes the flaccid nose to flop from one side of the red face to the other.

So as we sat there, not five metres from that male Proboscis monkey, he had chewed and his nose had swayed, flop, flop, flop, from one side of his curious face to the other. As he finished one seedling and espied another particularly juicy one above his head, he had reached up for it with his long muscular arm and, as he did so, looked up towards the heavens to view the forthcoming delicacy. His nose quivered, wobbled precariously, markedly changed shape and then flopped backwards across his forehead to smack him between the eyes. The seedling procured, he had looked down and, while this most majestic of Proboscis monkeys must have been a leader among his own, he seemed to glance at us with a momentary hint of the embarrassment that one might expect such a nose to evoke.

The light was closing in as we started to prepare our supper of dried prawns and rice back at Kampong Menunggol. Supper-time was also rapidly becoming a ceremonial occasion for the application of ointment to our innumerable mosquito bites and antiseptic cream to our increasingly septic hands and feet, scarred from battle with the barnacle-coated pneumatophores. Having dealt with our various medicaments and, for once, gained a slight strategic advantage in our continuing battle with the Tilley lamp, we sat back to discuss the day and enjoy our after-dinner coffee.

Almost at once, however, we heard the lapping of water which signified that somebody was crossing the logs from the mainland to our house. Sure enough the floorboards sprang up and down as the fisherman who had previously owned the house came along the verandah and into our little room. We still knew absolutely no Malay and remained uncertain whether our last encounter over the revolting tea had been anything other than a complete failure. (It is strange to recall my mixed feelings of social uncertainty as this young man filled the doorway of our house, when I think of how soon he was to become a valued friend.) Unable to communicate in any other way, we grinned and beckoned the fisherman to sit down. He entered the room hesitantly, glancing at us and then discreetly back to the floor again. Finally he edged in and squatted down. Ages seemed to pass with all of us staring intently into the hissing lamp, occasionally looking up and smiling nervously. We were delighted that our neighbour should visit us, and were distraught at our social ineptitude and inability to speak his language. Our attempts to learn some key words proved useless as our visitor clearly found our mispronounced syllables incomprehensible. However strange he might think our zoological aims, his help would be vital and we were all too aware of the fragility of such gestures of friendship.

The Tilley lamp provided some common ground for as its light dimmed Mark began to pump it. The fisherman obviously understood the predicament as he watched Mark's feverish efforts to generate more light. Satisfied, Mark sat back, sweat pouring off his forearms and brow. The fisherman cautiously reached towards the lamp, looking questioningly around our faces for approval. He picked it up and moved it towards him, and pumped vigorously and rhythmically for some minutes, the muscles of his forearm bulging. The resulting glow was many times brighter than we had ever realized such a lamp could generate. He had so easily belittled our efforts that we might have felt embarrassment, but this never entered our heads. The ice was broken. We pointed merrily at the offending lamp and mimicked Mark's dwarfed efforts. But such exuberant gaiety could not last for long, and just in time Andrew had the idea of unearthing the Malay dictionary that had lodged deep in our baggage since we had bought it in Singapore. We were soon to learn that official Malay (or at least our pronunciation of it) was significantly different from the dialect spoken in this isolated kampong. However, the fisherman soon understood that the small book provided us with a means of limited communication and so, as we all gathered closer around the again fading light, we tried to think of strategic words that would allow us to exchange simple messages.

As we had come to Borneo principally to look for Proboscis monkeys and as the success of the afternoon was still pounding in our minds, it was about this that we tried to talk. It was extremely fortunate that of all the words in the English and Malay languages, the one for monkey should have strong phonetic similarity in both tongues, for as the evening progressed it seemed that we had spent rather too long thumbing through the crumpled pages of the dictionary. Periodically we found a word so simple that it seemed almost impossible to mispronounce, but each time we saw yet again in the hissing shadows of our Tilley lamp that embarrassed grin, that told once more that the Malay language dictionary bore little relation to the dialect spoken by these people. But at last we struck lucky and the

grin positively exploded into laughter. 'Monyet.' We leant forward into the
fading glow pointing frantically at our noses, happily babbling back at
him monyet, monyet. The fisherman's pleasure visibly faded as another
veil of incomprehension spread across his face. I feared that he would
leave soon, clambering out of our bark-wood home and off into the
swamp, taking with him his unspoken offer of friendship and help, leaving
behind three apparently lunatic zoologists chanting 'monyet' and
frantically pointing at their variously shaped snouts. Luck was on our
side, though, and it suddenly came to him. 'Bangkatan.' He patted his own
nose and repeated 'Bangkatan.' 'Monyet besar hedong, monyet nama
bangkatan.' 'The monkey with the big nose, the monkey called
bangkatan.' The next bit was relatively easy: we pointed towards the
mangrove, now engulfed in the night, pointing at our eyes, pointing again
at the trees, saying 'bangkatan' over and over again. Soon he understood
that we had seen a bangkatan on the other side of the swamp. The fact that
there was a bangkatan there and that we had seen it was probably of very
little surprise to him and of even less importance, but he was kind enough
to look interested. Overwhelmed by this crescendo of comprehension we
all sat back against the bark walls, laughed happily, and made yet another
cup of coffee to celebrate.

By the end of the evening we had built on this small start so that we
had a vocabulary of about twenty words. We had discovered that the
fisherman was twenty-two years old, that he had six brothers and two sisters and we had also managed to understand, after a great and complicated lexical feat, that the thing he loathed most in the world was the army.
We knew that the word for house was 'rumah', that water was 'ayer', birds
were called 'burong' and that to go to sleep was 'tidor'. The fisherman had
learnt our names but we had not found out his and fearing, I think
correctly, that it would be socially ingracious to ask unless the information was volunteered, we did not do so.

Hours had gone by and the lamp had been battered by many a pump
when our friend rose saying 'Salmat malam, saya tidor' – 'Goodnight, I'm
going to sleep'. He stepped quietly out of the room and onto the verandah
and we heard him pause before he padded back again into the light; grinning and pointing at us he said 'Orang puteh chakap bagus melayu' –
'White men talk good Malay'. He disappeared into the shadows of the
night. As we snuggled into the contours of the bamboo floor that night, I
think we all felt that we were beginning to make progress.

We began to develop a strict routine. One of us in turn had to be the
first person up in the morning and, as the light rose above the swamp, he
had to leap forth from his bedding, dash out on to our verandah and down
the steps to the boat; oversleeping by half an hour would have meant

disaster. By dawn, the water pouring into the boat through the holes in the hull reached within a couple of centimetres of the point at which it sank. Any remnant of sleep would be driven from the unfortunate individual on duty as he used a rusty can to bale out all the water and rescue our craft from a watery death. This done and feeling vastly superior to his two slumbering colleagues, the early-bird of the day would make the ritual Complan, a powdered food supplement.

We found that a week on rice was enough to provoke even the most stalwart carbohydrate addict into being prepared to make any sacrifice in exchange for a single spoonful of protein-rich Complan powder. And so every morning the man on duty would spoon two teaspoonsful into each of our three billy cans and mix this with a suitable amount of water for our individual tastes. There would then follow a short, almost religious period as each of us retired into his own secret thoughts, revelling in the delightfully squidgy white paste. The ceremony over, the mosquito nets and bed rolls were tidied away and the day could commence properly.

An unrelenting diet of rice has involved me in a variety of surprising incidents. A particularly unforgettable occasion occurred during one of my first trips overseas when I spent an entire summer in Kashmir, studying the flocks of birds found in the foothills of the Himalayas. For most of this time I lived in a small Government Rest House on the periphery of a shepherding village in the hills. This remote bungalow, often empty for months at a time, was staffed by three men – a sweeper, a cook and a 'chaukidar' (or general boss) who did absolutely nothing other than supervise the other two. Every day the cook provided lunch of rice and curried egg. After several weeks of this diet the cook offered an alternative – chicken curry instead of egg curry. The thought of fresh meat was irresistible and so I accepted at once. A couple of days later the chicken curry arrived, and although the chicken must have been an extremely old and skinny specimen, it was much appreciated. The next day neither egg nor chicken curry was forthcoming, merely a plate of rice. On inquiry, the cook answered quite simply, 'Eat chicken, no eggs'.

On the morning following our first lengthy chat with the fisherman, we finished our Complan, loaded the gear into the bailed boat and set sail for Bandar Seri Begawan, Brunei's capital town, from which our camp was about thirty-five minutes by river. This excursion back into town was necessary in spite of the pressing need to find more and better places to watch monkeys, firstly because of the gradually deteriorating petrol valve on the engine (which belonged to the Museum) and secondly because of our shortage of an ever-increasing number of necessary store items.

Arrival at Bandar Seri Begawan was, however, soon followed by despair because, having limped the last mile or so towards the town's jetty with Mark adroitly handling a nearly defunct engine, we found to our dismay that the only other engine the Museum owned had been stolen earlier that week. There was no replacement for ours, and nobody around who could mend the faulty one. It was with fairly low spirits that we made our way into town to the Government Rest House from where, as a last resort, I telephoned the army camp where the Royal Brunei Malay Regiment was based. The next few moments had a dreamlike quality and firmly revived my faith in miracles. Getting through to the switchboard I asked the operator for the name of the CO, to which the answer was a Gurkha colonel called Runce Rooney. I asked to be put through to Rooney, and waited while the phone buzzed. Eventually a clipped military voice answered 'Rooney here'. In what I hoped was my most persuasive voice I began to explain why three young zoologists were wandering around the swamps in an attempt to find Proboscis monkeys, why we wanted to learn about their habits and why I thought he might help us out of the perished petrol valve predicament, although he had neither met nor heard of us before.

I was not halfway through my first carefully designed sentence when Rooney interrupted me, barking down the phone, 'For God's sake man, don't beat about the bush. What is it you want?' Shaken, I was forced to resort to the unveiled truth, 'I had hoped, sir,' I said, 'that you might be able to help us because we have no engine for our boat and this makes observing the monkeys impossible, we can't travel among the swamps.' 'What horsepower?' Rooney asked 'Well,' I mumbled, 'almost anything would do as long as it is not too expensive, of course, because we have very little money, and you see . . .' 'What horsepower?' roared the colonel in aggravation. 'Twenty,' I stammered. 'What, is that enough?' It was, since we needed a quiet engine to get about the swamp without disturbing the monkeys. Too much power could have a more disturbing effect on them than was worthwhile. Colonel Rooney accepted this explanation; I did not tell him that compared with our dilapidated Seagull engine, a twenty horsepower engine was as a Rolls Royce to a Moped.

My ears strained nervously down the phone as I heard Rooney's pen scratch out engine — twenty horsepower on his notepad. 'What else do you want?' came the voice. 'I wondered,' I began. 'What?' The exclamation severed my words. 'Food,' I said, adopting what I hoped was a suitably precise approach. 'How many men?' he asked. 'Three,' I replied, straining my ears as his pen scratched its course across the notepad again. 'Weeks?' 'Twelve.' 'All right,' he said. 'Be here by nine o'clock tomorrow morning and we'll try to fix you up.'

'There was one more thing,' I interjected. 'Oh yes,' he replied sternly. 'It would be a great help,' I started nervously, 'if we could have some aerial photos of the area we are working in.' 'When do you want the chopper?' came the reply. For a moment I did not connect our requirement for aerial photographs with a helicopter. When the true relationship between question and answer dawned on me I realized that he thought I wanted to take aerial photographs myself. This was a privilege I'd never dreamed of. We speedily arranged that a helicopter would probably be available the following week. 'O.K.,' said Rooney, 'we'll see what we can do. Be here at nine o'clock.' The phone went dead.

Funds are invariably very short on university expeditions and even the slightest extravagance might be frowned on. However, after this telephone call with a real live fairy godmother, the three of us made our way down to a street café. A celebration seemed justified.

The centre of Bandar Seri Begawan is arranged along a series of parallel streets lined with open-fronted shops, each an Aladdin's Cave crammed with coils of rope, barrels of dried food, buttons, plastic toys, straw hats and spare shear-pins. Here and there between the shops are cafés like the one we went to now. A handful of rickety tables stretched back into the dim cavern of the café. Some were covered with coloured vinyl plastic, grazed dull from many a scouring. An ancient fan laboriously clunked overhead, sending a gentle breeze among the droning flypapers which hung from the ceiling, rippling with ensnared victims. Everyone in the place seemed to sweat copiously, and none more than the proprietor who prepared the delicious pancake-like creations called parathas. I revelled in these cafés. They were places to watch the world of Bandar Seri Begawan go round, places to exchange smiles with gold-crowned teeth and to wriggle slowly into the local community. The atmosphere was as rich and sweet as the coffee – it was served in clear glass cups or glasses, one-third pure Nestlé's milk to two-thirds coffee. Viewed in profile the thick white goo oozed to the bottom of this obscene concoction: the spoon really did stand up in it. Throughout the expedition, our urgent trips out of the swamp were often little more than thinly veiled excuses to savour parathas and sickly coffee, together with the contrasting worlds that came with them.

Bandar Seri Begawan is a small place and people know each other's business. It was not long before our exploits in pursuit of monkeys were well rumoured. It became ever more easy to join conversations; as we sat in a café stray words from neighbouring tables drifted across the room – 'monkeys', 'photographs', 'England'. We'd nod and reply 'monyet', like some secret password, and would soon be surrounded by an eager audience who, it seemed, could never be convinced that our purpose in Borneo was really to look for animals. If they asked us what we were doing often enough perhaps we'd slip up and confess our real motives!

The next morning the miracle of the army camp really did come true. We spent several pleasant hours with a congenial crowd all of whom seemed eager to be convinced that they had been committing an original sin in their failure to note down each occasion on which their patrols had spotted Proboscis monkeys. In future platoons would be equipped with a notebook for this purpose. We left the camp greatly indebted to Colonel Rooney's generosity and laden with rations which had slightly passed their date for legitimate consumption, a twenty horsepower engine and much important advice, and showered with offers of help from latent Proboscis monkey enthusiasts.

We arrived back at Kampong Menunggol to find that we were not, after all, the sole occupants of our house; as we traipsed back and forth, decanting our supplies from the boat, up the stairs and into the house, a large buzzing insect came and went through the door just about as many times as we did. However, it travelled so fast that other than noting timorously that it sounded like an infuriated bee, we could not identify it.

Our gear unloaded, we positioned ourselves in strategic corners of the house to await the next arrival of this ferocious-sounding insect. Only minutes later the ominous buzzing sounded outside and the silhouette of a black dancing form appeared in the glaring light of the doorway. A quick circuit of the room, causing us all to duck, seemed to reassure our visitor that we were comparatively harmless, or if not, that it was certainly a match for us all, so it settled on the bark wall of the house. We could then see that it was slightly bigger than the average queen bumble bee and had an entirely black body except for a ring of bright red around the pointed end of its abdomen. This sinister ring left little doubt as to the effectiveness of the barb that assuredly lay within.

Again the beast paused to survey us and waggled its abdomen as if to make sure we understood the status quo. Then strode purposefully fifteen centimetres across the wall to a little pile of glistening mud that adhered to the bark. This preoccupied the creature which pranced around, chewing and working at the mud with its forelimbs. Soon it was obvious that the pile was growing. Our new visitor was a Potter wasp, one species out of a large family of wasps which, with monumental architectural prowess, builds sepulchres in which their eggs are laid.

Having palpated the mud which it was sticking to the wall of our house, the wasp flew off again. A quick scrabble followed as we grabbed cameras, tripods and flash guns; by the time the visitor reappeared the room had been transformed into a photographic artillery base. These modifications seemed to displease the wasp and it made an inspection of each of our cameras, causing us to withdraw in turn lest it took serious offence. Apparently satisfied, it returned to the wall and with a few derisive whips of its abdomen in our direction, stalked back to its building site. Visit by visit the new home grew and soon a construction shaped like half an egg cup stuck our a clear two centimetres from the surface of the bark wall. When the egg cup was completed it formed a hemisphere in which only a tiny opening to the outside world remained.

There are many sorts of Potter wasp and the way in which they use their buildings to rear their young varies from species to species. In Britain there is a genus (*Eumones*) which makes beautiful vaselike cells, sometimes seen attached to the stems of, for instance, heather. Within each of the cells made by *Eumones* there hangs a single egg suspended from the roof of the cell by a thin thread. Below the egg are placed several small caterpillars. These caterpillars will have previously been stung and paralysed, although not killed, by the parent wasp. The young larval wasp devours the first and topmost caterpillar as it hangs from the end of the thread that suspended its egg. The larva thereafter breaks free from the shell and descends to eat the rest of its living meal. Perhaps suspending the egg above these cached caterpillars obviates the danger that the occasional twitches of the immobilized caterpillars will damage the fragile wasp egg. Not all species of wasp use their sting to paralyse the victims as they gather food for their impending brood; some may actually poison the victim fatally but have antiseptic qualities in their sting which prevent the prey from decomposing before the young larval wasp hatches and eats it.

It seemed, however, that the arrival of the Potter wasp had not gone unnoticed by eyes other than ours. As she was putting the final touches to

the new nursery for her offspring a short rounded snout emerged, milli-
metre by millimetre, from the chinks in the banana bark wall. This snout
wiggled cautiously towards her, in and out between the crevices of the
bark, appearing, disappearing, then appearing once more, each time
slightly nearer the industrious wasp. Finally, when no more cover remained, the snout edged forward to be followed by a pair of eyes and the
whole head of a house gecko, presumably a more long-standing member
of our household menagerie than the wasp. Moving in slow motion the
gecko edged its way towards the intruder. A confrontation seemed
inevitable. Only a few finishing touches were necessary to the wasp's
nursery; as she flew back out of the door the gecko emerged from his
camouflaged crack and moved the remaining distance to conceal himself
in ambush immediately adjacent to the nursery.

Minutes ticked by and we began to wonder whether the gecko had
been thwarted and we had missed the battle, our cameras still poised. At
last the heavy drone came into earshot and the Potter wasp swung
through the door of the house into the room. Throwing caution to the
winds she neglected her customary circuits of the room and flew straight
to the new nursery, where she immediately started fashioning the final sections of the porch above the entrance to the mud chamber. Only a tiny
porthole now remained through which to lay her eggs, having first inserted
the paralysed grub as a birthday feast for her children.

The tension mounted. If the gecko did not strike soon the wasp would
be gone again. Perhaps her crimson abdomen was as much a deterrent to
him as it was to us. A sudden rustle, rasping claws and crackling wings:
the wasp flew up in the air and, humming fiendishly, dived back to where
the gecko's lurking form had been but a second before. The gecko had
fumbled its attack and scuttled back into the sanctuary of the bark, not to
reappear again until after the wasp had laid her clutch and finally sealed
the chamber.

The drama past, we dismantled our various cameras and tripods,
returning the flash guns to their carefully packed boxes of silica gel just in
time to hear the slurping of water on the logs which heralded the arrival of
the fisherman and his family for tea. This was now becoming a daily ritual.
The fisherman's initial shyness was receding quickly and, seeing that we
had been active, he entered the house to find out what had caused the
excitement. We led him to the little ceramic masterpiece on the wall. To
my horror he drew his parang to smash it. Managing to restrain him, I
asked the Malay name of the creature that had built this architectural
marvel. Totally unimpressed and oblivious of my enthusiasm he answered
in a very offhand fashion that it was made by a 'burong'. We had previously worked out, and confirmed by recourse to the dictionary, that

Our home at Kampong Menunggol

Proboscis monkey picking mangrove leaves

Fruit bats hanging in the shade of a banana leaf

Flowering tree trunks: the phenomenon of cauliflory
or flowering on the trunk

A fragile fungus of the forest floor

A mangrove denuded of leaves stands above a carpet of Nipa palm fronds

burong meant birds. Now we were starting to be exposed to the subtleties of zoological Malay which were soon to frustrate us in many of our efforts. It seemed that the fisherman used the word burong to describe a bird, and anything else with wings as well, and thus a strange and non-biological classification emerges whereby butterflies, birds and our Potter wasp fall under the same umbrella. However, we became even more confused when we later discovered that wasps were also called penjenjak. I tried to explain that to me the wasp's chamber was beautiful, but our vocabulary was still built by analogies and I had to abandon this when he mistook me to say that the wasp's nest was like his wife's face!

The fisherman had brought three large green fruits with him for tea, each the size of a very big football. We thought he told us that they were called 'grappa', as he pointed to the trees outside, but time has told that the name is kelapa. The trees were coconut palms, but if the fruits were coconuts, they bore no resemblance to the coconuts I was familiar with, nor for that matter to the coconuts that Andrew, Mark and I had eaten several days earlier to the great merriment of everybody around. With a couple of swift slashes of his parang the fisherman made a neat incision in a nut: inside the husk was a sparkling milky fluid. This 'milk' tasted delicious – almost fizzy – and was quite unlike that which I had drained from coconuts bought in greengrocers' shops at home. The juice finished, the fisherman cut a thin sliver of strong green 'skin' from the nut in order to make a sort of spatula which was wiped around the inside of the nut to scrape off the soft, tender coconut 'meat'. This was almost the consistency of a thick skin of cream rather than the leathery, oil-drenched stuff to which we were more accustomed. Slowly it dawned on us why it had caused so much wholehearted merriment when we had eaten the withered coconuts a few mornings before. They were the seeds that were being kept for planting to raise new coconut palms in future years and were, in local opinion, far too old and overripe to be worth eating at all. I wondered how many of the other fruits that we buy in our shops in the belief that they are delicacies are actually miserable shadows of the gastronomic delights enjoyed in their native countries. It was doubly embarrassing that we had eaten somebody's seeds! Indeed it is horrifying to think back on our brazen naïveté. To us the woodland around the kampong initially looked a wild uncultivated place. As the weeks passed we soon learnt that we were on 'farmland', albeit quite different from Constable's agricultural landscape. Those first coconuts we had taken were somebody's produce. I tremble to think of what response a British farmer might show to a directly comparable way of behaving – imagine a Malay visitor to Britain happily setting up camp in an orchard and self-assuredly plundering the apple trees. We were lucky not to have been shot!

Afternoon tea on our verandah with the fisherman and his family was now a very relaxed affair. We no longer stared forlornly across the silence between us, but laughed with each other at our inadequacies as we mishandled an engine or a fish trap, or he held a book upside down. The fisherman's wife seemed quite relaxed too, though she never spoke to us, and always sat a little apart. We knew the Malay word for wife was 'isteri' and between ourselves and in conversation with the fisherman she was always referred to as the Isteri. On the afternoon of the coconuts she was particularly forthcoming and openly smiled at our conversation as she sat methodically picking a large scab off her baby's leg with the point of a rusty nail. At one stage she moved and knocked a fish trap, provoking an unhappy squeak which, it transpired, emanated from a nest of baby rats nestled therein. We carefully rearranged the traps and while we never actually saw their mother, the rat pups continued to grow and became our pets as the weeks passed.

At night we cooked on a primus stove. For the most part we ate rice, complemented by powdered curry scavenged from the expired-date army rations. Afterwards we drank tea or coffee – they seemed to taste the same – laced on special occasions with a measured nip of Scotch. These tropical evenings were almost blissful, but I must confess they were equally close to hell, for we were plagued by mosquitoes in numbers which those who have not spent nights in the swamps could not conceive. The Malay name for mosquitoes is 'nyamok', and even the word sounds itchy. They coated our sweating brows and, scorched by the steam, they fell by their hundreds into our boiling rice. We staged competitions to see who could scratch the least or kill the most. The itching came in frantic waves, although goodness knows why it should, and by ten o'clock at night the waves reached such tempestuous proportions that we were verging on hysteria. And yet as the days passed we seemed to acquire some sort of immunity to these wretched creatures and before long they were no more than tiresome.

By day we became progressively more adept at finding and watching Proboscis monkeys. We began to accumulate systematic notes on their lifestyle: on finding a troop, we would try to count the number of individuals present, noting their sex and approximate age. Even at a distance this was not too difficult as they were such large beasts that the adults were fairly easy to distinguish from the juveniles and infants. We recorded where the monkeys were in the trees, what they were eating, how quickly they were eating, and any social interactions between individuals which we saw. Nevertheless, more often than not we were still thwarted by some wary individual taking exception to our boat. We were always at the mercy of currents, drifting too close or too far away, or directly behind some unhelpful tree which obscured our view. These difficulties meant that our periods of observation, while more frequent, were rarely protracted.

At one point we decided that salvation lay in the construction of some sort of hide. However, the monkeys were fairly unpredictable in their movements and so our attempts at permanent hides in promising trees proved fruitless. After I had spent one particularly long day wedged in the elbow of a mangrove tree without the slightest sight or sound of a monkey, I decided that some sort of mobile hide was necessary. We decided to modify our leaking launch for this purpose. First, we cut a series of thick palm poles and tied them into a scaffolding framework which was wedged into the boat. The palm fronds sliced our skin, and sweat and salty swamp water bit into the cuts, so that lashing together the pole framework soon became a test of endurance. We worked throughout the morning, ever more infatuated with the belief that the fruits of our labours would enable us to make prolonged observations of the monkeys.

The scaffolding erected, we crossed the swamp to cut fronds of palm leaves to strap to the frame, thus turning the boat into something that we hoped would closely resemble a floating clump of Nipa palm. The choice of this design was not without foundation; due to the erosive tides quite large islets of Nipa palm do occasionally break off and float downriver, their roots still embedded in the mud. At last the boat, now well filled with water from its unrelenting leaks, was completely covered in artistically arranged waving fronds, jutting from the boat at what we hoped were authentic angles. A quick 'road test' confirmed that the structure was sound, although it had dramatically altered the aeronautical properties of the craft. We bailed out and with high hopes chugged off in search of monkeys.

It was high tide before we located a troop of monkeys on the hide's maiden voyage. They were spread among the crowns of adjacent mangrove trees in a gratifyingly visible situation. In the distance we could see that several individuals were involved in a slight squabble and our hopes of watching the outcome from our floating sanctuary were soaring. Normally the monkeys allowed our boat to drift downstream towards them until it was within a hundred or so metres before taking flight. The hide certainly made a significant difference to their response: we must have been something like 250 metres away when every monkey in the troop stopped whatever it was doing and stared with unabashed astonishment at our approaching craft; then with wild shrieks and honkings they threw themselves from the tops of the mangrove trees into the Nipa palm below to thunder off as if convinced that we represented some demon on a recruiting drive from Hades.

Slowly and sadly we returned to Menunggol and stripped all the palm leaves from our boat, uncut the twine that had so deeply incised our fingers and removed the Nipa palm scaffolding. Our daily wanderings in pursuit of monkeys continued but in an uncamouflaged craft, although we did eventually find a method for making fairly prolonged observations. This required the tide to be approaching its lower limits, whereupon, if visibility permitted, we would run the boat aground on the mud about seventy metres from the monkeys and were then able to make extended observations on their foraging behaviour.

As the days passed we quickly began to feel at home in the swamp and became more adventurous, travelling further afield in search of our beasts. On one excursion we journeyed far into Limbang, the limb of Sarawak that bisects Brunei. That afternoon was a particularly hot one, following two unusually cool and humid days, and having motored along for some hours with only occasional glimpses of bands of Proboscis monkeys in the distance, we decided to ground our boat and to explore a little on the mud. Finding a tiny weathered cove with convenient fallen trees to which we could tie the boat, we clambered ashore. The mangrove here was quite different from that which grew around us at Kampong Menunggol; there, the roots cascaded down to form a series of arches and alcoves, like a waterfall solidified in mid air. The roots of the trees we were now among, a genus known as *Rhizophora*, formed solid wafers of wood resembling ornamental trays of turned metal balanced on their sides and buttressing the tree in the soft mud. The shapes so formed were beautiful, and in search of ever more ornate designs we slowly climbed from root to root deeper into the forest.

Everywhere we walked would be submerged at high tide and the roots were covered with slime which made handholds a necessity. But each surface was armed with strategically placed barnacles that impaled our hands and feet. Our progress had been so painful that, on reaching the shore diagonally across the islet from the cove where our boat was moored, we were reluctant to retrace our steps. We determined instead to walk around the head of the peninsula, via the mud beach, but even a few metres of this was sufficient to make us reject that idea too. Smooth though this route might look, there were enough mangrove pneumatophores fiendishly arranged below the mud surface that wherever one stepped at least one foot became almost irretrievably skewered. We paused to think, and looked closely at the barnacle-studded roots.

These barnacles are as fascinating as they are painful. For a long time their hard shells and immobile existence made people think that they were molluscs, like limpets. However, in 1829, J.V.Thompson studied their breeding behaviour and found that they produce larvae which, like those of many marine creatures, spend their infancy in the plankton – the community of small creatures that drifts in the surface waters of the sea. Close inspection of these barnacle larvae revealed that they were very like the so-called nauplius larvae of crabs (and other *Crustacea*) and, correspondingly, quite different from any known molluscan larvae. Biologists had been duped by the sedentary life of parent barnacles; their true affinities were with crabs and lobsters. Today barnacles as a group are known as *Cirripedes* – they have six pairs of filamentous appendages called cirri (think of filamentous cirrus clouds) which they dangle in the current to ensnare passing food particles. With the benefit of hindsight, anatomists can now see that five pairs of these cirri correspond with the five pairs of walking legs of a crab.

Every mangrove pneumatophore in the swamp was coated with dozens of these barnacles, so there must have been hundreds of them in every square metre, and at high tide each one would be busily sifting through the water for edible debris. On one estimate there may be two thousand milllion barnacles per mile of coastline! Barnacles have an ingenious method of colonizing new pneumatophores, or rocks. When a larva has been through half a dozen moults in the plankton it becomes transformed into a cigar-shaped creature, called a cypris, which settles on a root or rock. If it detects a barnacle already in residence it moves on till it finds an unoccupied gap to colonize. At this stage the cypris is walking on its head, trundling along on what would have been its antennae had it grown into a more conventional crustacean! When it finally settles down and metamorphoses into an adult it does so by reorganizing its body while standing on its head. The biology of these invertebrate creatures which we deign to call 'simple' animals reduces the most elaborate fairy tale to urbanity by comparison.

At this point we were distracted from the problem of retrieving our boat and avoiding barnacles by the sight of some large tracks in the mud. They were reptilian and we thought perhaps they belonged to a small crocodile. So we squelched along in the direction that the tracks took us, going still further from our boat. The tracks led us back into the mangrove and a further twenty minutes of clambering about on all fours among cascading roots found us at a murky stream. Eyes straining, we could just make out a scurrying form and then came the inevitable plop as a large Monitor lizard, well over a metre long, dived into the water and hastily made his way out into the main estuary. The excitement of seeing this enormous lizard compensated for his failure to be a crocodile, but left us with the problem of picking our way back to the shore and reconsidering how to retrieve our boat.

It seemed that the most sensible solution was to wade out into the

estuary and then to swim round the promontory back to the boat. It was
decided that this should be the task of one of us, who would then bring the
boat back to pick up the remaining two. Mark volunteered for the job.
Handing me his camera, safely wrapped in his dry shorts, Mark waded
naked into the mud and had not gone far before he was sinking to the
knees with every step. When he was still only a matter of metres from the
shoreline he stopped for a much-deserved breather; he had reached a
depth of mud which only relinquished his legs with a rending gulp at each
pace. At this moment we heard an approaching engine.

Mark turned back to us, surprised, shouting, 'Sounds like there's a
boat coming'. We agreed, and Mark returned to his mission of retrieving
our craft. Two or three paces forward and correspondingly deeper in the
mud, the horrible truth suddenly hit him. He was trapped, naked and knee-
deep in mud, in full view of the approaching boat. A moment later the boat
rounded the bend. Mark gyrated helplessly in an effort to advance, retreat
or do anything, but this only resulted in his collapsing full face in the mud.
He struggled to his feet, waving his arms in an attempt to remain upright,
and then we saw the reason for his concern: the boat was a waterborne
school bus, loaded to the hilt with youthful Malay schoolgirls. It chugged
along the shoreline at a leisurely observation pace, while its cargo of
bewildered pupils gazed in disbelief at this mud-streaked naked Orang
Puteh.

As the school bus disappeared from sight Mark staggered back to us
to commiserate on his misfortune. His composure regained, he set out
once again across the mud. He had almost reached the spot at which his
first unhappy exposure had occurred and was once again thoroughly
entrenched when an ominous engine noise was heard again. Almost un-
believably this was a speed boat, containing three tropical-besuited white
men, gentlemen of some eminence from their appearance and obviously
on a tour of inspection. On sighting Mark their astonishment was obvious.
They cut the throttle of their boat and tried to drift closer, perhaps
wondering whether illusions were a symptom of cirrhosis of the liver or
some other occupational disease of the diplomatic service. As they drifted
towards Mark we could hear their distressed nasal murmurs. Mark
managed to pull himself to his full height – at least his height from the
knees upwards – and waved heartily towards them in true Brighton beach
postcard style, at the same time bellowing 'Jolly good show, eh?' At this
the throttle was speedily pulled out and the boat disappeared over the
horizon amid a cloud of white spray and doubtless carrying three new
converts to teetotalism.

This Dr Livingstone episode over, Mark swam round to collect our
boat, and Andrew and I used the opportunity for further exploration on

the beach. We found a place where the mud was criss-crossed by what looked suspiciously like miniature tank tracks. Yard after yard we followed these little trails, weaving back and forth on themselves in an apparently meaningless fashion. We mused on the possibility of a microcosmic war raging among the local elves and pixies until our pursuit reached a line of tracks so fresh that the water still seeped from their edges. Then we saw one of the culprits before it hurtled between us to the safety of the water. The leprechaun theory was no less plausible than the truth, for the tracks had been made by a fish which was, proverbially, out of water. It was a Mud Skipper, an amphibious creature whose whole bodily appearance and way of life are so extraordinarily improbable as to deserve further mention.

Mud Skippers of various species are found by the hundred thousand along the swamp muds of mangrove forests. They, like the mangrove tree itself, have had to evolve physiological and anatomical strategies to overcome the difficulties of living in this ever-changing briny habitat. Mud Skippers spend half their life in the water like 'proper' fish and the other half clambering about on flippers, like miniature seals. This schizophrenic existence raises a problem of how to breathe. Obviously the conventional fish method of respiring through gills will be inappropriate during their sorties on to dry, or even wet, land. Evolution has solved this conundrum in an extremely elegant way. The Mud Skippers' gills are enclosed in a large chamber into which they gulp water before surfacing for a terrestrial excursion. While on *terra firma* they are able to breathe through their gills, as they normally would, by carrying this little reservoir of water with them which facilitates oxygen exchange with their tissues (they also have an unusually good supply of blood vessels to the roof of the mouth to aid absorption of oxygen). They are, however, faced with many more problems related to their terrestrial wanderings. For instance, their skin has to be kept moist and this is achieved by indulging in gyrations upon the mud. So, as they sit with the sun burning down on them, Mud Skippers will periodically fling themselves into the air with a flip of the tail and roll over into the wet mud; an instant later they fling themselves the other way to dampen the other side.

The reason for their sorties on to land is to exploit a food source that would otherwise be inaccessible to them, the detritus stranded in the mud. They chew through the mangrove mud, spitting out the mineral component that is of no use to them and extracting vegetable matter. Once accustomed to the novelty of seeing fish on land, their next most spectacular behaviour is aggressive flag-waving. Each Mud Skipper has a large sail-like dorsal fin running along its back which is collapsible, rather like an ornate Japanese fan, and normally lies flush with the surface of the back.

When two Mud Skippers are about to engage in an aggressive dispute, they face each other some centimetres apart and flash their crests up and down like besotted semaphore enthusiasts. The colouration of these fishes varies from one species to the next. At a distance they mostly seem to be an uninteresting fishy brown, but on close inspection many are dotted with spots of brilliant luminous green, and these dots are concentrated on the dorsal fin.

My meditations on Mud Skipper behaviour were interrupted by Mark's arrival in the boat and we were soon speeding back to Kampong Menunggol, in time for our evening visit from the fisherman. Our nightly conversations with him were now becoming much more involved as we improved our grasp of the language, or at least a 'pidgin' version of it. The fisherman had now told us his name, Yahyah, a gesture which we took to be a significant compliment. Every night when we had just about finished our supper Yahyah would arrive, sometimes accompanied by some of his numerous smaller brothers, to sit for a couple of hours as we puzzled out new words and the names for animals we had seen or hoped to see.

Sometimes in the evenings we suffered a curious ailment. One finger, or perhaps a toe, would begin to swell and continue to do so to alarming proportion. The end result was like an infuriated chilblain, which would always subside by the next morning. Presumably it was caused by an insect bite, maybe bedbugs or perhaps an urticating plant, but Yahyah never seemed to be affected and had no explanation for us.

One evening we were able to describe a new sort of monkey to him, although he did not seem to have any name other than 'common monkey' for it. We had spotted these monkeys as we drifted home after roasting in the sunshine for over an hour as we watched a male Proboscis monkey snoring sonorously through twitching snout. We rounded the bend at a sandy spit where the mangrove saplings grew to the height of a man and seemed to form a shaded alcove which ran back into the dense stands of Nipa. Framed within this alcove, seated or standing on the ground, was a troop of brown monkeys. We were no more than ten metres from them before we spotted them, and from the look of surprise on their faces I guess that they had been as oblivious of our approach. The biggest of their number was sitting with his back to us; he swung around, still sitting, his long face momentarily expressionless and his mouth a trifle open. An instant later he half stood, shoulders hunched, staring straight at us. He coughed once, quietly, then again, more emphatically. Miraculously, the boat hit a spur of mud, grounded and remained still. We froze. Ten seconds slipped past. An infant monkey tiptoed towards an adult, another grabbed at it as it passed. The first infant forgot its caution, pinched its companion's tail and fled. A game was on. The big male slowly dropped his glance to look at the scampering youngsters, turned back to us and relaxed. He stood up and moved a couple of paces before finding another comfortable seat. He was about half a metre long, with his tail more than doubling that length. His ears were prominent and his face a warm hypertensive puce. Although heavy by comparison with his companions, he was rangily athletic in comparison with the Proboscis monkeys. These monkeys were long-tailed macaques (sometimes called Crab-eating monkeys because of their beachcombing habits), and we counted about a dozen of them. In addition to the two small infants, there were two half-grown juveniles, four adult females and two or perhaps three males beside the big male who seemed to lead the troop.

Tiring of their game of tag, the two infants strolled, tails arched, to the water's edge and stared inquisitively at us. One then bounced up on to a pineapple-shaped fruit which stood on a stiff stalk perhaps a metre off the ground. This was a Nipa palm fruit. Spiky and tough on the outside, the football-sized structure contains many grape-sized nuts (like lychees in flavour). Soon the baby monkey, perched on top of the fruit, was picking out these succulent morsels. He fed noisily and messily, casting torn shreds of the orange-coloured rind to the ground. Meanwhile the other infant was pestering two of the females, dashing from one to the other, pulling tails. One of the smaller males approached the big one, but shrank away when he moved. The whole group seemed relaxed and placid in one another's company.

A shutter clicked in one of our cameras and the big male seemed to jolt back from a daydream. He stood up again, looking around the troop. They all stood up and as a closeknit unit moved back into the palm fronds. The two babies scampered after them, clambering aboard the females' backs as they disappeared from view.

We described the whole episode to Yahyah who had a patient, if puzzled, knack of struggling with our zoological vocabulary. During another evening of conversation we had guessed at length about something called an 'ular'. Yahyah had been in a particularly jovial mood that night and between laughing with his brothers over whether or not the 'ular' could be said to be 'banyak bagus', i.e. very good, or 'tidak bagus', not very good at all, we did not actually progress very far in diagnosing whether an ular was animal, vegetable or mineral – and the dictionary was little help. However, game for anything, I asked Yahyah if he could possibly get us an ular, so that we might have an opportunity of discovering what it was and perhaps photographing it. Such was Yahyah's merriment at this suggestion that it was fairly certain that we were about to commit a *faux pas* of a similar magnitude to the coconut episode. However, there is nothing better to do with ignorance than to admit to it, and so it was with curiosity mingled with apprehension that we later peered at Yahyah through the floor slats as he splashed about, armed with a paraffin light, in the waters below our house. Soon he came in dripping with water, clasping his hands secretively behind his back. Grinning broadly he thrust the unfortunate ular under my nose. The ular turned out to be a snake, creatures for which I normally have a great affection.

On the assumption that had it been even remotely dangerous Yahyah would not have handled the ular himself with such abandon, I took it from him with profuse thanks and converted a little wooden box into a new home for it. Yahyah was beside himself with merriment at the notion of keeping an ular inside the house and was astonished that we should decline his repeated offers to chop its head off. He set off for home, presumably to tell the rest of the kampong about our latest prank.

I had brought with me to Brunei a detailed guide to the snakes of the region. Snakes, when one gets down to their finer points, are distinguished from one another by the shape, pattern and position of a variety of scales on and around the head and belly. Eye-straining details – for instance whether the edges of a given scale are rounded or pointed – can be important when distinguishing between closely related species. Working with the key we set about trying to identify our snake. It soon became apparent that, according to the key, this snake did not exist at all. By a process of elimination we made a weak guess that it was a baby python as the adults were quite common among the mangrove swamps, actually being among the supposed predators of infant Proboscis monkeys. The snake was duly christened Monty. A considerable amount of effort was expended in trying to make him feel at home, providing him with all the things which I thought a python would like.

Monty's arrival happened to coincide with a night on which I was writing home to my family, and in the letter I mentioned the difficulty of identifying him and described some of his features. Three weeks later an emergency telegram was delivered at our kampong by an army patrol boat. With trepidation I tore open the cable to read the extraordinary message from my father, who had been busying himself with guides to snake identification. 'Monty is dangerous. Get rid of at once. Father.' In the meantime I had finally identified Monty as nothing more than a harmless dog-faced water snake!

Yahyah assured me that what Monty would like to eat best of all was a Mud Skipper. It seemed to be a stroke of luck that such apparently abundant prey would suit the snake and hence make my job of feeding him easier; I set about catching a supply of Mud Skippers. But a whole morning spent fumbling about in the mud while failing to catch a single fish, and being repeatedly outsmarted by even the silliest three centimetre long infant Skipper made me less optimistic. A further afternoon's endeavour and I had devised a method. First find a rivulet crossing the mud on which two or three baby Mud Skippers are basking. Then crawl on one's stomach across the mud, arms spreadeagled to the side, so extending the line of attack. When confronted with this apparition the Mud Skippers, not surprisingly, retreat gradually up the rivulet. Then suddenly the moment comes when their minuscule Mud Skipper brains twig that further retreat will only take them from frying pan to fire and they dash headlong towards their spreadeagled foe. At this point one springs as best as circumstances permit on the fleeing Skipper. An hour or so of this intriguing pursuit enabled me to catch two, two centimetre long Mud Skippers. These I proudly took back, wriggling, to Monty. He swallowed the first Mud Skipper that I had caught in one gulp. Much heartened I put him on the bamboo floor of the house and handed him the second one. Gently, like a retriever taking a duck, he grasped hold of the tiny wriggling fish and looked at me so gratefully that I felt sure some warm relationship was about to break the poikilothermic barrier between us. Then to my horror he leant forward over the slats of the bamboo floor, holding the fish in his mouth. I screamed at Monty that I had spent three-quarters of an hour trying to catch this single wriggling morsel. He carefully put the fish down so it straddled the gap in the floor. Monty's curiosity had apparently been aroused and he watched with an academic expression as the fish plopped back into the stream from which I had caught it. That evening I let Monty go.

Mud Skippers are not unique among fish in breathing air. In fact, to be strictly accurate, they do not even breathe air, they simply carry their water with them. But another South East Asian fish, the Climbing Perch, can lay real claim to being a genuine air-breather. The Climbing Perch has a large area of folded tissue in a convoluted labyrinth above its conventional gill chamber. When it clambers from one root to another (walking, in part, on its reinforced gill covers!) it can breathe using this labyrinth organ which is richly supplied with blood vessels for oxygen exchange. A similar principle is used by a catfish which breathes by gulping air into a section of its gut which is especially endowed with blood vessels for oxygen exchange, and then expelling the used-up air at intervals at its vent.

The swamps abound with intriguing fish. Among the most beautiful are the Bat Fish. They have stubby bodies and greatly elongated fins. As they swim through the dark waters their long fins make them look like spookily aquatic bats. These fish use their unorthodox anatomy to good effect: when predators threaten them they stop swimming and drift, marvellously disguised as fallen leaves!

It was during another evening chat with Yahyah that he inquired whether we liked 'ketam'. Still mentally bruised from the ular episode we cautiously confessed only indifference to ketam and were caught out when Yahyah said he was surprised that we were not more enthusiastic about them. This immediately suggested that whatever ketam might be, it must be edible. On inquiring this proved to be the case. Ketam was indeed 'banyak bagus makan' – very good food. So the next night, after a fruitful afternoon of monkey watching, Yahyah turned up at our house after dark carrying a thick pole which, on closer inspection, turned out to be a segment of bamboo trunk about a metre in length. The bamboo is hollow and its stem is segmented. Yahyah had cut the stem once directly below the division membrane of one segment and again below the next one. This left him with a long hollow tube, open at one end but closed at the other. At the

closed end he had carved out a forked handle. The tube of bamboo was filled with paraffin and a rag had been jammed into the open end. It was lighted and made an admirable torch that would burn for over an hour. Thus equipped we set forth in search of a ketam, still without the remotest notion as to what it could be.

We walked down to the edge of the swamp, the tide lapping at our feet, and Yahyah waded out until he was knee deep in the water. We followed, creeping slowly through the water, under the overhanging mangrove leaves. Ahead of us I could see Yahyah, in the flickering light of his paraffin bamboo torch, his muscular body crouched. In his right hand he carried his parang. At intervals he would freeze, holding the torch high, his parang aloft ready to strike, much after the manner of an agitated heron poised over an elusive sprat in a rock pool. On he stalked, parang raised.

Thwack, his knife hammered on the water's surface and down to the swamp bed below. 'Ketam,' he anounced. We crowded forward into the light of his paraffin lamp as he brought to the surface a large crab, twenty centimetres or more across its carapace but neatly severed in two by the blow. Slightly worried that this slaughter might be solely for our entertainment, I tried to confirm that 'ketam bagus makan'. 'Bagus, bagus,' Yahyah answered. So on we went in search of our dinner. Half a dozen ketam later we returned to the house and Yahyah, bundling up all the crabs, retired to his home where his wife would cook them. He would return with them later so that we could share the feast.

One point that had preyed increasingly on all our thoughts: we had never been into the kampong proper, never been inside Yahyah's new house, nor seen how he really lived. We were cripplingly keen to play the game according to local rules, not to enter where we were not asked and not to break the local mores (which involved an indirect approach to everything). So we resolved to wait until Yahyah invited us before we explored further into the village and his life; the fear at the back of our minds was that the invitation might never come. A couple of hours later we were all seated around the Tilley lamp happily chewing on the bits of crab cooked in a delicious curry sauce. We made much of his wife's talents as a cook, partly in the hope that our enthusiasm might prompt him to invite us to his house.

Although Yahyah did not issue an invitation on that occasion, we were certainly settling into the kampong. We were privileged with time to stand and stare at our surroundings; the monkeys took up most of our time, but the rest was empty of telephones or taxman and we spent many an hour fruitfully pottering. One afternoon I perched on one of the logs joining our house to the shore. It was high tide, so the log floated freely, rocking me back and forth as I watched a pair of Sunbirds through my binoculars. These tiny creatures are the Old World analogue of America's hummingbirds, although they do not hover like hummers. The Sunbirds darted from blossom to blossom above me, metallic green plumage flickering in the sun. They were little bigger than a large beetle and agonizingly frail. In the same tree a pair of larger birds foraged lower down. Apart from their size and less colourful appearance, they looked like bigger versions of the Sunbirds, sharing the long curved bill. These were Spider Hunters, gleaning the trees for prey.

The palm trees behind our house were alive with interest that afternoon. Two squirrels engaged in hide-and-seek amid the dense fronds which cossetted the ripening coconuts at the very tip of the tree. I could only glimpse them as they scuttled back and forth in the foliage. They were tiny and striped. The description seemed to match up with Striped

Ground squirrels, but if that is what they were they had no fear of heights. Lower down, among the bushes, two drab warblers were building a nest. I suddenly realized to my delight that they were Tailorbirds, animals which perform a remarkable feat of homebuilding by sewing together leaves to make a snug cup in which their nest is built. They puncture the leaves with their bills, thread grasses through the holes to sew the two edges together and then tie a knot to secure them. It was breathtaking to watch them.

The good thing about fieldwork around the house, or out in the estuary, is that even when your particular subject is elusive, there is always plenty to watch or investigate. For instance, as we scanned the trees for monkeys we frequently saw strange bulbous plants growing from the branches of overhanging trees. Plants which grow on other plants are called epiphytes, and many of them get their nutrients from puddles forming in the hollows of branches. However, one type which we often saw – ant plants – had evolved a very elegant way of getting food, as they hung like upended turnips from the mangrove boughs. The body of this plant is like a turnip in colour and approximate shape. Out of its upside-down crown droops a cluster of blade-like leaves. The mystery begins when one looks inside. One firm blow with a sharp knife splits a thriving metropolis in two: the inside of the plant is a maze of passageways which teem with ants! It seems that the ends of some of the passageways are used by the ants as middens, providing a rich source of nutrients for the host plant. In turn one might guess that the ants gain free accommodation, with all household maintenance and repairs attended to by the growth of the plant.

Another interesting thing which we noticed hanging from a tree, when no monkeys were in view to distract us, was a squirrel's nest. It hung pendulously from the narrowest tip of the branch, reaching well out over the water below. Presumably the risks of an incautious slip leading to a swim are outweighed by the difficulties a predator, for example a python, would have in reaching such a precarious nest.

It was getting late in the afternoon on which we had dissected the ant plant when we rounded a bend to be faced with twenty young Proboscis monkeys sitting in the small mangrove saplings which were almost submerged at high tide. These monkeys were no more than babies and the saplings could not have supported more than their minimal weight. However, the leaves were particularly juicy and to be able to feed on them was presumably a great advantage for the infants. Adults were debarred from doing so, firstly because they would sink into the mud while trying to reach the little saplings and would then have to maintain an equally uncomfortable and exposed position while feeding. Secondly, it would probably be impossible for them even to reach the leaves because of the springiness and flexibility of the saplings.

We managed to beach the boat upstream from the Proboscis monkey babies and after a few moments they continued to browse, unconcerned by our attention. In appearance they presented a very different picture from the adults. The infants were bright red fluffy bundles with perfectly normal monkey faces, except for a slightly snub nose which was the only indication of the magnificent snouts that the males among them would sport one day. In the course of the next three-quarters of an hour fifty-five Proboscis monkeys, mostly adults, appeared in the tall mangrove trees immediately behind the feeding babies. We were stunned by this enormous gathering and the beautiful setting for, as the night drew in, the shades of the sky grew more pastel and fell on the monkeys with sensationally rich colours. As we were leaving the troop the sky was a tremendous slur of pinks, blues and lilacs through which threaded silver-grey bundles of smoky cloud, all framed by what remained of the deep blue daytime sky. Against this picture protruded the tops of the palm fronds, dark green and black knives lacerating the gentle sky. It had been a wonderful hour.

It was late by the time we reached Kampong Menunggol. We were all tired and, after a quick meal, prepared to go to sleep. At this point, and after an excess of cups of tea, I staggered out on to the verandah to obey the call of nature. However, it was high tide and as my eyes were not accustomed to the dark, I did not feel inclined to do the tightrope trick across the logs to dry land. Since the tidal waters lapped the legs of the house a foot below the floor, I decided to solve the problem there and then. I was astonished when, as a result, the water below appeared to burst into flame. Cascades of sparks erupted in a Guy Fawkes' display, shooting here and there across the water's surface. Another experiment, with the aid of a cup of water producing its own cascade of sparks, revealed that the swamp was full of phosphorescent bacteria and small shrimps equipped with luminous patches on their bodies which emitted light at any disturbance of the water. The intricate patterns we could conjure in the water by trailing a piece of string across the surface provided hours of starlit distraction in the weeks that followed.

Shining a torch into the swamp to explore the night life of the water below our home I saw what seemed at first glance to be a pitifully deformed minnow, about six centimetres long, thin and pipe-like in shape. The fish had a peculiar elongated lower jaw, protruding about a centimetre from its snout. The upper jaw was also elongated but only to about a third the extent of the lower jaw. Casting around with the beam of the torch I saw a whole school of these weird fish and so abandoned the idea that the first one had acquired its disquieting appearance through a nasty accident. In fact these were Half-beaks. Half-beaks are relatives of flying fish and share with them the feature of an enlarged lower lobe to their tail-fins, which enables them to skiff across the water's surface. I gently poked a stick at them and several immediately broke the surface as they dashed away. Nobody can really say for certain why these fish have such odd jaws, but they are known to forage near the surface. Perhaps their beaks somehow aid them in surface feeding. Whatever the case may be, they are used in Thailand as fighting fish. Wagers are placed on the outcome of contests in which two Half-beaks grapple with each other's beaks.

Any thoughts of sleep that evening had been banished by the discovery of all this nocturnal activity around the legs of our home, so Mark and I took the opportunity to try to approach the Proboscis monkeys by night, something we had been planning for several days. The monkeys were opposite the kampong; indeed one was occasionally silhouetted against the moon. We climbed carefully into the little dugout and paddled as silently as we could across the swamp. Reaching the other side, surrounded by bushes flashing like beacons as they were bedecked in fireflies, we could hear the monkeys above us. In the stillness of the night the extraordinary nature of their voices was exaggerated. They groaned and murmured uncouthly in their slumber and every so often a male uttered a nasal twang. We paddled further upstream, away from the monkeys and into the silence. Pausing beside a glowing bush we picked a handful of bright green fireflies to send to Ivan Polunin, the firefly expert in Singapore, before letting the current ease us back towards the kampong. It seemed that the monkeys had stirred in the meantime, for as we neared them a male let out a roaring grunt and there were sounds of rapid movement in the branches. Moments later all was still again, save for the occasional belch. We paddled back across the current to our six-legged house, casting insect-like shadows on the moonlit waters.

The day had been crammed with so many new experiences from the swamp that it seemed wrong to retreat from it. That night I lay ouside on the verandah, alongside Yahyah's fishing traps, and fell asleep to the crashings and honkings of the troop of Proboscis monkeys whose silhouettes I could just discern in the tops of the trees on the far bank, as the moon hung behind them.

4

Macaques and Swimming Monkeys

The largest male macaque ran forward, a short swerving feint with tail raised. His followers, about fifteen strong, shuffled behind him. Two other males were close at hand. Twenty metres away the biggest male of a smaller troop jostled sideways, assertively barging one of his companions who was barely in his way. The tide was so low that the rivulet which normally separated these two troops was no more than a trickle and the smaller troop was on the 'wrong' side of it. The males of the bigger troop charged forward again and the smaller team wheeled around and splattered their way back across the rivulet at a canter, awkwardly punctuated by glances back over their shoulders. They lifted their feet so nimbly as they fled that they barely had time to sink in the mud. On reaching 'their' side they fled straight up a mangrove tree before pausing to chatter at their intimidators who were already trotting back into the woodland opposite our home. I edged around on the verandah to get a better view, binoculars resting on top of the steps. I had named that clump of tall trees Macaque Wood. As the sun was setting the big troop would probably sleep the night there – they normally did. Maybe it was only the unusually low tide that had tempted the smaller group to venture to the north of the swampy island which I believed delineated their territory. Now they moved a couple of hundred metres to the south to sleep, as was their habit. Almost without trying we had learnt the borders to the territories of the macaques, whereas we seemed unable to recognize any such boundaries for the Proboscis monkey; perhaps they were more flexible in their tenure of land.

As the weeks passed we had become familiar with the swamp and its denizens. We had explored every stream and probed every rivulet up which the boat could be punted, and travelled many kilometres inland up each of the larger rivers. The prospect of the forthcoming helicopter flight became daily more exciting as we grew ever more confused about the geography of the swamp. The flight would afford us an opportunity to put into perspective the contorted courses of the waterways which, at boat level, rapidly obliterated any sense of distance and direction. We had seen monkeys in many different places and we needed the aerial photographs to map these in relation to each other, to get a better idea of the distances the troops were covering.

The morning of the flight dawned. We excavated our one pair each of 'town' trousers from polythene bags, pressed into the contours of a rucksac, dragged a reluctant comb through our salt-towsled locks and headed the boat for Bandar Seri Begawan. About halfway there the boat bucked violently, the engine roared then coughed into an emasculated whine and we rocked to a halt. The propeller blades had caught a water-logged Nipa root and fractured the shear-pin. This mishap recurred once every day or two and, as the first few instances had involved a very long paddle, we routinely carried a stock of spare pins. On this occasion the transplant was almost complete when the wind began to tease the palm fronds and sprint through the rivulets – a storm was brewing and we were barely underway again when the curtain of rain bore down towards us. Being stranded in a tropical rainstorm is actually more invigorating than it is unpleasant, except, that is, when you are wearing the only set of reason-able clothes you possess. In moments we were drenched and bailing the boat which threatened to sink under the continued onslaught of water from the skies and through the normal leaks. Ten minutes later the sky was clear and the sun bright. As we reached Bandar Seri Begawan, racing the boat at top speed through the hot wind, our clothes were almost dry, if markedly crumpled. In the aftermath of the rain the sky was pure blue and loops of colour circled the sun, like a heavenly Catherine wheel.

The approach to a mooring in the town is across a wide bay. We entered the bay, narrowly missed colliding with half a dozen lunatic drivers who were racing to the floating petrol station, and crossed the bay to Hell's Gate. Hell's Gate was our name for the low, narrow-spanned bridge that barred the entrance to the moorings. Two, or perhaps three small boats like ours could squeeze below it simultaneously – dozens often tried to do so. Much of the life around Bandar Seri Begawan is waterborne and most of this traffic channels towards and beneath Hell's Gate – a sort of North Circular of the swamps! The confident helmsman simply revs his engine and rushes the opening in the conviction that somebody else will get out of the way – but often they don't. More prudent, we would lurk in the swell waiting for a lull in the traffic. Today we were in a hurry, and perhaps we did not lurk for quite long enough. We were under the bridge when two other boats approached from the other side at full throttle. With team co-ordination they took us, one either side, amid a mountain of spray. We were still leaving wet footprints as we arrived at the helicopter, even more crumpled than before.

None of us had flown in a helicopter before, and as we scrambled into the machine I was surprised how small it was. When the motors started to turn it was obvious how the helicopter came to get its colloquial name, for apart from their decapitating potential, the rotating blades sounded exactly like someone repeating the word 'chopper' at high speed.

We flew in an arc across Bandar Seri Begawan. Old Brunei town swept into view – acre after acre of kampong-style houses built in the water and raised above the surface on stilt legs. This old part of Bandar Seri Begawan was named Kampong Ayer – the Water Village. Adjacent to Kampong Ayer on the mainland are the new districts of Bandar Seri Begawan, much of it built on the proceeds of Brunei's affluence that came after the discovery of oil off her coast. From the air, the new buildings such as the Mosque of Omar Saifuddin, the biggest mosque in South East Asia, and the Museum, similarly the record holder for size, all stood out, their architecture an amicable, if unexpected, marriage of old and new, east and west. But as we circled higher it was Kampong Ayer that held my attention. From the air we could see clearly that the water village was divided into little communities, clusters of waterborne homes joined by ribbons of duckboards along which miniature people scuttled. We hovered above the kampong and watched as dozens of tiny motor launches traced waspish courses through the waves. Hell's Gate was no less daunting from the air; the boats seemed to hurl themselves through the impossibly narrow gap, burrowing below the bridge in a squall of spray. Others were more sedate – the floating shops, laden with fish or groceries. The crews seemed too small to be real: they were transformed into animated models in some sophisticated cartoon replica of life in a kampong. But when we swept low over these boats and spray whipped up from the draughts of our blades, the figures sprang to life shaking their fists furiously at the pilot, who hung out of the cockpit door to screech greetings to the drenched individuals that he recognized.

Apart from the engines on the boats and the occasional corrugated galvanized iron roof, it was easy to let one's eyes drift from focus and imagine that Kampong Ayer had changed little from the descriptions of sixteenth-century explorers. At that time the ruler of Brunei was also the monarch of all western Borneo and further afield too. Nowadays Brunei is a fraction of its former size. The Sultan Omar Ali Saifuddin Washa'dul Khairi Wad-din was crowned ruler of the British protectorate in 1951, and is overlord of just over 100,000 people scattered in 5565 square kilometres. Modern Brunei exports crude oil, rubber and sago, and has prospered since the oil rigs at Seria began to suck out the devil's blood. When the first Sultan came to power in the fifteenth century neither oil nor Islam had arrived in South East Asia and his sultanate was a dependency of Java. Java was then under Hindu influence and, by way of tribute, the Sultan of Brunei paid annually one jar of areca juice to the ruler of Java. However, by 1478 the Mohammedans had overwhelmed the kingdom of Java, and so the Sultan of Brunei was converted to Islam. By the sixteenth century Brunei was being visited, and written about, by a steady trickle of European explorers. One Sultan built a wall across the mouth of the Brunei river, and from the description we guessed that it stretched across the bay just below and to the north of our monkey-watching area. The sea wall was built by sinking forty junks, each filled with stones, across the entrance to the bay and thereafter building a rampart on top of them. It seems that in 1521 Magellan saw this Hadrianic structure when he passed by. During these centuries Brunei was rich, but she began to crumble, perhaps through the attentions of European colonialists. Later, the Spanish occupied Brunei and although they relinquished their hold, it seemed that this was the end of Brunei's golden age, for by the nineteenth century pirates and slave traders had infiltrated the capital which became a colourful centre of banditry. Brunei became a British protectorate in 1881 and was administered by the Governor of Sarawak, Rajah Sir James Brooke. In 1906 the Sultan agreed to an administration under the auspices of a British resident and ever since, with a brief interruption during the Second World War when it was occupied by the Japanese, Brunei had been a British protectorate.

The pilot of our helicopter looped out over the forest on the outskirts of town. A heavily built black and white bird flapped away through the treetops and disappeared from sight. It was a hornbill, symbol of much augury among the people of Borneo's interior. Hornbills are intriguing birds (no relatives of the Guinness-is-Good-for-You Toucans of the New World) with cumbersome long bills, topped with casques. In all species except the Helmeted hornbill of Borneo the casque is filled with lightweight spongy tissue. The casque (a large embellishment on top of the beak) of the Helmeted hornbill is solid, filled with golden horny material, coated in brilliant red, and prized as a headdress. The hornbill's casque is a mystery, but the long heavy beak is used to handle the dangerous prey which supplement their fruity diet: a snake or scorpion is kneaded back and forth through the hornbill's beak and thoroughly crushed before being eaten.

Below us the hornbill burst from cover again. This time four of them scurried out of the treetops below us. I still could not tell what species they were, but the sight of several apparently adult birds together suggested a social species. The family life of all hornbills is peculiar in that the female is physically incarcerated during the breeding season. She nests inside a hollow in a tree, where she is sealed in using a cement made largely of her own faeces and sometimes supplemented by mud supplied by the male. Safely walled in from predators, the incubating female hornbill is fed through a slit out of which she also attends to nest sanitation by defecating with considerable accuracy and at high velocity. In some species the

female even moults within the safety of her prison. Unfortunately, before I
had more than glimpsed these birds they had scuttled back into the
canopy and the helicopter had sped past them. The kaleidoscope of shape
and colour on the forest roof whirled below us faster than thoughts could
keep pace. It was dizzily exciting.

The route to Kampong Menunggol followed the river that we customarily used in the boat. We photographed our study area in a series of
overlapping pictures which thereafter enabled us to draw a detailed map
of the district. The distribution of vegetation came as a revelation: the jux-
taposition of Nipa forest and mangrove trees seen from above was very
different from our impressions, peering in at the edges. The mangrove was
rather unevenly distributed, either along the water's edge or in small
clumps with large expanses of Nipa palm between. The area covered by
mangrove trees which the monkeys could utilize was far less expansive
than we had imagined and the monkeys would have to travel through relatively barren areas to reach these islands of food. Furthermore, there were
more kampongs than we had realized amid the islands, each one associated with clearings and plantations which, from our boat, were quite
hidden by the curtain of mangroves and Nipa that fringed the coastline.

Our mapping completed, we swept out further down the Brunei river
and out to sea before turning north along the coast and above the skeleton
of the deserted kampong we had passed during our first day of monkey
watching. The pilot pointed to a small island in the distance. Jutting out of
the dazzling bright sea, it looked almost black. At first I thought the colour
was an illusion caused by the blinding sunlight, but as we drew closer the
surface of the island remained unrelentingly black, even as the shapes and
forms of trees became discernible. The stark outline seemed to have been
ravaged by fire, leaving only an epitaph of charred vegetation. As the helicopter circled wide around the island I puzzled over how such a serious
fire could have raged amid lush foliage. We could not ask the pilot for an
explanation over the noise of the motor. Then, coming down in an arc, and
almost before I knew it, we were flying directly over the island. As the
charred trees flashed faster and faster below, the whole island erupted as a
cloud of milling forms became airborne. There had been no fire at all; the
trees were green and lush but thousands upon thousands of bats hung
from them, masking their greenery with a blanket of bodies.

The doors of the helicopter were open and we were tied around the
waist by 'monkey straps'. We craned out of the open doors to see better.
Further and further I strained out in an effort to see and photograph these
extraordinary creatures as they flapped and milled below. As the pilot
dropped lower and the bats rose higher we were suddenly engulfed in a
cloud of them. These fruit bats, or Flying Foxes as they are called because

of their rather fox-like faces and slow flapping flight, are quite large animals with a wing span which may measure over a metre. Every attempt I made to focus my gaze on a particular bat was distracted by the hundreds of other individuals that glided between us. A benefit that may accrue to some birds that fly in tightly knit flocks became suddenly vivid. Any predator attempting to select any one member of the flock is so confused by the profusion of other flapping bodies that it is unable to make an accurate strike. Quite apart from that, hurtling at the speed of, say, a peregrine falcon, into such a mass of airborne prey could easily result in a crippling collision for the predator. At the same instant it struck me how disastrous it might be if one of these animated doodle bugs struck the blades of the helicopter. I signalled to the pilot to fly higher for I was anxious to minimize the disturbance to the bats and was concerned for our safety. As we rose, the bats began to return to their resting places, settling on the trees like a cloud of soot.

Flying Foxes set out each evening from their rookery, in twos and threes, and fly to fruit plantations and banana crops to munch their way contentedly through the night to the great infuriation of the people whose crops they steadily obliterate. Almost every day, from my sleeping place on the verandah of our house at Kampong Menunggol, I had dreamily seen these other-wordly creatures flapping overhead at dawn or silhouetted by a full moon. I had never imagined that such a concentration of their numbers as we had just witnessed could be seen. Borneo is an island of bats – some seventy species live there. Indeed, because of their nocturnal habits and largely tropical distribution, few people realize how large a proportion of the world's mammalian species are bats; there are over 800 species of bats among just over 4000 species of mammals. That means that almost a quarter of mammalian species can fly!

As we swept up the coast, away from Bat Island, I spotted what seemed to be a discontinuity in the sea bed about a hundred metres out from the shore. Perhaps it was the edge of a shelf causing wave turbulence. I motioned to the pilot who swept low over the thin white line traced below the surface of the waves and stretching unbroken along the coast. As we raced towards it, I realized that the line was actually a band of huge opaque jellyfish. It was very hard, from the air and at an unknown height, to judge their real size, but these jellyfish certainly seemed to be the best part of a metre across. I wondered whether these were the notorious 'sea wasps', a family of jellyfish (called *Cubomedusae)* which have a highly venomous sting. Some are absolutely deadly. Apparently the sting is particularly effective when applied to skin which is already coated with mucus from fish, and for this reason fishermen are at greatest risk.

Peering down at the ocean surface, something ahead caught our attention – a form appeared and then submerged. We gestured to the pilot to get closer. Sure enough, a few minutes later a turtle appeared and swam briefly at the surface, its huge shell just centimetres below the waves, clearly visible to us as we hung out of the helicopter. The study, and conservation, of these Green turtles around the coasts of Borneo became a crusade of the late Curator of the Sarawak Museum, Tom Harrisson. Influential Malay families had the right to collect the eggs from turtles which laid at particular locations. As generations passed the question of who had which right became increasingly complex, especially with the spread of Islam among the Malays and the consequent complexity of the laws of inheritance. For these reasons Charles Vyner Brooke, the third Rajah of Sarawak, bought out all the rights to turtle egg collection in 1941 and gave them to the Sarawak Museum. First efforts at conservation or study were inevitably thwarted during the Japanese occupation of Borneo between 1941 and 1945, when the turtles were slaughtered as a ready source of meat for the occupying troops. After the war Tom Harrisson began to salvage what was left of the turtle population. Traditionally two million eggs had been harvested each year; this figure had been decided upon by more or less casual observations of the numbers of turtles crawling up the beach to lay their eggs. Harrisson had the disquieting thought that if each female clambered up the beach to lay eggs on more than one occasion, then the whole harvest would be based upon an inappropriate calculation. To test this he tagged female turtles with numbered clips which enabled him to recognize individuals from year to year. By 1956 he was able to report preliminary results which showed that at least three years elapsed before many turtles returned to lay on his study beaches, and that each female might make several trips during a season to lay eggs. The calculated egg production (and hence the permissible harvest) of the population had been hopelessly overestimated.

We hovered above the turtle for several minutes as it repeatedly surfaced and then slid below the waves, gliding like a greenish shadow through the surface waters. Then, after a final reconnaissance of our study area, we returned to base.

Aerial views of the expansive swamp lands with kampongs dotted here and there emphasized a point that had been intriguing me since arriving at Kampong Menunggol. It was astonishing that people could manage to scrape any sort of existence in a zone where acre after acre appeared able to support only the harsh, coarse Nipa palm and a handful of other plants adapted to a saline environment. Yet we had asked Yahyah many times where he had got particularly delectable titbits of food. He would wave vaguely towards the swamp in answer. Sometimes there was a comparatively straightforward source, for instance the sweet, rich-tasting fruit similar to lychees which came from the Nipa palm.

Most of the kampong's daily ration came from the swamp waters. The men were all fishermen; almost every day Yahyah and his two younger brothers, Ramli and Bacal, and sometimes two of his elder brothers, Abdullah and Ahmad, would leave the kampong in their dugout canoes, unstable crafts, narrower at the midpoint than a man's shoulders! Fish were caught with a technique unsurpassable as a union of function and grace. With ten-year-old Bacal paddling the canoe Yahyah would stand at the prow holding a large folded net in his arms. When fully extended the net, called a jahla, was shaped like a parachute. The rim of the net was weighted with lead and the biggest ones must have weighed at least twenty kilograms when dry. As the canoe drifted slowly across the swamp waters Yahyah would twist his body like a discus thrower winding up for a throw, poise on the narrow prow of his canoe and launch the net far into the air. The weights carried it spreadeagled over the water to drift down with hypnotic perfection to the surface, into which it melted with criss-cross ripples. To cast the net not only required careful co-ordination, but also immense strength.

After each cast Yahyah allowed the net to sink for several minutes before gradually pulling it in. Its fascinating contents, drawn from the surface waters of the swamp, were then emptied out into the boat. Much, of course, was inedible and hence was useless to him but nevertheless enthralling to us. He frequently caught the Sharp-nosed Puffer, for instance, a squat and dumpy little fish about ten centimetres in length, whose tiny fins each appeared to be suffering from its own independent panic at the prospect of propelling their totally unstreamlined owner along. In the face of danger the Puffer Fish responds by inflating itself into an animated balloon, making its fins seem even more ludicrously inadequate. The function of this behaviour is perhaps to intimidate a predator through the mistaken impression that the Puffer Fish is bigger than it really is. However, they are also extremely poisonous, so they have little need to be shy of predators.

When the tides permitted, Yahyah would be continually casting his net, letting it sink and pulling it back again. The prawns he caught were a supplement to his staple diet of rice, grown in the kampong further back on the mainland. Surplus shrimps were taken to Bandar Seri Begawan and sold or exchanged for other foods. Yahyah told us that this was a new feature of Malay life in the swamps and that in the recent past fish would have been the mainstay of the village.

One morning I perched on the ledge of the verandah watching Yahyah fishing. The sun scorched the day to perfection and his net was wet with drops of water from previous casts. The net glided through the sunlit air, falling in a cascade of sparks. Apparently satisfied with his haul, Yahyah paddled to the jetty. Soon he and several of his brothers, together with his wife and Ruslan, the baby, congregated on our verandah to drink the ritually awful tea. I admired his catch and, choosing three or four of his largest prawns, he handed them to me, saying in Malay, 'There you are, a present, eat them'. Surprised, I replied that I had not realized that prawns were eaten raw. Yahyah and his brothers explained with the tolerant air of experts confronted with an untutored idiot that when this special variety of prawn was freshly caught and had only just stopped wriggling they were a great delicacy raw. To cook them would be gastronomic sacrilege. Yahyah did suggest, however, that the heads were an acquired taste. Swept along on the tide of doing as Romans do, I discarded the head and, looking bravely around, crunched into the sporadically twitching prawn. Logically, one must always allow the possibility that something could be more revolting – but only just. I managed to gulp down two or three small mouthfuls as I squinted through watering eyes. Andrew and Mark looked on in horror, realizing that their turn would follow soon. Meanwhile, Yahyah and his brothers chatted about whether they should go fishing again to catch more of these delicious 'oudang' for us. It took the best part of two retching minutes for me to eat the prawn before my benefactors burst into convulsive laughter. Surely in Britain people knew that prawns should always be cooked!

The fish traps that lined the verandah were used once every month when the tide was 'right', that is, when it was highest a sufficient time before dawn to ensure that the ebb was well on its way out to sea as the sun came up. The traps were long wickerwork fences made of split bamboo canes tied together with strips of Nipa palm leaf. As preparations mounted for a suitable high tide these traps were collected from our verandah and secured to stakes driven into the mud along the shoreline, angled in such a way that they formed a 'V' with the border of the swamp. The arrowhead of the 'V' pointed seawards so that, as the tide receded, any fish that were on the landward side of the traps were swept down the funnel towards the arrowhead and were ultimately stranded on the mud as they were unable to get through the fencing. It was a couple of days' work to get the traps up in the right position; if the tide was not just right or if the sun came up a little too soon, the whole operation was in vain, reputedly because the fish could see the traps and swim around them. When all went well it was the job of Ramli, Yahyah's younger brother, to go out with a longboat stacked high with rolled up fence-traps, each ten to fifteen metres long, and to plant them along the edge of the swamps.

I wondered what fate would befall the friendly gecko which resided in the fence traps and ventured forth every night as I lay on the verandah. I relished the night time, lying between the fish traps with my head resting on a folded pair of jeans wedged between the top of the steps leading down to the water; nothing could have been more tranquil. Sometimes I read or scribbled notes by the glow of the Tilley lamp and then the gecko would creep out and sit by the lamp, its eyes moving with an eerie independence as they followed circling insects in the glow. Often I left the lamp burning long after the time when my eyes could focus on the printed page, because I felt reluctant to disrupt my little comrade's predatory vigil. The first time Yahyah moved the fish traps I felt sure the gecko had been carried to a watery death, but at night it emerged safe from the bark – although my companions refused to believe that I could recognize my particular gecko personally.

Unbeknown to us, there was another inmate of the stored fish traps. It was our habit as we went to bed at night that one person would extinguish the Tilley lamp before going under his mosquito net, having seen to it that the other two were securely tied in. On this occasion two of us were already encased in our mossie nets, talking as we finished our last cup of tea in the fading glow of the lamp. It was one of those dreamy, half-asleep moments when one looks about, investigating the grain of the bark on the walls or the shadows of the lamp, wondering how they happened to be the way they are. The peaceful instant was shattered by a throaty whisper from Mark, the only one still free from his net. 'Look at that!' he croaked, peering intently at Andrew's foot. Andrew's foot, especially out of its sock, was indeed a fairly gruesome sight, but I was surprised at the lapse in Mark's tact. In his efforts to see what was being pointed out, Andrew removed the offending foot and we scanned in vain for some alternative item of interest. 'Dash it,' said Mark. 'If you hadn't moved, it would have stayed there.' 'What?' we demanded.

While the description that followed was neither specific nor savoury, it seemed that Mark had seen a spider of such gigantic proportions that even he, a man never separated for long from his catching net, was somewhat taken aback. While we lurked beside its crevice for an hour or more this spider, who came to be known as Fred, failed to materialize again. The next night, as bedtime approached, we lurked in the hope that Fred would reappear. Our efforts were rewarded for, as we peered hopefully at a sizeable crack in the slatted floor, a couple of hairy legs gradually appeared. These legs grew longer and longer and with each additional centimetre Mark's expletives became more profound. Slowly the legs emerged and equally slowly Mark advanced on them, armed with an upturned biscuit tin and net, circling to approach the spider from a blind side. There was a pause – perhaps Fred sensed that he was the centre of attention – then slowly, whisker by whisker, segment by segment, the remainder of his legs and body emerged.

The magnificent Fred was a solitary hunting spider, pursuing and hunting his quarry rather than building webs to ensare his victims. A violent creaking and it seemed as if the floor would give way as Mark thundered over and hammered his inverted biscuit tin down on the unfortunate spider. Carefully a piece of paper was slipped under the tin to entrap Fred within. We peered cautiously through a crack in the paper; Fred had been too quick for Mark and had slipped back between the bamboo, leaving only an empty tin.

Andrew had managed to secure an extremely pleasant sleeping space near to the wall of the house. It was from this very same wall that Fred had emerged. Poor Andrew was greatly exercised in an attempt to think of reasons why he must swop his sleeping place that night. Neither of us was prepared to oblige. The next night, however, Mark's aim was better and Fred was inspected in detail.

The kampong Malays managed to wrest a good living from the superficially sterile mangrove swamps and their ingenuity was nowhere better illustrated than one day when we were travelling with Yahyah. We steered the boat down a river which we had cruised along many times before. As we were negotiating a familiar bend at a place where we had often seen Proboscis monkeys, Yahyah turned the boat and headed straight for the bank. To my surprise we did not run aground but instead ploughed on through an arcade of overhanging mangrove leaves behind which opened a tiny tributary whose existence I had never suspected. Yahyah slowly guided the boat up this narrow course, around interminable bends and shallows, through a forest of Nipa palm overhanging on either side and sometimes falling down so low that we had to crouch in the boat to avoid our heads being whipped by the overhanging fronds. Then the tiny tributary widened out. It seemed to have been artificially enlarged: spade marks and angular sides replaced the intricately etched pattern of eroded mud and root. Around us the Nipa palm was thinning and its distribution began to take on an orderly appearance, almost as if it had been cultivated. But why should anyone have chosen to cultivate a plant whose cutting fronds I had come to view with the affection appropriate to this botanical equivalent of mosquitoes? Nevertheless, the Nipa palms were unquestionably arranged in a geometric pattern that only a human hand could have fashioned.

We came to a mooring. Yahyah secured the boat and we clambered out. The mud was heavily worked and the irrigation ditches formed, which were spanned by thin planks, were threaded between the trees. We teetered in pursuit of Yahyah's agile lead, his bare feet balancing on the slippery wood from which we slipped with scuff and graze, until we found a rounded hut with bark walls and a palm leaf roof built on a patch of dry land. The middle-aged man within obviously knew Yahyah who soon explained with a nod and a wink that we were three lunatics who had come to watch monkeys and would be interested to see him at work – not that any of us, except Yahyah, had the slightest idea of what it was that we had come to see. The man agreed to show us, and our restricted Malay vocabulary made it easier to sound enthusiastic about whatever it was that we were about to be shown.

Taking a truncheon-shaped instrument made of wood, the pitted surface of which testified to the striking of many a blow, our host sped off across the spindly bridges from one island to another with Yahyah close after. The three of us struggled along behind, slipping and slithering. At last we came to a halt beside a pineapple-sized Nipa palm fruit, the same delicacy that we had seen the baby macaque feast on. The fruit's surface was studded with a pattern of spiky prisms, each containing a separate fruit. These are compound fruits (rather like a scaled-up raspberry), comprising dozens of small fruits within the one big structure. Sweeping his truncheon in a large back-swing and with his bare toes digging into the mud for purchase, our guide started assaulting what we had assumed to be his most prized produce. The buffetted fruit swayed unhappily on its half metre long stalk. Soon it was battered and mutilated and he stood back to view his handiwork with some satisfaction. After ten minutes the man drew his sharp parang from its scabbard and sliced off the pummelled mess just at the top of its stalk. Next he fetched a bamboo casque, a length of hollow bamboo forming a long tube that was blocked at one end and

open at the other. The tube had been charred to preserve it and was wedged at an angle immediately below the sliced top of the severed stalk, so that as sap oozed from the cut it dribbled down into the casque and collected as a pool of sticky white fluid. Our host now led us to several more islands where similar casques had been in position under lacerated fruit stems for several days. Finding at one that the trickle of sap had come to a halt, he set about bludgeoning the top of the stalk with punishing blows of his truncheon. The beating over, a new cut was made to remove the top few inches of the stalk so that the sap flowed again, pumped up as part of the plant's attempt to repair the bruised tissue.

Further on and several beaten stalks later, the man began collecting casques that were already full. We took these back to the little hut where he explained that their contents would be poured into the cauldron made of mud and bark which was bubbling ferociously in the centre of the room. The base of this cylindrical cauldron was made of dry mud, which had been baked hard, and a fire was lit beneath it. Inside the hollow a hard bark barrel made the whole structure watertight. The whitish sap from the bamboo casques was poured in and heated from the fire below. For two days this brew would be boiled and gradually transformed into a reddish syrup which is finally collected in small flat pans where it cools and crystallizes. The resulting crystalline solid is called 'gula nipah', the sugar of the Nipa. Sometimes it is called 'gula melaka' after the locality in which it is especially common on the Malay peninsula (Malacca). Gula melaka, a product of quite extraordinary ingenuity, is sweet and rich. We watched, entranced, as this farmer tended his seething cauldron. How strange to reflect that in bygone days the Portuguese had fought wars to secure rights to gula melaka and various spices.

In fact Malacca first came to prominence when Indian Moslem traders (from Gujarat, on the east coast of India) made it one of their bases in the thirteenth century. It became a thriving centre of commerce. For the previous millennium Indian culture, in the form of Buddhism and Brahminism, had exerted an enormous impact on much of South East Asia, but in the fifteenth century European eyes, particularly those of the Portuguese, turned towards this centre of the spice trade. Perhaps they were motivated partly by a desire for spices and partly by the possibility that some of the honour lost by so many European kingdoms during the Crusades could be regained by another onslaught on Islam. So, in the time of Marco Polo, the Portuguese set out on what almost constituted another Crusade. They captured Malacca and, by the end of the sixteenth century, controlled an empire in the South Pacific. The wars and brutality associated with this empire and, to a lesser extent, with the conquests of later invaders such as the Dutch and English, seem ludicrous considering that the trophies were no more than spices and sugars. Nevertheless, the lust for commerce and imperial expansion which drew Europeans to the East Indies has left the twentieth century with an inheritance of imbalance between the influence of East and West in South East Asia.

Gula melaka is often served with sago, a less tasty but equally extraordinary example of a food source. Sago is made from the pith of a tree. This particular type of palm tree *(Metroxylon)* is a rather short stumpy species seldom reaching more than ten metres in height. It does not reproduce until it is fifteen years old, whereupon it produces a massive compound inflorescence of over ten metres. As a preparation for flowering the pith running through the centre stem of the palm becomes completely engorged with rich starch. As the fruit ripens this starch is moved completely up into the fruiting body, leaving the stem an empty shell. Once the fruits have ripened, the stem dies. People dependent on the cultivation or cropping of sago palms wait until the flower spike just begins to emerge, then they cut the tree down and, splitting the pith into sections, grate it into a fine powder. The powder is kneaded with water over strainers through which the starch passes, leaving behind a residue of inedible woody fibres. A couple more washings and the sago is ready for local cooks to make into cakes and pastries. Any sago which is to be exported is made into a further paste with water and then rubbed through sieves, the end product being the little dried pellets with which we are familiar – the 'frogs' spawn' of school dinners.

While we marvelled at the ingenuity of these people, coaxing a livelihood from what at first sight seems a barren environment, we could not fail to be struck by the large proportion of their time that is spent doing nothing. Hours ticked by as men sat on tree stumps, watching the tide come and go until it was of a suitable depth for fishing; mornings slid past while chewing lazily on mildly stupefying betelnut in preparation for mending fish traps; substantial portions of the day were idled away under the blistering sun. Indeed inactivity, adapted to the tropical heat, is so typical of kampong culture that it provides an amusing contrast to the styles of thinking fashioned by the temperate climate of Europe. The British Forestry Officer in Brunei told me a story about one of his colleagues who, recently fledged from agricultural college, was given the job of touring certain Malay kampongs in Sarawak. His enthusiasm and knowledge had infected some of the local people and the villagers had tried out his schemes. His particular concern had been to increase the yield of the rice crop and in one village where his following was particularly strong he managed to double the annual productivity of the paddy fields. Delighted by this success the district officer returned to his head office to report. The results seemed so exemplary that several VIPs went back the next year to inspect the same kampong. Arriving there these Europeans were horrified to see everybody sitting around with not the slightest sign of any agricultural endeavour under way. The fields were not planted nor did they show any sign that they would be; the men chewed betelnut, the women footled with fish traps and the water buffalo wallowed. The forestry official, writhing in embarrassment, demanded an explanation. The answer was simple and significant. 'You taught us last year how to grow twice as much rice in one year, so now we do not have to work for one year out of two.'

We struggled to master as much as we could of kampong life, but we were never able to perfect – or anything like it – Yahyah's fishing technique with his jahla casting nets. Our attempts to emulate him did no more than provide harmless entertainment for the professionals. However, early one morning we did have one near-success with fishing. The kampong cockerels had barely cleared their throats when we were awoken by Andrew shouting something about catfish. In spite of our mutterings that his responsibility lay more with our morning Complan than with the finer points of ichthyology, Andrew demanded that we inspect his discovery. Through the bamboo slats of the floor we could see a large catfish just below the water's surface. Thought of our dwindling rations shook the sleep from our heads and we began to lure the catfish from under the floor of the house to an exposed position by the steps with the aid of military biscuits under the label of 'Biscuits – Sweet'. There, as it was high tide, the catfish was within easy range of a swift blow from a parang. Apparently the catfish found the 'Biscuits – Sweet' unappetizing, for it was not prepared to risk much to reach the morsels we threw to lure it. However, a sortie into our supplies unearthed packets austerely labelled 'Biscuits – Plain'. Clearly the catfish greatly preferred some flavoursome nuance of these biscuits, for it rose to take them with gay abandon.

Mark, delighted by the chance to prove to Yahyah that we were not totally inadequate as food providers, changed his tactics and manufactured a fishing hook on which he impaled a lump of 'Biscuits – Plain'. This lure attracted considerable attention and, eventually, a bite. Mark, delirious with pride, landed a catfish that must have been a good fifty centimetres from head to tail. We immersed the front of this unfortunate fish in a water-filled bucket from which its tail protruded, flapping energetically. Drenched in a seemingly endless fountain of slime and trying to persuade the fish to keep its head in the water, we set off in great spirits in search of Yahyah, to show him our prize.

It was the first time we had ventured into the heart of the kampong and to Yahyah's house, for the long-awaited invitation had never come. However, the fish had forced our hand and seemed to merit a departure from routine decorum. Arriving at Yahyah's house we shouted gaily beneath his window: Yahyah's head poked sleepily out from between the folds of a half-finished fishing net which spanned the window. Not a little astonished, he viewed us clasping our upended trophy. He came out to the top of the steps to his house, but we sensed he did not share our delight. 'Ikan tidak bagus, ikan tidak bagus, bau.' Well, we knew 'ikan tidak bagus' meant that the fish was no good, but we were mystified by the word 'bau', although it presumably qualified the no-goodness. Yahyah, now perforce an expert at lexical miming, pointed at the fish, then held his nose and swooned dramatically across his verandah. 'Bau', we realized, meant smelly. Yahyah stood at the window of his house and watched three disgruntled would-be fishermen stumble barefoot down the hill, across prickles which seemed much sharper than they had done five minutes earlier. We returned a much-irritated catfish to his home waters, and presented him with a whole packet of 'Biscuits – Plain' by way of compensation.

To live in the swamplands required other skills besides finding food, for instance the construction of homes suitable for ever-changing tides. We had an opportunity of watching this in progress during our stay in Kampong Menunggol. We had been away for several days with Yahyah and his family, on a visit to Limbang, and on our return we found that our house no longer stood alone in the waters of the swamp. Adjacent to it, and separated by a gap of only three metres, was a new house being constructed by Abdullah. He had only just finished the framework when we returned. In the course of the next two days we were able to watch him complete the whole of the remainder of his new house.

The preliminary stages of the house could be built only when the tide was at its lowest ebb because it was then that the mud was completely exposed and the main struts could be sunk into position. Furthermore, the principal uprights had to be high enough not only to accommodate the height of the house, but also the further two metres or so through which the tide fluctuated daily. There were six such struts made of iron wood. (I never understood how the villagers managed to work with this apparently indestructible material.) Once positioned in the mud the six uprights were fastened together with transverse poles which formed the perimeter of the oblong floor and which were strapped with time to the main uprights. Next came the bamboo floor. Lengths of split bamboo were cut to the appropriate shape and individually tied down across the floor. This, when completed, was used as a surface for work during the remaining construction of the house.

So far all this work had been undertaken by Abdullah alone, but once the floor was finished other members of his family were recruited. Dozens of fronds were stripped from Nipa palm trees, each one having a backbone from which long sword-like leaves hung as ribs on either side. Abdullah's wife, sitting cross-legged with a jungle or 'ulu' cigarette hanging loosely from her lips, deftly used her parang to strip these leaves from the central backbone and gradually accumulated heaps of stripped leaves around her. She sorted the leaves into piles, keeping the largest and discarding the shorter ones that grew near the tip. Great rods of bamboo were then cut to span the length of the roof and the long leaves cut from the Nipa palm fronds were wound around them, folded along the whole length of each bamboo pole to produce a giant comb-like structure. This was then laid flat on the floor while Abdullah's wife began to lace more leaves between the teeth of the 'comb'. More and more long Nipa palm leaves were woven to create a latticework fence. Each completed unit was fairly strong and was then heaved up on to the roof and manoeuvred into position. Successive units were staggered down the width of the roof until, at the end of two days' work, it was completely covered and the fresh green house was finished. Instead of having walls of bark, like our home, the new house was enclosed only by hand rails around it. As Yahyah sat idly watching Abdullah heaving a monstrously heavy log into place, he explained that he had designed it for storage and not for domestic habitation. When we returned home the next evening the new house was filled with stacks of fishing traps and attendant paraphernalia and was already taking on the muddy hue that adorned everything in the swamp.

Abdullah built his storehouse during a period when the Proboscis monkeys often frequented the bank opposite the kampong. Perhaps they, too, were attracted by the novelty in the landscape, and we were able to watch both the monkeys and progress on the house simultaneously. We were also able to keep a weather eye on the monkeys when we were busy in the kampong, writing notes or tinkering with the infernal petrol valve. But many of these fleeting glimpses of Proboscis monkeys had to be discounted from our notes when we came to trying to assess even simple things like how big a troop of monkeys was. The first problem that beset us was that the number of monkeys we counted appeared to be related to the length of time we watched; in general we saw more monkeys in a troop the longer we were able to watch it. Of course this was because a fair proportion of each troop was normally hidden from view among the foliage. Sometimes there were exceptions to this, however, as for example when the number of monkeys in view would decrease as we watched and then stabilize at a new level, which emphasizes how easily we could have been deceived into recording an artifically low troop size had we arrived on the scene a few minutes later. Sometimes the number of monkeys changed because some animals really moved away; but sometimes they simply moved out of sight. We were forced to conclude that the troops were actually very fluid in composition and variable in size.

Sometimes we saw what we were almost certain was the same individual in the same place on two days, but in different sized troops on each occasion. This raised the question of whether the foraging groups were necessarily the total social unit. If not, was it more sensible to think of larger troops fragmenting into foraging parties, or of small troops occasionally coalescing for other social functions? In an effort to develop a valid description of Proboscis monkey groups we adopted a stringent criterion in our analysis of group size, including only groups that we had watched for half an hour or longer. During our observations we repeatedly counted all the monkeys in sight, noted where they appeared and disappeared, and tried to estimate the minimum number that must be present. Occasionally our task of making accurate counts was made easier, as for example when the whole troop might cross between two large trees and we could count them as they leapt the gap.

When all such observations are totted up they amount to only a fraction of the total number of times we saw monkeys and give a sample of only forty-three satisfactory observations. Of these, the average number of monkeys in a troop was thirteen to fourteen, which includes adults and juveniles, but may exclude some infants still clinging to their mother and hidden from our view. However, this figure of almost fourteen monkeys in the average troop creates the wrong impression of what we actually saw: in most cases we counted fewer than fourteen monkeys and the average is boosted by the inclusion of a small number of occasions when we watched really large troops. The troop size we saw most commonly was six to ten monkeys and the next most common category was one to five, and these two categories together comprised well over half our observations. This really does raise doubts about the stability of Proboscis monkey troops, since many of these observations were made along the same stretch of river and very probably involved the same individuals. If troop sizes within our small study area varied between such wide limits (from a handful of monkeys to five dozen or more) then it seems likely that they are unstable associations which merge and split.

One day there was a particularly good example of the apparent number of monkeys in the troop being biased by problems of visibility. We found the monkeys halfway between our house and the bay at 9 am and they were scattered lethargically among the mangrove tops. The mangrove crowns were peculiarly defoliated on some of these trees and this made it easier to count the monkeys. Even so, there were some reddish forms amid leafy branches which we could see, but not well enough to age or sex them. We managed to set the throttle of our engine against the current, so we could hover in the estuary, keeping the monkeys in view. We counted eight animals. Five were quite clearly adult females while a further two were also female, but probably not quite full-grown. There was one other monkey we simply could not get a clear view of. During the next quarter of an hour we managed to keep our position without disturbing our subjects; many of the monkeys stayed in the trees where we had originally spotted them. Some moved from one branch to the next, others stayed still, but all seemed largely preoccupied with browsing. At 9.15 I counted again, and scored thirteen monkeys in sight. This time the count comprised a fair-sized male, five definitely adult females, another two which were probably adult females, and five more monkeys of unidentifiable ages, but which were probably well-grown juveniles. Several monkeys had appeared during this quarter of an hour in trees to the seaward of our first sighting, and several of those we had originally spotted had disappeared from view, but in this case we could not be certain how many of the same individuals were involved.

Another problem facing us was what criteria to use to decide whether monkeys feeding in different but neighbouring clumps were members of the same troop. We began by defining a foraging group as all the monkeys that we could see at any one time, but the vagaries of meanders in the rivers reduced this definition to absurdity, so we polished it to the form that a feeding group comprised all the monkeys that could be counted within a continuous group of trees and any monkeys that were in sight in the next group of mangrove trees. Thus monkeys who were in clumps of mangrove separated from each other by a third and 'empty' clump were categorized as separate feeding troops. Operationally this definition did not seem to lead to absurd compromises, and I used it in calculating the average foraging group size of just under fourteen monkeys. This problem of definitions might seem trifling to a non-biologist, but when one is exploring another species' society it is important to make descriptions explicit.

While we were counting the monkeys we also tried to get an idea of the mixture of ages and sexes that comprised each group. It was one thing to see a monkey as a flash of fur racing through the leaves – quite another to be certain of its sex and even approximate age. The sample of feeding groups for which we could confidently categorize each individual is even more paltry than the one from which we assessed the average troop size. In only nine cases, ranging between feeding groups comprising from two to twenty-five animals, were we able to get these figures. The ratio of adult males to females was 1:2·6. Considering the amount of variation in feeding group size this ratio of males to females was comparatively constant. When we watched feeding groups the males and females were for the most part distributed similarly in the trees (this is only approximately true as females could get to more slender branches than males, and males tended, I think, to sit in more prominent positions). Even when we could see only fragments of feeding groups they generally contained about three females for every one male. We also made an attempt to count the juveniles and infants, of which there were just over two-thirds as many as females (1:0·68). This would give an overall structure to the Probiscis monkey feeding groups of 1 male per 2·6 females per 1·8 youngsters. However, I fear the figure for youngsters is almost meaningless, it is so riddled with bias. Sometimes we saw quite large groups of Proboscis monkeys which included several adult females and no youngsters at all. Sometimes, after we had watched a group for a while, a whole host of infants would emerge from the Nipa and begin to eat mangrove saplings on the shore – but only if the tide were low enough to grant them access. These youngsters may have been out of sight below the troop and uncounted by us. Or they might have formed a crèche, moving together with one party of adults while their parents foraged away from them. Either, or a combination of these and other ideas might explain what we saw.

In each of the larger feeding groups we saw more than one male and several females of reproductive age. Sometimes infants were in sight too, and they seemed, at least superficially, to frolic with equal disrespect among all of the males present. How do these societies tick? Who is whose father or mate? In many species of animal there is competition for mates. Indeed the ultimate measure of biological success is the number of surviving offspring an individual leaves. One might imagine that each of these males in the Proboscis groups would be in fierce competition, especially when considering that some species of monkey live in harems where only one male commands the affections of a covey of females. Why are there so many male Proboscis monkeys in a group? If Proboscis monkeys were members of a hierarchically arranged society then, although several males were present, one of them (the most dominant) might in effect be the only breeder present. However, signs of any hierarchy were certainly not obvious. The question of why Proboscis monkeys have several males in a group whereas others do not is not an easy one to answer definitely. A clue may lie in the large size of the males: the old ones are more than twice the bulk of female. Strong-arm monkeys may be important to the troop's defence, either from predators or from neighbouring troops, though we did not see any sign of antagonism between neighbours. Rumour had it that Clouded leopards lived in the mangrove swamp, but we saw no trace of them. It is arguable that the presence of several powerful males might help safeguard a troop from such predators, but this begs the question of why troops of some species of monkey only include one adult male.

Each day as we chugged back from monkey watching and rounded the last bend to the kampong we were greeted by our house, old and brown, and Abdullah's new one, still green from the fresh materials from which it had been built. The more we learnt about kampong life, the more we enjoyed it. Still one thing frustrated us; we had never been invited to Yahyah's home. This grew out of proportion in our minds, and became an ulcer on our ambition to become as integrated as possible into the kampong community. True, every night Yahyah would come to visit us and now he regularly brought some delicacy with him. His wife would deliberately prepare a little extra food every day so that we could sample a new Malay dish. One night the gift was a few curried prawns, the next a piece of crab. We always waited for Yahyah before making the coffee after our evening meal. Then, when he arrived, we would stretch out on the floor, sipping coffee, nibbling the titbits he had brought and lazily slapping mosquitoes. It took ages to exhaust a single topic of conversation since our stumbling knowledge of Malay necessitated a circuitous route to the most simple conversational destination. We mimed, imitated and sketched pictures and I think we eventually said everything we wanted to say.

The hours we spent sitting in our house talking with Yahyah were always filled with laughter and excitement, and laced with intriguing snippets of information. We felt sure that his friendship for us was genuine, but it was marred by a sad blemish. Yahyah had the entrenched idea that, as whites, we were somehow better than he. We had waited for him to tell us his name rather than asking him and now we would wait until he invited us into the heart of the kampong. But we had to do battle with the recurrent theme that he thought we might not want to associate with him. Yahyah was familiar with the cinema and had several times seen films during his trading trips to the town. One night, with his head hung low and toes wriggling uneasily, he explained with painfully naked logic that white women must be more beautiful, or somehow better, than Malay women because the female stars of films were invariably white. Our attempts to argue were fruitless, our vocabulary simply could not cope with that one.

The day was fast approaching when we would have to spend less time with Yahyah as we started to visit different habitats in search of the other beasts which we hoped to find in Borneo. So there was some urgency when, one evening, we decided that our friendship was such that even if we were to break all the conventional rules, it would probably not be held against us for long. The very next day we would visit Yahyah's house with some offering of food. What was the offering to be? It was one thing for him to bring us deliciously cooked prawns, but another for us to dispense soggy 'Biscuits – Plain'! We finally decided to sacrifice a prized trophy; hidden deep in our supplies was a single tin of fruit cocktail. The cherished tin was opened and the three of us set forth up the hill to Yahyah's home.

A hundred metres inland and we were in the small clearing surrounding Yahyah's house where he had thrashed down the jungle undergrowth and planted small banana trees and coconuts that would, in his middle age, bear fruit. Although sited on dry land, his house was nevertheless built on stilts with a notched log ladder running up to the entrance. We climbed up to the verandah that opened directly into a small section of the house which was used exclusively as a kitchen. Yahyah's wife was working there when we reached the top step. She scurried into the back of the house from whence animated conversation was soon heard. Attack is reputed to be the best form of defence, so I shouted hello to Yahyah who appeared, looking thoroughly disconcerted. It was too late for us to retreat so we announced that we had brought him some food and handed over the opened tin of fruit cocktail. As Yahyah stood in silent amazement, gingerly clasping the offering, our limited vocabulary left us with no recourse to subtle chit-chat. We jumped straight in and explained that we wanted to eat our 'best food' with him. Yahyah obviously understood, but was clearly nonplussed. Nevertheless he got a bowl and emptied the contents of the can into it. The Isteri lurked in the background and we were left still perilously perched on the verandah outside. For a while it looked as if that was where we were going to stay! The only words in my vocabulary that could be organized into an approximately plausible explanation of why we did not want to remain on the verandah was that we were scared of it. So, with a wan smile, I announced that we were frightened of the verandah! It worked. Yahyah's eyes widened, but he invited us in.

His house, like ours, comprised only two parts with a partition between them. There was the kitchen, big enough for one person only, and the rest of the house was given over to a main room. It was more solidly built than our home, bark walls and bamboo floor having been replaced by timber, and the floor covered with two unmatching strips of spotlessly clean linoleum. There was no furniture in the room and the floor was utterly bare except for a pile of cushions in one corner; one shelf was fixed at head height to the wall, from which hung the only other possession in evidence – an amply sized black and purple brassière delicately trimmed with gold brocade.

Spoons are necessary to eat juicy canned fruit and like idiots we had forgotten to bring any. By and large the kampong Malays eat rice-based dishes and as their food is predominantly dry it is best eaten with the hand. Since arriving in the kampong we had also been following the same habit. It seemed that disaster had struck when Yahyah began to explain that he had no spoons, but after protracted and embarrassing rummaging in the kitchen, his wife unearthed a motley selection of five spoons. We began to eat the few tiny squares of fruit that a five-way split of the tin allowed. Yahyah's wife moved into the kitchen and ate separately from us. In the following weeks we ate almost every day with Yahyah, but his wife never entered the main room while we were there, except to sleep, and she never in the whole time we were in the kampong addressed a single word to us or looked us directly in the face. Yahyah obviously found fruit cocktail tolerable and so our first visit seemed to be a moderate success. Feeling much heartened we set forth again in search of Proboscis monkeys.

It was that evening that we discovered a place that became known as Mesopotamia Lagoon. We had borrowed Yahyah's canoe in which we were by then proficient, and edged it slowly round the mangrove-covered promontory of Macaque Wood. As it was high tide we decided to investigate how far we could go up the little tributary running along the side of this wood. For about one hundred metres we edged carefully through what we later realized was the neck of a lagoon. Poking a paddle into the water on either side of the boat we probed a route forward, the hull grinding across the tops of hidden pneumatophores. We crouched low in the boat, brushed by the overhanging mangroves. Then the canoe found a deeper channel and, as if entering a lost world, we found ourselves in bright daylight in a tranquil lagoon, insulated from the tidal comings and goings of the main swamp.

The restricted water movement had allowed mangrove saplings to grow further out from the shore than they could have survived in the strong estuarine currents so that we were drifting between the trees of a waterborne forest. It was a place to talk in whispers. Quietly we paddled forward. The watery noises of the main estuary were muffled and the bell-like plop of each paddle stroke sounded loudly across the water's surface. A gem-studded kingfisher darted tantalizingly ahead of us, surfaced with a glistening sprat and whirred away into the bushes.

Several times in the shallow water we snagged on the pincushion of pneumatophores that protruded from the mud, necessitating a hazardous movement within the canoe as we tried to rock back and forth to free ourselves. So preoccupied were we with the problems of navigation and the pursuit of the kingfisher, together with the breathtaking beauty of our surroundings, that we all started with shock when we heard loud crashing just ahead of us in a clump of Nipa palm that overhung the water. A flash of red told us that a Proboscis monkey had been sitting by the water's edge and had been suprised as we were at our encounter. Paddling as quietly as we could we tried to creep forwards in the direction from which the sound had come and to follow the ensuing trail of crashings. Minutes ticked breathlessly past. We crouched low in the canoe, holding on to a clump of mangrove saplings to avoid drifting into an exposed position.

Mark tugged at my sleeve. Cautiously he pointed to the top of a mangrove about seventy metres to our right. I scanned the trees but could see no monkey. Mark's withering look told me I was missing something obvious. Then I saw it – a Fish Eagle. I had been scanning so intently for monkeys that I had not spotted the imperious bird as he stared critically down at us.

Fish Eagles are not uncommon in the swamplands bordering Brunei. They are big, heavy eagles with a band of white behind their necks and descending to their shoulders. With this superbly photogenic bird staring at us from above and the possibility of discoveries to be made about the Proboscis monkeys ahead, we were trapped in the naturalist's dilemma. What were we to do? As slowly and silently as was possible our telephoto lenses crept upwards to bring the eagle into view. The click of the shutter sounded like a rifle's firing but there was no panic from the monkeys ahead. Some minutes and several photographs later the eagle, bored with watching our antics, launched himself in a leisurely fashion into the air and drifted out of sight over the swamps.

Our attention drawn back to the monkeys, we paddled on, tiptoeing the boat through the water. We had nearly reached the bottleneck entrance to the lagoon when we spotted Proboscis monkeys high in the tops of the mangrove trees overhanging the water at the narrowest part of the lagoon. Mercifully they had not seen us and, as we peered out from beneath an overhanging bough, we could watch a gathering of about twenty monkeys. One adult female was so far out on the periphery of a wavering limb that it seemed impossible she could maintain her balance much longer. Then, to our astonishment, she threw herself far out into the air across the water, arms and legs spread wide as she crashed down on to the surface in an agonizing bellyflop. Spray fountained up in all directions. She had landed about two-thirds of the way across the narrow neck of the water and now immediately began to swim in a dog-paddle to the far bank. Arriving there she swiftly climbed up the nearest mangrove trunk, her red fur glistening a deep wet maroon and hanging in unbecoming sodden streaks. She shook herself as she scaled the tree and speedily leapt off into the woodland beyond. Then another monkey followed suit and another and another until they were raining down on the water's surface. Each one landed with its arms and legs spread to their fullest extent from a height of at least fifteen metres; and then only one monkey remained. A female, she fidgeted nervously about the edge of the bough, preparing to jump, and each time changing her mind with an expression on her face that we could easily sympathize with. Then I saw the reason for her despair, for clinging grimly to her tummy was a tiny infant. The crashings of the rest of the troop were rapidly receding into the distance and the mother's plight became more distressing by the second as she shifted her weight from one leg to the next in mounting despair. Suddenly she threw herself high into the air out over the water, the baby still hanging on. As she bellyflopped on the water I winced at the thought of the air knocked from the infant's lungs. When the monkey surfaced, she was already paddling forwards with the baby's head miraculously sticking up out of the water just in front of her shoulders.

Although seldom observed, such behaviour cannot be uncommon for the Proboscis monkey. Without an ability to cross water they would be restricted to extremely small feeding areas on the shifting islets of the estuary. Indeed, Proboscis monkeys are anatomically unique among the primates in having webs between their toes. Nevertheless, although I imagined that the young Proboscis baby that had been dunked into the swamp waters beneath its mother's stomach would be neither the first nor the last to experience this, I could only marvel at its resilience.

5

Lamplight Huntsmen

During evening chats with Yahyah we struggled to describe some of the other animals that we wanted to see. At the top of our list was a rarely seen animal, completely unstudied in the wild, the tarsier. The tarsier is a primate and so belongs to the same order as Proboscis monkeys, other monkeys and apes, and, of course, man. The beast appears to be no more than a rat-sized bundle of fluff, fitted with large protruding eyes, and looks rather like the more familiar bushbaby of Africa. Its hind legs are long and it can jump great distances with agility. Just as it seems that the Proboscis monkey's nose must be an embarrassment to it, so the tarsier has a blemish – a thin naked tail – suggesting that somewhere on the evolutionary conveyor belt an operator let his concentration slip; perhaps on an as yet undiscovered continent, there is a melancholy rat making its way round the jungle with a bushy tail.

The tarsier is not only intriguing to look at, it is also of considerable scientific interest. It has many anatomical similarities to apes and man (collectively called the *Anthropoidea*); in addition to its large forward-looking eyes and a structure in its retina remarkably like the sharp focusing area of the anthropoid eye, it has a small nose and a placenta similar to that of apes. In 1918 these features led R.I. Pocock to classify the tarsier in the same category as monkeys, apes and man, and separately from other primates such as lemurs and lorises. Later, C.G. Simpson disputed this and relegated the tarsier to the more 'primitive' primates (*Prosimii*) with tree shrews, lemurs and lorises. Most recently, the late Profesor N.A. Barnicot joined the fray. He argued that similarities in the protein structure of certain molecules, such as haemoglobin, of different species could give clues to their evolutionary past. Before leaving for Borneo, I visited Barnicot and his colleagues in London at a time when their analyses of tarsier blood showed greater similarity to anthropoids than to lorises. Hence the tarsier has been promoted again to the upper drawer of primate taxonomy.

In spite of this active debate nobody had studied the tarsier in the field nor knew how rare or how common they were; we were hoping at least to find them. As we quizzed Yahyah about tarsiers, we stumbled into confusion at once. In the Malay archipelago there is another small primate, also with millpond eyes, called the Slow Loris. They are comparatively com-

mon. The Slow Loris has no tail at all, in contrast with the rat-like tail of
the tarsier, and rather than being a leaper, it moves with slothful precision
from one step to the next as it stalks purposefully after insects and fruit. In
answer to our first queries about tarsiers, Yahyah announced that they
were plentiful and that he could readily show us 'kukang'. Luckily, when
naming the Slow Loris, a far-sighted biologist had borrowed its Malay
name. To science the Slow Loris is known as *Nycticebus coucang,* so my
suspicions were aroused that Yahyah was confusing the common Slow
Loris with the beast we really wanted. It was some evenings later, after
asking among his friends, that Yahyah eventually announced that the
animal we wanted was not a 'kukang' at all, but a creature which mas-
queraded under the enchanting name of 'tampolili'. To find a tampolili
was a more difficult proposition for Yahyah who, having spent his life
around the swamp, was unfamiliar with the secondary jungle in which
tarsiers reputedly secrete themselves. However, some days later he arrived
with the news that tampolili were to be found in large numbers in Limbang. Limbang is a strip of land dividing Brunei and belonging nowadays
to the neighbouring country, Sarawak. This boundary prohibits travel
between one segment of Brunei and the other without a bevy of visas and
documents. Yahyah's wife came from Limbang as did several of the frequent visitors to our kampong so we had heard many stories about the
area. Yahyah said that he and his family were going to visit his in-laws for
a three-day trip during the coming week and if we went too, he could
guarantee to show us some tampolili. Delighted, we agreed.

The morning of our departure dawned and our preparations were
complete. At first light Yahyah set off into Bandar Seri Begawan with our
passports, supposedly to get the visas necessary for our crossing to Limbang. He returned soon, reporting that no visas were necessary after all.
This statement later turned out to be rather optimistic. After much dither-
ing as to whether we should go in the morning, the afternoon or perhaps
the following day, we eventually wobbled into Yahyah's overloaded boat
and, powered by our engine, slowly chugged off into the swamp. We soon
crossed the border that divided the uncharted maze of channels through
the swamp, but it was some hours before we were to reach the nearest
immigration post at Limbang town itself.

The journey to Limbang was filled with expectation and novelty.
Yahyah was excited at the prospect of seeing his relatives, and for us every
twist of the river brought a new landscape into view. Occasionally we were
passed by drifting rafts of logs, tied together with rattans, on their way
from logging camps to the sawmills downstream. Hardwoods from Borneo are exported in large quantities to Japan, Taiwan, Korea, Hong Kong,
Australia and several European countries including the UK. Virgin

tropical rain forest is dwindling on a world-wide scale at about ten hectares a minute (five million hectares per year) and these rafts of logs were a vivid reminder that we were travelling to an area whose beauty future generations would probably never see. There are three main blocks of tropical rain forest, the biggest being centred on the Amazon basin, the smallest on the Zaire basin, with the Indo-Malayan forests encompassing an intermediate 250 million hectares.

We had already been in the swamps for two months, during which time a gradual metamorphosis had taken place in our appearance. Shorts were old and ragged, and shoes and shirts discarded. Our skins were heavily tanned. Shoddily clad we cruised into Limbang town and found a customs point projecting from the river's edge where we clambered ashore up the dusty steps. Yahyah and his wife insisted that they had nothing to say to the official within, a decision which hindsight showed to be very prudent. We were no more than halfway across the official compound when a gnomish character slunk up to us and demanded our passports. Uncertain, but suspecting that all he wanted to do was to sell them elsewhere, we declined. Inside the customs point more troubles lay in store.

A Chinaman armed with a badge saying 'Official' pinned to his ragged shirt started muttering something about illegal immigrants and waving a stamp in the air which, when viewed upside down, read something like 'undesirable aliens', an epithet which I was anxious should not be stamped on my passport. There followed an hour of arm waving with aggrieved fists smashing on tables amid general protest, which centred initially around the fact that the official refused to believe that we were British because of our sadly ragged appearance. When we had nearly won the poor man over he asked for our destination; I answered that we were heading for a kampong named Meritam. Unfortunately he had never heard of the place and assumed I had invented it as part of an elaborate conspiracy. In the end a document of dubious legality was stapled into each of our passports and with considerable wrath we were waved out of the customs office under the threat that if we were not back within a specified time the sins of the universe would be vested on our shoulders.

Once past Limbang town the countryside began to change more rapidly. We left estuarine coastal scenery and glided up an inland tributary. With each succeeding kilometre the vegetation changed. The most notable transition was in the species of mangrove trees which shrouded the banks. This succession of species results from the decreasing salinity of the water as the river stretches inland. Around Kampong Menunggol, for instance, the coastal swamp was bordered by mangroves named *Sonneratia* and *Rhizophora*, both species with a very high salt tolerance. As we travelled further inland these gave way to *Bruguiera,* distinguishable

from its salt-tolerant cousins by its pneumatophores which form a series
of little loops as they wander beneath the mud, instead of the sharp spikes
of *Sonneratia*. The end result is that *Bruguiera* trees are encircled by
hoards of miniature humped-backed bridges, snaking their way across the
mudflats.

We had found that fireflies were common in the coastal mangroves
such as *Sonneratia*. These insects are luminous and glow in the dark, and
the ones we saw around Menunggol were particularly striking, for they
could turn their lights on and off. In fact, some genera of fireflies, for
instance *Pteroptyx*, not only flash their lights on and off but will congregate in large numbers on one bush and then, by some mysterious
mechanism and for some unfathomable reason, synchronize their flashes.
The pattern and sequence of flashes is probably useful to courting fireflies,
to ensure that they mate with a partner from the correct species.

As we travelled on through the mangrove swamps I remembered the
exciting travelogue which Mary Kingsley wrote in the nineteenth century
of her love-hate relationship with the West African swamps. In one
passage she wrote:

> You are liable to get tide-trapped away in the swamps, the water falling
> around you when you are away in some deep pool or lagoon and you
> find you cannot get back to the main river. You stop in your lagoon until
> the tide rises again; most of your attention is directed to dealing with an
> 'at home' to crocodiles, mangrove flies and the fearful stench of slime
> around you. What little time you have over you will employ in wonder-
> ing why you came to West Africa and why, after having reached this
> point of absurdity, you need have gone and painted the lily and adorned
> the rose, by being such a colossal ass as to come fooling about in mang-
> rove swamps. On one occasion a mighty Silurian, as the *Daily
> Telegraph* would call him, chose to get his front paws over the stern of
> my canoe and endeavoured to improve our acquaintance. I had to retire
> to the bows to keep the balance right, and fetch him a clip on the snout
> with a paddle.

I rather envied Mary Kingsley her encounters with the 'mighty Silurian'
for the only reptilian passers-by we saw that day were Monitor lizards,
and these only fleetingly.

At last we turned off the main river and began the final leg of the trip to
Meritam. By now the riverside scenery was transformed and we were in
true rain forest. A couple of shear-pins later, and with the engine turned off
and heaved back into the boat to avoid further snagging in the shallow
water, we paddled through an avenue of towering jungle trees overhung
by creepers and lianas. A curtain of rustling leaves deprived us of the sun,
so that overhanging boughs sprang out from the gloom only centimetres

from our faces. As we rounded each bend our eyes were peeled in the hope that a wild pig or a Banteng might be drinking from the river. The Banteng is a wild ox, standing the best part of two metres tall, with heavy horns and white-stockinged legs. If they are still numerous anywhere then it is said to be in Borneo, but sadly we saw no trace of them.

At last we could go no further and, firmly grounded in the mud, we disembarked, tied up and set forth along a small, twisting path through thick rain forest, damp leaves stroking and cutting us as we brushed past. A plant with large green leaves jutted into the path, and on one of the leaves grew what I mistook for two fungi. They were white and covered in pale filaments which cascaded all around the 'things', like the tentacles of a sea anemone. I touched one gingerly and the tentacles fell away like ash from a cigarette. This was not a fungus at all, but an insect – the nymph of a bug called *Phrommia* – which had exuded these trailing filaments, presumably as some form of protection against predators. When knocked, the filaments disintegrate, but more are soon exuded.

The forest stretched at least thirty metres above us, each tree draped with thick-stemmed lianas from which sprouted lush epiphytes with delicate fronds. All plant life struggles upwards in the jungle, in pursuit of the sun's energy. The trees carry the soil's nutrients upwards too, storing them and leaving the ground barren below. Eventually the nutrients return to the soil, as fallen boughs and leaves decay, but they are soon taken up again in an unending cycle – unending, that was, until man began to fell the trees and hence to steal their nutrient stores, leaving barren ground as a testimony to this folly.

The tropical rain forests of the Far East have a unique flora which scarcely intermingles with that of neighbouring regions. A botanist named van Steenis emphasized this in 1950 when he counted 200 genera which reached their southern limit on the Malay peninsula, while another 375 genera reached their northern limit there – a climatic battle front along which 575 genera align but do not cross. The plants thriving on the islands of the Sunda shelf and east to Bismarck together form a floristic empire known to botanists as Malesia which houses about 10 per cent of the world's flora (32,900 species). The botanist T.C. Whitmore has contrasted this with Britain's flora with only 1430 species. Although the land areas are not equivalent, the contrast does give some measure of the extraordinary richness which engulfed us as we left the boat amid trees, some of whose eccentricities involve growing up to four metres a year, or flowering only once in forty years, and struggling vines whose crowns may reach the sunlight some one hundred metres from their roots!

As we walked the most striking feature of the rain forest was the extraordinary diversity of species in a single patch of trees within the jungle. Each tree seemed to be different from its neighbour. One possible explanation for this may lie in the behaviour of insects. Each time a tree sheds its fruit there is an invasion by hordes of insects which destroy the crop. Another tree fruiting at the same time nearby would have its crop quickly laid to waste as it would be 'infected' by the army that was already in residence next door. One might speculate, rather wildly, that one reason why so many tropical tree species are widely spaced out from others of their kind is that this ensures that they are sufficiently far apart to minimize the risk of insects eating them and then moving quickly between neighbouring trees. The insects are unlikely to be able to eat the fruit of a variety of species of trees since so many have chemical defences in the form of poisons in their leaves and fruit. Each species of tree can be eaten by only one, or a few, highly specialized species of insect.

I was already looking for signs of the tarsier. There was only the tiniest chance that we would spot a greasy patch on a tree trunk where a tarsier had smeared a scent mark, and it was really a hopeless task. Tarsiers have two sets of glands, which they use for scent marking. One set around the stomach (called the epigastric gland) can be rubbed onto bark. The application of scent from the second set of glands conjures up an evocative picture, for the tarsier 'kisses' tree trunks to smear the secretion of its lip

glands on them. What messages these traces of 'lipstick' leave are un-known.

The walk was long, nerve-wracking and bedevilled by a multitude of single tree trunk bridges across which Yahyah and his by now obviously pregnant wife, baby in arms, trotted at a disconcerting speed, leaving us to struggle waveringly behind. The last of these bridges spanned at least three metres and comprised only a narrow tilted plank. By the time we reached this infernal structure Yahyah was already across and we were just in time to catch sight of his wife, her baby on one arm and heaps of bedding in the other, nimbly jumping the last few centimetres. The three of us stopped forlornly, and viewed the bridge with acute distrust. We decided the only thing to do was to rush it and hope that our momentum would carry us to the other side before disaster overtook us. I only just managed to accomplish this but my two colleagues were less fortunate and they, together with our gear, had to be retrieved from the muddy water below.

We found ourselves almost amid Kampong Meritam when we struggled up the other bank of the gully. It was quite a contrast to our familiar Kampong Menunggol. Sited in a jungle clearing, the houses rose on their stilts amid lush vegetation, coconut palms and high grasses. The noise of the jungle insects and birds around all combined to arouse in us a thrilling sense of anticipation which was to be more than fulfilled during the coming days.

Following a narrow path around the clumps of coconut palms, Yahyah made his way towards the biggest house in the village. It was built in the same style as our own home in Kampong Menunggol but was about twice the size. This was the home of Yahyah's father-in-law, whom it was soon clear was an eminent man. He was not only the village chieftain but also the spiritual leader of the community, bearing the honoured title of Haji. The word haji derives from the Arabic Darb al-Haji, meaning the Road of Pilgrimage. This road leads from such centres of Islam as Damascus and Baghdad, down to Mecca and Medina, the first and second most important centres in the Moslem world, being respectively where the prophet Mohammed was born and buried. (Incidentally, he ascended to heaven from Jerusalem.) Once in a lifetime it is necessary for devout Moslems to make a pilgrimage to one of these religious centres and thus to earn the title haji. However, it seemed unlikely that anybody from this remote kampong could ever have made such a journey. The use of the term haji in these kampongs probably arrived with Islam, when it was conveyed by Indian traders to the Malay people in the Middle Ages.

As we approached his house the Tua (kampong headman) stood inside the doorway. He had probably had no warning of our arrival, but he received us with great dignity, shaking hands with each of us in turn; after grasping each of our hands he touched his chest indicating that the spirit of friendship embodied in the handshake is taken to the heart. We followed suit with this greeting. A few awkward moments followed until Yahyah broke the smile-laden silence by announcing to the Tua, whose family peered coyly from behind him, that we spoke 'bagus Melayu'. Taking this as a cue we gabbled away, while Yahyah hovered around like a compère orchestrating his star act. In a frantic bid to break the ice we re-enacted, in exaggerated detail, the horrible saga of the bridges on the way to Kampong Meritam, while Mark, as a renowned expert in tomfoolery, threw himself dramatically to the ground in graphic illustration of the evils that had beset us. Soon everybody was dissolved into hoots of merriment and, far from feeling embarrassed by the strange guests he had introduced, Yahyah clearly felt quite proud of us! Once we entered the Tua's house the women and girls were bustled off into the back room, and we sat cross-legged on the floor of a big anteroom.

The Tua was a tranquil-faced man; old and respected as he was, he still had a superb physique. We talked for hours, plied with innumerable cups of black coffee, thick with indecent quantities of sugar. A host of his brightly clad daughters padded to and fro, their faces averted from us, as they shyly refilled our cups. The Tua was anxious to learn about the land we came from, a topic that gave Mark scope to shiver convulsively as he mimed through the rigours of the British winter. With mounting humour the Tua's eyes twinkled happily around the room from face to face. Every so often he would lean forward and shake each of us warmly by the hand announcing gravely that we spoke very good Malay, although the compliment was diluted each time by being followed by a burst of laughter.

Now and again I ventured into the realms of zoological inquiry, mentioning the tampolili, but it was difficult to raise any enthusiasm about this topic. I had asked Yahyah to explain to the Tua that the main purpose of our visit was to find this beast, but it seemed that every effort was being made to steer the conversation away from that topic. However, as the day drew on and darkness began to cloak the village, I persisted in my inquiries. Yes, they all knew of tampolili and had seen them in the district. We had certainly come to the right place, they said, but of course they had not seen them for many years. However, they had not been out at night for some time, and certainly not with the express purpose of looking for tampolili. For reasons that were only slowly unfolded these people were even more reluctant to talk about tampolili than about most other animals.

Dinner arrived in the form of huge platters of rice and a series of bowls containing various dried fish. There was some twittering in the background before a girl sidled to the Tua and handed him three twisted old spoons; finding them had probably involved ransacking the whole kampong. These the Tua hesitantly offered to us. With exaggerated disdain we refused them. Delighted, the Tua summoned the young girl and crossly thrust the spoons back at her, rebuking her by announcing that his friends did not use such things. The topic of the spoons, supplemented by occasional anecdotes about forks, kept us going for a large part of the meal.

As the meal drew to a close, I increased my efforts to bring the conversation round towards tampolili and at last Yahyah conceded that after supper it was planned to go in search of them. However, after the meal I was dismayed to see Yahyah heave himself into a corner of the room and immediately fall asleep. One soon learns that it is not Malay custom to hurry and thus the only thing to do was to wait and hope. It was about nine o'clock before Yahyah yawned, stretched himself and got up. He disappeared purposefully into the room behind the one in which we all sat and to my amazement emerged with an old single-barrel twenty bore shotgun. Apart from its antiquity, this weapon was particularly noteworthy because the barrel was seemingly tied on to the stock with pieces of string.

We set off, calling at almost every other house in the village to muster people for what seemed about to develop into a hunting party for fresh meat. Finding tampolili was clearly a peripheral aim. Eventually we discovered another man who had a gun and the party of us set off from the kampong into the jungle beyond. Yahyah and his hunter friend were in the lead and each carried a Tilley lamp. These were the only sources of light, so we straggled in a thin line through the jungle, blindly following the bobbing yellow light ahead as we slipped off bridges, slithered into ditches and grasped for spiny handholds. We had not gone far when the leader stopped and it was decided that we should split into two parties, each taking a gun. Andrew and I were to go with Ahmad, who was one of Yahyah's brothers, and the hunter whom we had acquired in the kampong; Mark and Yahyah and the others were to go in the second group. To my dismay Yahyah swapped weapons with our hunter so that my party was armed with the gun held together by string.

We walked on in our different directions. Our group marched for well over an hour, out of the kampong through patches of jungle and across clearings, many of which smelt strongly of wild pig, prompting the hunter to sniff close to the ground reading the signs that were at first mysterious to us. We came to a small rise above a piece of boggy ground and there we stopped to load the gun. Loading was a complicated procedure, because the hunter could not get the string untied in order to get the barrel off. It took him over fifteen minutes to work his way through the little knots before he was faced with the new and equally serious problem of how to get the cartridge, which was too big, to fit into the bore of the gun. Undaunted he unsheathed his parang and, bit by bit, whittled away the cardboard case of the cartridge until it was pared down to a smaller diameter. I watched horrified from a safe distance. At last the cartridge was thin enough to be squeezed into the barrel, and the string was tied up once more. The entire inflammable operation was performed within in-ches of the faltering Tilley lamp, in order that the hunter should see clearly what he was doing.

On we went, quietly now, or at least as quietly as we could manage, for although Ahmad and the hunter moved like shadows through the jungle, Andrew and I were finding that the route was a tough one, up and down rocky river courses; spiny creepers carefully positioned by some malig-nant elf gave the impression of being the perfect handhold, yet viciously lacerated us, piercing the cloth of our army combat trousers and ripping the skin beneath. The gun, however, came into its own. It was used as a walking stick, as a handhold, and as a lever; as the hunter climbed up one particularly slippery bank from a slimy river bed, he turned and held the gun back towards Ahmad who grasped the barrel and was pulled up by it. Andrew and I followed suit. My heel, which had a bad blister at the start of the exercise, started throbbing in spite of the layers of bandage I had tried to protect it with. Thus started one of the most hellish nights of the whole trip, and also one of the most memorable and exciting.

After interminable plodding, we heard a shot far off into the jungle from Yahyah's group. Our hunter and Ahmad compared notes and it seemed that the most likely victim was a 'pelandok', or Mouse-deer, and

indeed from their point of view this was the main quarry of the night. On we went and every so often I tried to struggle forward to whisper 'tam-polili' in the hunter's ear. Were we going to find some tampolili? The only answer was a slight change in his rhythmic breathing. Many minutes later, all of us having been reduced to hands and knees to get under a barrage of prickles which spanned our path, the hunter signalled a halt. He crept quietly forward, every step measured, like a dog setting scent, his foot poised above the ground before it came silently down. Fifteen metres ahead of us he halted and held the light high in one hand, his flickering shadow casting a red glow through the jungle behind him. His other hand held the shotgun. All that we could see was his black silhouette. He crept forward down the little gully in front of us and stopped halfway up the other side to listen. A crackle of leaves and the shotgun moved into action, held in one hand. A thundering bang and he ran forward with a shout of success. As we scrambled up the bank after him he stood above a strange creature. 'Angkis,' he said, pointing to his quarry. A beast the size of a rabbit lay in the lamplight, covered in short prickly spines out of which, rather incongruously, protruded a long thin rat-like tail, the end of which was tipped with a little bob of spines. In a fit of zoological hysteria, no doubt precipitated by the combined excitement of the chase and the agony of his feet, Andrew exclaimed, 'Good heavens, is that what a Mouse-deer looks like?' However, the angkis was in reality a Long-tailed porcupine. It is interesting that the hunter used the word angkis, which I believe is the Iban name and not the Malay one.

We had to pause for some moments as the shot had singed off some of the string which held the barrel in position and it was quite a task to salvage enough short lengths of string to make one bit long enough to re-secure it. This done we shouldered the angkis and plodded on. The going remained rough and was made all the worse by our efforts to move quietly. By now we were covered in mud and our clothes, drenched in sweat, stuck tenaciously to our bodies; my whisperings about tampolili were becoming more plaintive. By this stage my leg was throbbing so badly from the blister that it was all I could do to hobble along to keep up with the others.

One palm dealt me a double blow; as I strove to disentangle my impaled flesh from the palm's three centimetre long spines, the whole tree began to rattle and hiss most alarmingly. Close inspection revealed that the fronds were busy highways for thousands of ants. Each time the tree was tapped all these *Campanotus* ants paused in their harried travels and synchronously rubbed together a pair of their legs – the effect simulated a most aggrieved snake! In some cases at least this type of association between ant and plant does seem to be vital to the plants' survival and doubtless to the ants also. In an ingenious experiment on the Swollen-thorn acacia tree in Central America each and every one of its resident ants was carefully removed. The ants normally hide within the so-called swollen thorns. Within three months of this compulsory divorce the trees died – they were literally shredded by herbivores which ate them alive but which had previously been deterred by the presence of the ants. Species of acacia which have resident ants to defend them do not, as many others do, load their leaves with toxic chemicals. A similar difference in defence strategy between close relatives exists in the case of the familiar British hedgehog and his tiny cousin the shrew. The shrew has glands which produce a substance that makes foxes and other predators feel decidedly green around the gills, while hedgehogs, although most tasty, are bedecked in spines. In any event, the combination of palm thorn and ant certainly unnerved us.

About an hour passed before we miraculously met up with Yahyah's group. He had got a pelandok, with his one shot. These really are extraordinary animals: little antelope on short spindly legs, they are not much bigger than a chihuahua. Mouse-deer or chevrotains are the smallest living hoofed animals, being only twenty-five centimetres high and weighing not much more than a large rabbit. In many ways they look more like large rodents, and from what little is known of them, they probably live rather solitary existences, defending territories and forming pairs during the breeding season. They are included in that section of the cloven hooved animals known as the ruminants, but within that group (or sub-order) they are separated from all the other existing species because of certain primitive characteristics. Indeed they do not even have the complicated four-chambered stomach of the more advanced ruminants such as sheep, cows and deer, but retain instead a more primitive three-chambered stomach (also found today in pigs and camels) which does not permit regurgitation and 'chewing the cud'. Incidentally it is quite probable that the habit of chewing the cud, facilitated by this complicated stomach, is one of the principal features which has contributed to the enormous success of the more modern ruminant creatures. It enables animals such as deer and antelope to feed quickly in the thick vegetation that harbours dangerous predators and then to retreat to a safe place to chew the cud and digest their meal at leisure. The absence of such sophisticated anatomical features in the chevrotain combined with their similarity to certain fossil forms going back as far as the Eocene geological period (fifty-four to thirty-eight million years ago) suggest that perhaps they are quite similar to the extinct ancestors of present-day ruminant animals.

Mouse-deer have caught the imagination of the jungle people too. The Kelabit people tell how one day a Mouse-deer fell into a deep pit and was in danger of starving to death. Other animals came and peered down at him and he told each in turn that he was hiding there because the sky would fall down and kill everybody on the surface. Soon, pigs and deer had jumped in with him to shelter. The Mouse-deer then persuaded them to stand on each other's backs, with him on top so he might pick grass for them. Of course he leapt from his unsuspecting saviours and left them to starve. In fact this Mouse-deer, named Agan Pelandok, was not always so lucky. In a sequel the Kelabits tell how the Mouse-deer was challenged to a race by a fish. But the fish mustered all his friends to swim in relay and Agan Pelandok was fooled by their similar appearance. So he ran and ran until he died of exhaustion.

Lonely jungle nights were fitting circumstances to remember these myths, indeed, almost to believe them. In shrouded whispers the two hunting parties chatted about their respective fortunes. I felt a bit better when I glimpsed Mark's face in the light of the Tilley lamp – streaked with mud and sweat, his route had obviously been as arduous as ours. It seemed that they had trailed along similar terrain to ourselves and that Yahyah had shot his Mouse-deer by firing into complete darkness at a rustling sound made by the animal as it ran.

Our two groups split up again and hours passed without sign of a tampolili, or any other quarry. For my part I began to doubt whether I could make it the whole way back to the kampong on my mangled foot, not that I knew where we were or how long the journey was. Nevertheless, just as we had perversely enjoyed the engine room of that steamer across the South China Sea, so now I felt thrilled, if numbed, as we scratched and clawed our way through the tropical jungle. It was just before dawn, having travelled in a wide arc, that we came upon a small clearing in which stood a little kampong house. Around the house we dimly made out a small area of cultivated land with pineapple, sugar cane and some paddy. Our hunter paused below the door, climbed the notched log which functioned as a staircase and shouted loudly to wake the sleeping occupants. There were muffled grunts from within, and the hunter shouted again. An old man's head appeared at the door wearing an understandably irritated expression. On spotting us his frown faded and there followed an unforgettable exhibition of hospitality.

The head disappeared and the old man's voice boomed orders to his slumbering family. A lamp flickered into life as the hunter beckoned us up the notched log to the house. This was no easy task for me since I had only one functional foot. The house was similar to our home at Menunggol. One main room was about five metres long with an annex behind adding about a metre and acting as a kitchen. Two layers of solid wooden bunks raised off the floor lined one side of the main room and these were crowded with sleeping bodies, or more accurately, rudely awakened bodies. Quickly spoken instructions were soon given to the women, who scurried out to the kitchen, while sleepy-eyed men sat up cross-legged, rocking gently back and forth in a polite battle against sleep and smiling wearily at us. Andrew and I, together with the hunter and Ahmad, sat on the floor with the head of the household. The women bustled back with cut sugar cane and pineapples which were quickly sliced into sections and sprinkled with the coarse sugar crystals. From the kitchen a huge pot of hot, sweet coffee materialized; it was possibly the most welcome cup of coffee I have ever drunk.

Just as the fresh coconut we ate at Menunggol bore no relation to its withered shadow sold in the United Kingdom, so this pineapple was more succulent and tender than any I had eaten before. The sugar cane was equally welcome. It grows rather like bamboo cane in thick stalks, perhaps an inch to an inch and a half in diameter, and is eaten by ripping lumps of fibre and pith from the stalk with one's teeth and chewing and chewing as the delicious juices trickle out. The residual mass of fibre is then spat out.

I protested at the disturbance to this man whom we had never seen before and who had no idea what we were doing in Borneo or Meritam and who was now feeding us before dawn in his house. He replied in a torrent of Malay, welcoming us into his home and finishing with the remark, 'Before I was asleep, but now you are here and I am pleased to be awake'.

A woman appeared carrying a plate of rice and curry. Feebly apologizing for the inconvenience we were causing, we gorged ourselves. An hour later I said that we must leave as we had intruded too long. Dismay crossed the hunter's face and that of our host. Their smiles vanished as they stared with agitated embarrassment at their hands. The hunter explained in a whisper that our hosts would be deeply insulted if we were to go now; as guests we must stay a while and sleep before continuing our journey. So Andrew and I stretched out at the end of the bunks on the wooden floor. An hour and a half later, when we woke, the sun was nearly up; my sweat-soaked clothing was now freezing cold and I was shivering. My right foot and lower leg were excruciatingly painful, badly swollen and locked into my boot. I could barely flex the leg at the knee as we climbed down the log, still profusely thanking our hosts for their hospitality as we staggered through the dewy dawn.

I was thankful that we had stayed those few hours in the little house for the walk back to the kampong was even longer than I had anticipated. We had walked for perhaps fifteen or twenty minutes, by which time I was hobbling far behind the others, when we came across an eerie place, a hundred and fifty metres across, where no vegetation grew. The sun was still low in the sky and there was a general greyness in the air, with long shadows creeping over the ground, when we stepped into the clearing. The ground was covered with grey, powdery soil, caked hard in places with large cracks running a mosaic patchwork across its surface. Scattered here and there were mounds like fairytale mole hills; the central core of each was filled with bubbling grey mud. The dry mud had a soft texture like graphite, but that in the cores was fluid, bubbling, popping and gulping melodically as I peered into this outlet of the bowels of the earth. I hobbled to the edge of the muddy area and fetched a dead branch which measured over two metres. Carrying it back to one of the larger holes, I sank it into the mud. It disappeared out of sight, leaving an epitaph of bubbles gulping their way frantically to the surface.

To my surprise, when I gingerly dipped a finger, the fluid mud was cold to touch. As I limped across the barren patch, serenaded by plops and gulps as if from a choir of nostalgic frogs, and occasionally splashed on the leg by mud showered out by some over-enthusiastic bubble, I wondered insecurely how thick was the crust on which I was walking. It was with relief that I found myself back in the jungle.

Now, in daylight, I could see much that had been invisible in the night. A weird tree caught my attention. Brightly coloured protuberances grew up its trunk, below the height of its lowest branches. Each protuberance resembled a collection of a dozen or more old fashioned hat pins – all a vivid pink! The tree, actually called *Polyalthia cauliflora* – was one of a large number of so-called cauliflorous trees which, instead of flowering at their crown, keep their reproductive organs on their trunks. Theory has it that it is much easier for creatures pollinating these trees to locate the flowers and to travel between them among this world of bare trunks than it would be in the wilderness of the canopy. A few paces further and I saw another example of the same phenomenon: growing from the trunk of another tree was a spray of scarlet rods. Each of these rods had four ridges along its length and a dark constriction near the top. This was a relation of mistletoe (called *Macrosolen nobilis*) with an extraordinary method of pollination – small birds called Spider-hunters brush against the cluster of flowering red rods as they forage. As the rods touch the bird's breast their topmost section explodes, showering the bird with pollen. Subsequently, when the Spider-hunter visits other trees, the pollen is brushed onto the female plant and fertilization is accomplished.

The peace of the forest was overwhelming and I paused to stare around. I tried to locate the buzzing cicadas, but they seemed to be excellent ventriloquists. Many secretive animals have calls at frequencies which are hard to pinpoint. As I gazed around I noticed a series of V-shaped cuts in the bark of a tree towering above me. The villagers were extracting jelutong, a sort of latex. I was struck by the irony that large quantities of this material are exported to the USA as the base for bubble gum, a product which seems to symbolize much that is foreign to the jungle.

Back at the kampong we found Mark and Yahyah asleep, having ultimately shot two pelandok. Mark's trip had involved two sad casualties, one of which nestled forlornly in the hands of Yahyah's son. Shining the lantern into the lower branches of a tree Yahyah had dazzled a roosting bird, which he had picked from the branch and carried home, plucking its primary wing feathers to ensure that it had no chance of escape. Yahyah assured us that these birds made good pets. The mutilated creature was a trogon – an insect-eating bird. Even in this desecrated condition it had the most beautiful colouring I had ever seen on a bird. Its head was chocolate brown, its back and breast orange, its rump pink and what remained of its wings was an intricately barred grey. The trogon was swathed in finery to the last detail; even its eyelids were bright blue. The second disaster had occurred when the lamplight had picked up the reflection of a pair of eyes. Yahyah had whispered to Mark who had not understood what was said and so grunted neutrally. At this Yahyah brought up his gun and, before Mark could stop him, he had fired and a civet fell to the ground. It was a linsang, more slenderly built than the other Malaysian civets, and the first we had seen.

On the homeward journey Yahyah had dispensed with the Tilley lamp. Mark could see absolutely nothing except the low glow of a white cloth which Yahyah was carrying. Bumped and bruised, Mark struggled to keep the cloth directly in front of him all the way home. The story is reminiscent of the way the Penan, one of Borneo's native peoples, helped the British troops during the confrontation with the Japanese in the Second World War. The British used the Penan as scouts for nocturnal raids and, considering that they are never normally abroad in the jungle by night, they proved so remarkably adept that the soldiers had trouble keeping up with them. So, each man tied a luminous fungus to his back for the man behind to follow. The Penan in front was quite able to find his way, unaided, in the darkness.

The rest of that day passed in a curious mixture of sleep, fever, festering and extreme gratification. The latter came in the afternoon when all the others had gone out leaving me, asleep and feverish, with my raw foot, now devoid of most of its sole. I woke to find myself in a room full of women: Yahyah's wife, her ancient mother, a couple of other old women and several of her younger sisters were talking in the centre of the room. This was indeed a rare opportunity for, as I have explained before, throughout the whole of our stay in Brunei, the women kept strictly to themselves. Yahyah's wife held the floor, recounting tales of our strange ways back in Kampong Menunggol; her audience was in a jovial mood. I pulled myself into a sitting position, propped against the wall. To my sur-

prise, perhaps because there was no other man present, the women did not scatter into the background, but grinned back and even passed a few remarks. One pretty girl kept dissolving into laughter and the others were obviously teasing her. At last she disappeared into the back of the house to come back holding a tattered book entitled in English *Elementary Spelling*. Shyly looking away, amid riotous hoots and giggles from the other women, she presented this to me. As I thumbed through it, she managed to muster courage and turned it to the page which she had reached in her studies. My exclamations of enthusiasm were greeted with roars of laughter. Then, her nerve cracking, the girl darted back into the group of women who mercilessly shoved her towards me again.

I was overjoyed to compare all this with their normally subdued behaviour towards us. Even Yahyah's wife was laughing and chattering. Perhaps pressing my luck but anxious not to miss an opportunity, I started mentioning 'gambar' – photographs. I had only three flash bulbs left, so there was not much room for error. Everybody shyly giggled and then started arranging their hair. However, at the sight of the camera, most of them lost their nerve and ran off. Some stayed, and I was able to get three pictures of Yahyah's wife and my friend with the spelling book. Although the women withdrew the mood of hilarity persisted when Mark and Andrew returned with Yahyah. Yahyah was weak from laughing for Mark had reputedly fallen off every bridge on the road and was completely caked in drying mud.

Mark had suffered an additional misadventure. A large and manifestly hungry leech had latched onto his thigh. Leeches may go for a year without a meal, so when they do eat they make the most of it, and this leech had already gorged itself on Mark's blood when he noticed it. It had been persuaded to let go its hold by the application of a lighted cigarette, but the result looked gruesome. As leeches feed they inject an anti-coagulant into the wound to prevent their meal from being interrupted by clotting. Once the leech has been detached, voluntarily or otherwise, the anti-coagulant continues to function for an hour or more during which time blood flows in a steady trickle from the wound. The result is more unsightly than painful, and many people are filled with a disproportionate fear and hatred of these creatures which are, at least, preferable to mosquitoes.

With Yahyah's arrival several women scuttled to the other side of the room and others retreated outside. Some stayed and the girl with the spelling book made innumerable excuses for bringing us cups of tea and coffee.

For a while I sat on the steps, gazing out at the jungle. Sunbirds flitted like jewels in the sun, and a hoard of butterflies danced over a place where buffalo urine had seeped into the soil. I heard a whirring noise and two hornbills flew noisily overhead. I have already described how the hen bird is incarcerated while she incubates, but there is much more of interest in their private lives. The Bushy-crested hornbill, for example, lives in groups. This was first reported by T. Whitehead, an early naturalist, who noticed several of these birds around a concealed nest site. He shot three of them before noting: 'I was sorry that we had done so, and sent one of my boys to see if he could climb to the imprisoned female and let her loose.' The boy reported that on his return to the nest he had found several more hornbills feeding the widowed hen bird, so Whitehead continued: 'It is perhaps fortunate that the birds do not pair as any accident to the attendant male would mean death by slow starvation to the imprisoned hen.' In this remark Whitehead unwittingly posed an interesting question: why should other individuals help the captive female? (Actually she could easily break out for herself, but that does not make the question any less interesting.) Animal behaviour has been fashioned by natural selection for the good of the individual and its offspring, not for the good of the species, as is often mistakenly believed. Why should a whole gaggle of hornbills thus help this bereaved, imprisoned female when the result will be the survival of *her* offspring, not theirs? There are several possible answers. If all these birds were relatives then they would have a similar, but diluted, vested interest in the survival of the chicks, as would their mother. Alternatively, the mother might have been mated by all the male birds among the helpers, causing doubt about paternity, hence, so to speak, confusing all of them into helping. One might speculate that the female helpers can look forward to repayment in kind when they in turn are confined. Whatever the explanation, the noisy hornbills clattering about near the kampong held our attention for almost half an hour and when they finally left, Andrew and Mark again wandered off, leaving me alone with the Tua and the young girl with the spelling book. After a lengthy conversation the Tua looked me squarely in the eyes and invited me to stay at Kampong Meritam. I was overwhelmed by what I took as a great honour, but had not the courage to accept. As if to demonstrate the sincerity of his offer, he hinted that if I stayed his daughter could make a good wife. It all seemed like a tale from an old fashioned story-book, but I hadn't the courage to venture into the next chapter.

The next day found us paddling along Sungai Meritam on our way back to Kampong Menunggol. We were still without a glimpse of the tarsier but felt that we had learned a lot. Stopping at the customs post at Limbang we called into an open-fronted café. I was greatly pleased when the people there greeted us as the 'orang ulu' – men of the jungle.

6

Long-nosed Monkeys, Ghosts and Sharks

'Fifty-seven, fifty-eight, fifty-nine, sixty, dash it.' I squinted through my binoculars, failing to anticipate the unpredictable lurching of the craft while the Proboscis monkey on which my attention had been focused moved behind a thick bough, making further observations temporarily impossible. I had been counting the number of leaves this individual had plucked and eaten – sixty leaves in twelve minutes, in this case. For now, in spite of interruptions caused by trips in search of the tarsier, our monkey observations were going well.

The idea of counting the number of mouthfuls of food a Proboscis monkey eats may seem absurd, but if food supply is related to social life then nowhere are the details of that relationship going to be more clearly calculable than at the instant the food goes into the monkey. Just to say which trees the monkeys were feeding on would be grossly over-simple – Red Colobus and Black and White Colobus monkeys frequently feed in the same tree, but, as described in Chapter 2, they eat quite different food and consequently have different societies. Similarly, Proboscis monkeys and Long-tailed macaques would often sit in the same mangrove tree, sometimes at the same time, but that is not to say they were doing the same thing. The Proboscis monkeys were much stricter foliavors than the macaques. So, the Proboscis monkey whose every bite I was scrutinizing might have been eating leaves or branches or flowers or buds, or any combination of these. What she was actually eating would give her a different 'view' of the swamp depending on whether it was a leaf, of which there were many, or a hanging seedling, of which there were fewer and which were only occasionally available. As it happens this particular monkey was eating mature leaves.

You might believe that the biologist's passion for detail would be satisfied by this, but it is not, because even on one tree, on one bough, there is more to foliage than meets the eye. For example, leaves of different ages contain different nutrients, and, for that matter, different poisons. Some monkeys may select portions of leaves that are near the growing point and rich in proteins. Mature leaves are often those with the biggest concentrations of secondary compounds – the toxic chemicals that protect the leaf from browsers. In the case of mangroves the leaves are tainted with tannins. The Proboscis monkey that I was watching seemed to be eating

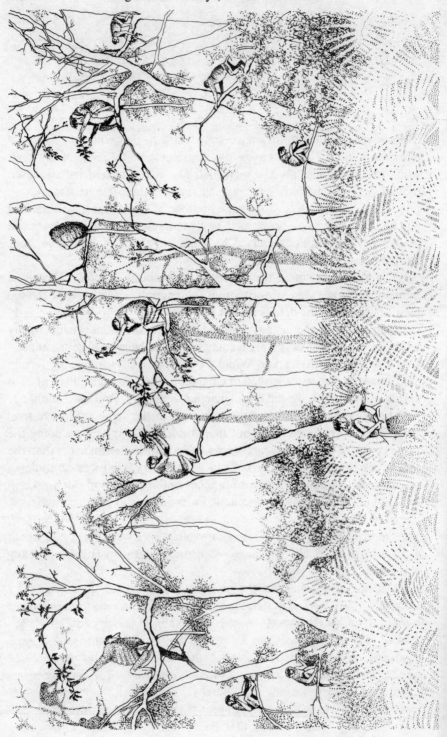

Top right The conspicuous warning coloration of a caterpillar of the moth *Thusea*

Right A lantern bug

Above A tarsier, photographed by R. Hanbury Tenison in Mulu

The Punan woman near Long Sukang

A view from the guano hill within the caves at Niah

Flying frog with its parasol-like feet

The Malay civet radio-tagged at Mulu

mature, and hence relatively poisonous, leaves. How could she get away with this? There are several possible explanations – perhaps mature leaves comprised only a small proportion of her diet, or perhaps she ate only a part of each leaf, with low concentrations of tannin. In fact, she was picking leaf after leaf and stuffing them into her mouth whole. Perhaps the monkey's digestive system is able to detoxify these plant poisons more effectively than we realize. There is, after all, the oft-quoted arms race going on between predator and prey as each develops, through natural selection, ever more resourceful methods of overcoming the other. Natural selection will favour the survival of mangroves whose heredity programmes them to produce leaves which Proboscis monkeys cannot stomach. Similarly, Proboscis monkeys who evolve intestines which can shrug off these nauseous chemicals will prosper compared with those who succumb to their influence. Since in over 90 per cent of our observations on Proboscis monkeys they were munching at mangrove leaves, it seems likely that they have evolved specialized digestive processes for handling these leaves.

There is another point which concerns the Proboscis monkey's stomach. All the Colobus monkeys (*Colobinae*) eat leaves, at least occasionally, and all leaves are composed in part of undigestible cellulose. Antelopes, and all other grazers, encounter the same problem: there's plenty of food about in the sense that the vegetation is made up of nutrients, but it is unassimilable because conventional digestive juices cannot penetrate the cellulose. The solution is to enter into a pact with bacteria which can digest the cellulose that encases plant cells, and thus liberate the nutrients. The pact is mutually beneficial: the host gets access to a menu which is otherwise out of reach, while the bacteria get free accommodation in a snug gut and a ready supply of food. These bacteria are deployed in two ways, both by ungulates and by monkeys. The even-toed ungulates, like the cow, have a special chamber at the front of the stomach which houses the bacteria and where the food is fermented before passing into the stomach. The Proboscis monkey has opted for a similar, if simpler, design. In contrast odd-toed ungulates, such as the horse, have a greatly expanded caecum (the portion of the gut to which the appendix is attached) and it is there that they store their bacteria and digest cellulose. It is said that the caecal system is only 70 per cent as effective as the fore-stomach one, and the fore-stomach may have another advantage too: the action of bacteria in the fore-stomach on the potentially poisonous food of the Proboscis monkey may actually neutralize the toxins *before* they get far enough down the gut to be absorbed into the bloodstream.

The Proboscis monkeys certainly seemed to favour a monotonous diet, eating leaf after leaf, hour after hour. Sometimes a monkey would sit on a branch and reach up to pull another branch towards it with one hand while stripping every leaf one by one with the other. Uninterrupted, the monkeys ate at a very constant, plodding rate. Taking an average from the cumulative total of almost five hours of such observations gives a figure of six leaves per minute.

A typical observation would be the one I made at 5 pm on 26 July. Two large male Proboscis monkeys were firmly seated in the forks of branches opposite our house, one above the other. Through a telescope I watched them for thirty-two minutes before either moved position. In that time each monkey had defoliated the branches within his reach, feeding at a very constant rate of one leaf per ten seconds. At 5.32 one of these big males stood up and, looking about, moved about three metres and sat down again; he seemed to be selecting a particular branch from which to eat next. Five minutes later the same monkey moved a further three metres. At 6 pm an adult female Proboscis monkey climbed into view on the same tree and eventually settled almost exactly between the two males, where she too began to browse. At 6.40 the male which had until then been stationary climbed about three metres to a new site. All these monkeys continued to pluck leaves at the same rate until 6.50 at which point we stopped watching them.

Another and unrelated difficulty that beset our monkey watching was that I was trying to divide my attention between observing and filming. At the time I was working freelance for the BBC and, armed with over a thousand feet of film, I was trying to get material for a Christmas wildlife spectacular in which the Proboscis monkey was scheduled to feature! The difficulties of getting this material were appalling: salt water smeared my filters, grit lurked in every crevice, but, worst of all, the combination of the rocking boat and long telephoto lenses resulted in the monkeys shooting about in the dimly lit viewfinder in an intolerably erratic way. We tried a variety of anchors, weights and tripods, but even the tiniest twitch in the water's surface was magnified to a horrific judder through a 400 milli-metre lens! At last we found that the only solution was to beach the boat as near as possible to the monkeys and to film as quickly as possible before they fled. The problem was, of course, that suitable opportunities for this manoeuvre were few and far between but, mercifully, sufficient of the beached material was steady enough to fill the slot on TV. There is certainly nothing more likely to taint one's enjoyment of nature than doing battle with a hand-cranked 16 millimetre camera in a mangrove swamp.

During the summer we spent at Kampong Menunggol we saw Proboscis monkeys at all times of the day. We watched them awake as the sun rose and fall asleep as it fell. However, our observations were not spread evenly throughout the daytime hours. Proboscis monkeys avoid the midday sun. Many of the trees they fed in were sparsely vegetated, and the monkeys sitting aloft were subjected to scorching temperatures, often in excess of 30°C. Probably because of this we saw monkeys most commonly at the beginning and end of the day. Another explanation might be that feeding bouts at either end of the day are the most efficient way of shunting large quantities of foliage through the digestive system. We were largely ignorant of what the Proboscis monkeys were doing when they were anywhere else save the edge of the swamp. From the air, we had seen that there was a ribbon of mangrove around these estuarine islands, but even in the interior there were substantial stands of mangroves amid the Nipa forest. Once in the interior of the swamp the monkeys were quite unassailable. Maybe they were contentedly eating throughout the midday period, when they were often out of our view, or perhaps they were eating something else during that time. We did try to find ways through the lacerating Nipa forest and we toyed with the idea of building a network of duckwalks, but time was too short and loss of blood too great. All I can say is that the monkeys we did see during the middle of the day were more likely to be loafing than eating.

Even when most members of a foraging group seemed intent on eating there were individuals who dozed off, wedged into the fork of a convenient branch. If our scanty data are reliable, then mangrove leaf eating is probably concentrated into less than five hours a day, and feeding is interspersed with plenty of gazing around and sleeping. This may once again be a consequence of the ready availability of food. In five hours a day a Proboscis monkey might consume the best part of 1800 leaves!

Other foods were rarely eaten. On five occasions I saw a big male eating mangrove seedlings plucked as they hung ready to spear the mud below. As I described in Chapter 3 they seemed to strip the skin from the seedlings as they ate, using the teeth, not the hand. On another occasion I watched a big male pick an epiphyte from a mossy branch and eat it, root and all. We began to suspect, on the basis of these six observations, that the males had a more varied diet than the females. One Bornean primate among which the sexes do have slightly different diets is the orang-utan. The male orang-utan eats less fruit than the female and more bark – this would seem to be a bad compromise, and may be related to the intriguing observations made by P. Rodman that in times of food shortage it is the males who move out of the area. Orangs make a good contrast to Proboscis monkeys in their dietary habits; they eat a much higher proportion of rich, but widely dispersed and fiddly foods such as fruit. The average orang probably spends almost half its daylight hours foraging, in contrast to the Proboscis monkeys which probably spend less than a quarter of their time foraging.

Perhaps the male orang eats seemingly unappetizing (and non-nutritious) foods like bark to minimize competition with his mate and offspring. The Proboscis monkey is, like every other creature, influenced by competition too. Not only did we quite often see Crab-eating macaques feeding in the same trees as the Proboscis monkeys, but there was also clearly competition from their own kind. There may be a lot of leaves on a mangrove tree, but there must also come a point when there simply are not enough to go around. A partial solution to this problem, at least on one level, is obvious the first moment one sees a sizeable troop of Proboscis monkeys. Individuals of each sex and of different ages eat in different places – not exclusively, but sufficiently to reduce the risk of their standing on each other's ecological toes. In biological jargon they have slightly different feeding niches. The most spectacular separation of feeding place is between adults and youngsters, and it is organized according to a formula which is fairly obviously to do with weight and mud! Along the shore, and largely immersed at high tide, are the young sapling mangroves. At a metre high the saplings have strong stems and a rich flurry of young leaves – the whole construction is just the right size to seat an infant Proboscis monkey without collapse. True, a heavier monkey could simply bend the sapling over to take the leaves, but to reach these young saplings a full-grown monkey would have to cross the pneumatophore-laden mud. The heavyweight adult monkeys would sink. In contrast, the young Proboscis monkeys scampered from bush to bush in a hail of salty spray, barely leaving a footprint behind. Larger saplings supported larger youngsters, but while we saw youngsters feeding on these shoreline saplings on twenty-nine occasions, we never saw an adult do so.

The difference between males and females was less clear cut. Certainly there was a wide overlap in their feeding stations in the bulk of the tree. However, old males are twice the weight of females (twenty kilos as against ten), so it is a mechanical certainty that some branches which will support a female will not support a male. In more realistic terms, females can venture further along the extremities of branches than males can, and higher up the tree too, and this is exactly what we saw happen.

There were some places where we found the monkeys very frequently, and we noticed that in these places the mangrove trees had a peculiar naked appearance. From a distance they looked dead, but on closer inspection they were fringed with fresh buds. The monkeys fed on young light green leaves on these trees, and often slept in their branches. The impression that the monkeys favoured these trees cannot be dismissed as arising solely from the increased likelihood of our spotting them in defoliated trees. We became more and more convinced of this association. One day, for instance, we explored the Limbang river. Ahead we spied a group of these naked trees. Half jokingly we said we had better just go and check there were no monkeys in them – but there were!

Initially I presumed that the trees lost the bulk of their foliage for some reason to do with their own physiology, as a deciduous tree sheds its leaves. However, we began to wonder whether the monkeys were directly responsible. The problem remains unsolved. Perhaps the monkeys browsed the trees too heavily, or perhaps because they used them as sleeping trees they poisoned them by drenching them with urine. Whatever the reason, the association seemed unquestionable and might benefit the monkeys as I assume the sprouting leaves on these trees were both nutritious and low in toxins.

Whatever the explanation, these musings on monkey diet led us to view the swamps and forests through more appropriately vegetarian eyes. For munching insects the forest is probably not so much a haven of lush greenery but more a frustrating mosaic of poisons – a huge green stomach ache. Much more than in temperate climates, trees in the tropics are loaded with chemicals to deter browsing creatures from eating them. Maybe, in a habitat where so much of the soil's richness is not in the soil but stored in the leaves of plants, the premium on defending each and every part of a tree's anatomy from vegetarian nibblers is particularly great. The leaves of mangrove trees are particularly rich in tannin, in concentrations which would make the most excessive tea drinker tremble, and yet, as mentioned earlier in this chapter, these monkeys were munching their way through hundreds of leaves every day.

There are really only two categories of solution for creatures eating from the jungle delicatessen. They must either follow the Proboscis monkey's example and specialize in a certain plant or part of a plant whose chemical armaments they have become adapted to. In the struggle between the eater and the eaten, vegetarian insects would in many cases seem to have a head start over their 'prey', since with several generations a year they can presumably evolve new ways of overcoming the plant's chemical defences more rapidly than the plant can retaliate with new variations of its poison. The second strategy which the browser might adopt would be to feed on a large variety of different plants, taking sufficiently little from each to avoid a build-up of ill effects. Some of the chemicals which tropical plants have evolved are certainly impressive. Vines may incorporate canavanine (an amino acid which gets painfully mixed up in the synthesis of proteins in the cells of anyone unlucky enough to eat it). Ten per cent of the dry weight of some vines is made up of this chemical which is impressive when you consider that rats confronted with a diet containing only one per cent of the same stuff will starve in preference to eating it!

Many of the substances which thwart creatures wanting to eat trees have actually been turned to other uses by jungle people. Mangrove bark is treated to extract tannin for the tanning industry, and the leaves and roots of another plant, the tuba, are squashed to produce a juice which native fishermen use: the juices of the crushed leaves poison fish, which drift defenceless to the surface. The chemicals involved are saponins, the same compounds from which we make soap, and the effect is the same too because they 'wash away' part of the fatty substances that coat and protect the gills of the fish. Another weapon in this chemical warfare is produced by a primitive group of plants called cycasids which produce material that induces cancers in the stomach of rats. Interestingly, this compound, cycasin, is known to have its unhealthy effects only when digestive enzymes produced by bacteria living naturally in the stomach of the rat begin to break down the toxic molecules. Rats who have been treated with antibiotics to remove the bacterial community from their guts are quite unaffected by the poison. Considering how filled with intrigue this battle is that pits gut against leaf, it is apparent that the nonchalant browsings of the Proboscis monkeys obscure some very complex processes.

While most of our time was concentrated on trying to solve the riddles of the monkeys' behaviour, we also encountered many other members of the fauna which thronged the swamp. On one occasion as we walked through the kampong towards the jungle, setting off on a day-long trek, I happened to glance up into the folded leaves of a banana tree to see two fruit bats hanging there. They were quite awake and, as we peered up at them suspended a metre above our heads, they defiantly answered our stares with round twinkling eyes. Periodically they turned their heads towards each other and sniffed noses as if to confirm each other's opinion of our presence. Averting our eyes in an attempt to assure the bats that we were not the slightest bit interested in them, we backtracked slowly down the hill until out of sight behind a banana tree, whereupon we sprinted for the house and our cameras.

Minutes later, stalking barefoot up the track again, we managed to reach the tree without disturbing the bats. We carefully opened the legs of our tripods, fitting the cameras in position as each bat lazily stretched one wing then another, periodically squinting down at us. Sweat poured off my brow and into the camera viewfinder making focusing almost impossible. Nevertheless, we managed to get four or five shots of the bats as they glared disdainfully at their admirers.

We determined to identify the species to which these bats belonged. After another stealthy retreat we returned with Lord Medway's key to Bornean mammals. It soon became apparent that we were not going to succeed in identifying the bats until we could examine them at close quarters, preferably in the hand. We had brought to Borneo several 'mist nets' of the type used by ornithologists for catching birds. These nets are about four metres in length, two metres high and are strung between two poles in a series of fine strings to support their almost invisible mesh in a succession of drooping folds. Once a bird has flown into the net, its momentum takes up sufficient slack to ensnare it, leaving the ornithologist to disentangle it, ring it and weigh it, prior to release. While these nets are designed for use in a fixed position, I had previously used them in portable fashion with one person supporting each pole, advancing on the quarry as if with an enlarged butterfly net. This was how we decided to capture the bats.

Stealthily setting up the net and the poles in a narrow jungle-edged path was no easy task. An hour later, sweating profusely and having several times entangled ourselves in the net, we began to advance on the bats. With Mark and myself at either end of the taut net, we sidled towards the banana leaf and edged the net into position. Throughout this manoeuvre the bats had scrutinized us with ever more perplexed frowns. Just as we were about to strike one of them stretched its wings and licked the other's nose. We held our collective breath. The tension passed as the wings were once again folded. Its companion repeated this performance. Again calamity passed. We edged another pace closer. The bats turned to each other, nuzzled noses, dropped together from under the leaf below the net and flew off up the hill!

Not all our attempts at catching animals for identification were so unsuccessful. About a week later when Andrew and I had gone into Bandar Seri Begawan to get some supplies, Mark found himself being pulled rapidly towards a palm tree by a band of chattering women. Many frenzied fingers pointed out a large and colourful snake entwined in the lower branches of the tree. Spurred on by the presence of so many admirers, Mark ventured forward, which prompted the snake to respond by spitting fiercely and striking out at him. This self-confessed ill nature on the part of the serpent might have sealed its fate: a parang was rapidly brought and Mark was instructed to despatch it. Declining to do so, Mark fashioned a long piece of bamboo with a piece of string tied with a slip knot round it at one end, to form a noose. Edging forward, Mark nudged the snake to provoke it to strike and, as it did so, he managed to slip the noose about its head and yanked it tight; landing the snake from the tree like a fish on a line was difficult and made all the more so by the onlookers' enthusiasm for destroying it and by the snake's own efforts to destroy Mark. Eventually, he managed to get it into a box with both parties unscathed.

The Cat snake, for this it was, was a truly beautiful specimen. Its basic light brown snaky colour was patterned, particularly around its head, with light shades of blue and green which glittered like sequins as it swayed its head. Under the chin were streaks of luminous blue and yellow which became more and more lustrous as it inflated its neck, with mounting anger. It struck repeatedly at the muslin covering of its box, its fangs protruding through the mesh and exuding drops of poison which left us in no doubt of its intentions. The snake was eventually transported to the live collection at the Museum, and displayed there.

At the Museum a letter awaited us from Ivan Polunin. He had received the fireflies and seemed excited by them: 'Either they are *Ptorgsteryx bearni*, a very ordinary species which isn't terribly interesting, or it may be an as yet unnamed species, which synchronizes its flashes at 120 flashes per minute – I'd be very very very keen to get live specimens.' The letter, scrawled across two large sheets of paper, explained how to resolve these two possibilities. The correct diagnosis included matching up the fireflies' pattern of flashes with Ivan's sketches of oscilloscope traces of their signals. Later we paddled the swamp by night trying to watch more of these creatures, timing their winking lights. We became nothing save mightily confused and tortured by mosquitoes. We simply could not find any that signalled the appropriate number of dots and dashes. Returning home I delved in my rucksac for Ivan's letter and the critical sketch from the oscilloscope, and suddenly I noticed a scribbled caption to the drawing: 'Ten individual subflashes are not discernible as separate by the human eye'! No wonder we had failed to find any, and the only solution was to send all our specimens back to Ivan in Singapore.

Yahyah still visited our house nightly and our conversation often revolved around other places where we might search for tarsiers, as we reminisced over the adventures of the trip to Meritam and his in-laws. During one conversation about Meritam, Yahyah told us how he had acquired his wife. It seemed that Yahyah had been disappointed with the moral decay of the young girls around his own and neighbouring kampongs, a decadence which we understood him to say stemmed largely from an increasing exposure of his generation to foreign ways. So when he had decided that he was ripe for marriage, he had forsaken the local beauties and travelled the rivers around Brunei and north into Limbang, in search of a suitable bride. He claimed to have explored every navigable river within twenty-four hours' journey and it was on one such trip that he had arrived at Kampong Meritam. We asked him what it was about his wife that had made him choose her out of the many prospective brides he had met. Try though we might, we could not fathom his explanation. We struggled with our limited vocabulary, with little bits of play acting, with drawings; the word 'displin' was the stumbling block to our comprehension, and the fault he found with all the girls. It was that they had 'tidak displin' that worried him. 'Tidak' means 'no'. The evening passed, and many a cup of sickly sweet tea was drunk, while Yahyah, his brow furrowed with that expression he always wore when he felt he was letting us down, tried to explain. Finally it dawned on us. His one word of English, gleaned from a brief sojourn in the army, was 'discipline'. What all these girls had lacked was discipline, and girls with none of it were no good!

A few nights later we were involved in another more serious breakdown in communication with Yahyah, again with his wife as the focal point. We had been eating supper at his house, as had now become our custom. As the hour grew late, Yahyah invited us to stay the night. The house had only one room and, thinking in European terms, we assumed that his wife would resent an intrusion into their bedroom, so we declined. Yahyah followed us home crestfallen. Once back in our house, he sat miserably in a corner. Eventually he announced that he could not stay in our house because his wife would be scared alone. What was he to do? Good friends should share a home. Distressed that we had wrongly interpreted a Malayan gesture we struggled to explain that a European woman might have resented our presence in her bedroom. Things went from bad to worse; Yahyah assumed that there was something wrong with his wife's standards. However, several cups of coffee later and the misunderstanding was largely repaired. We promised Yahyah that the following night we would be delighted to stay at his house.

The next day we went on a long excursion through the jungle at the back of the kampong, heading for the only hill on the horizon. Within a hundred metres the vegetation was completely different from that of the mangrove swamp – secondary jungle, interspersed with small clearings which had been slashed down and burnt in preparation for sowing banana trees or paddy. As we climbed, the forest became less and less disturbed. Going through some thick woodland we saw a belinkasa jump nimbly from one tree to another, then another. We had spent many hours watching these Green Calotes lizards, the species we had first encountered, on arrival in Menunggol, when one of them scaled Mark's boot. On this walk we must have seen two or three dozen, some green, others variously disguised in shades of brown. They were leaping between the trees, covering great distances at a bound. Occasionally one stopped to jerk its head up and down, pumping its slender forearms in vertical press-ups on the tree trunks, displaying the ownership of its patch to territorial neighbours.

The summit of the hill afforded a tremendous view over Brunei Bay. On one side of us, in the distance, we could see the Museum, situated on the outskirts of Kampong Ayer, while on the coastline on the other side we could see Kampong Menunggol and, standing by itself in the water, our own house. It was on this summit that we found the land crab and many strange goblet-shaped pitcher plants.

The leaves of the pitcher plant are shaped like a deep, cylindrical horn. These delicate pitchers are traps: the plant is a killer. The walls of the pitcher secrete a weak digestive enzyme which trickles down to accumulate as a pool of fluid trapped within the living vessel. This enzyme, like the ones in our own intestines, is capable of digesting meat, splitting large molecules into smaller ones that can be assimilated by the plant. The pitcher is coloured a pale green, flecked with shades of deep red. The colour may mimic an attractive flower and this, together with a strong smell emanating from the pool of fluid within, attracts insects. New arrivals land on the internal walls of the pitcher, which are covered with wax, so the hapless victims slip into the pool below and are slowly dissolved into the broth. The insect victims supply the plant with vital nitrates which are all too scarce in tropical soils. The pitcher plant is thus able to colonize soils where a normal non-predatory plant would starve to death, generating its own 'compost' wherever it grows, and in so doing it has created a new niche, inhabited in turn by a dare-devil member of the animal kingdom. The Pitcher-plant spider is only found inside these death traps: it waits there to snatch insects from one death, only to suck them dry itself. Presumably the spider is not a great inconvenience to its host plant, since it discards the shrivelled husks of its victims into the enzyme puddle below, where further goodness can be drained from them. Indeed, some insects can be seen successfully scrabbling out of the pitcher before it is too late, so perhaps the plant's overall efficiency even goes up with the arrival of a spider who makes sure that no such escapes occur.

Getting nutrients is a problem for all plants, of course, and the pitchers are not unique in becoming killers. The number of species of carnivorous plants found throughout the world runs into hundreds, but most, like the pitcher plants, are passive hunters in that the capture of prey involves no active movement on the part of the plant. The insects simply slither helplessly into the pitcher plant's open-air stomach or, in other passively carnivorous plants, the prey may be entangled in sticky substances secreted by the leaves, or may be caught by spiked hairs. By contrast, some plants are active killers and one of the most remarkable of these is the Venus Flytrap. Part of the Venus Flytrap's leaves are hinged down the middle and fringed with tentacles. When a fly lands on such a leaf the hinges close, the tentacles interlock and the book is closed for the captive within. Thereafter enzymes from the glands on the surface of the leaves and the tips of the tentacles slowly digest the struggling prisoner.

The sun began to sink and spread its warming rays more thinly over the hill top. We perched on some conveniently stool-shaped boulders on the summit, gazing across towards the Museum – thankful for time to stand and stare. Kota Batu, the 'Stone Fort' on which the Museum could be dimly seen, has figured largely in Brunei's history. It was probably a centre of civilization from the earliest times. Excavations have shown that Chinese coins are buried there from a dynasty which began in AD 618. Medieval Brunei was known as Po-ni, and there are records of envoys from Po-ni sending gifts and tributes to China in the 1400s. It is also clear that Brunei had important trade links with China; Marco Polo travelled throughout South East Asia in 1291 and mentioned a prosperous trade between the two nations. When the Chinese Emperor Yung-lo died in 1425 Chinese foreign policy was altered, with a change of emphasis towards internal affairs. Perhaps sensing this mood, the rulers of Po-ni changed allegiance and in 1430 became closely associated with the then Sultanate of Malacca.

Today Yahyah and the villagers of Menunggol and other Malay kampongs are largely Moslems. Their conversion stems from this time when Brunei drew closer to the Sultanate of Malacca, in response to Chinese disinterest. Iskandar Shah had been crowned Sultan of Malacca in 1413 and was the first Sultan to be converted to Islam. It was presumably his influence that, in 1476, led the leader of Brunei, Awang alak Betatar to change his name to Sultan Mohammad. In those days Brunei was an important and expanding power. As a nation she saw her golden age under the Sultan Bolkiah, fifth Sultan of Brunei (the present Sultan Bolkiah is the twenty-ninth of the line). Sultan Bolkiah travelled widely through the islands of the China Sea and eventually married a Javanese princess. Her followers returned with him to Brunei where they intermarried to produce, so it is said, the Moslem Kedayan who live in and around Bandar Seri Begawan today.

Through my binoculars I could make out a thick clump of vegetation which shrouded the site of Sultan Bolkiah's tomb. The ornate tomb is said to have been built by a suitor to the widowed Sultana. The story goes that Sultan Bolkiah and his wife were returning home from one of their sea voyages when she inadvertently scratched him with a golden pin. The scratch became infected and the Sultan died. The Sultana, even in her grief, was an outstandingly beautiful woman and various princes aboard the boat were soon plying her with offers of marriage which, considering the recency of her bereavement, she found distastefully premature. Returning to Brunei, the Sultana told her over-zealous suitors that she would marry the one who created the most beautiful grave and tomb for her late husband. The tomb was built, the dead Sultan buried and the

Sultana reputedly satisfied, at which point she promptly committed suicide, so cheating her suitors.

There is one wonderful account of the rulers of Brunei in their heyday, written in July 1521 by Antonio Pigafetta, the diarist aboard Ferdinand Magellan's ship, the *Mactan*. In fact Pigafetta wrote his account as the voyage continued after Magellan's death in the Philippines. It seems that they docked in Brunei Bay, under rather more glamorous circumstances than we had done. As I stared across the Bay towards Kota Batu the view which Pigafetta must have beheld over 350 years before sprang vividly to life: 'We remained about two hours in the prow, until the arrival of two elephants with silk trappings, and twelve men, each of whom carried a porcelain jar covered with silk in which to carry our presents. Thereupon we mounted the elephants while the twelve men preceded us afoot with the presents in the jars.' Pigafetta continued his account of his meeting with the Sultan, who was probably the great Bolkiah himself. It seems that the party of explorers was led up a ladder and into a large hall by the Governor; there they found a gathering of nobles. They passed into another room which was adorned with silk and populated by three hundred foot soldiers, each with a naked rapier to guard the king. At the end of this hall a large window opened into another chamber the entrance to which was hung with a brocade curtain, drawn aside. Pigafetta could see the ruler seated therein with his son, chewing betelnuts. A gathering was massed behind the ruler, but comprised only women, and it transpired each of these was the daughter of a chief. Pigafetta was forbidden to speak directly to the Sultan but had to make conversation through a chief. He in turn called a high-ranking dignitary who passed the message on to the brother of the Governor. This man spoke into a tube which passed from the hall through a hole in the wall to one who sat beside the Sultan in the little chamber. In this way Pigafetta informed the ruler that he represented the king of Spain and came in goodwill. After what must have been a rather disarticulated conversation, a trade agreement was made between the two countries and presents were exchanged. In Pigafetta's account he mentions how, when his party left the palace, they were again preceded by men carrying jars, this time filled with presents from Brunei's ruler to his visitors. I note that there were then only seven men carrying jars, perhaps indicating that while the Sultan was pleased enough to see his visitors he was sufficiently secure that the balance of goodwill was in his favour.

The evening mist cleared briefly as it drifted up from the trees around Kota Batu. I saw the grand Museum, the symbol of a still rich sultanate, but one that commanded a smaller territory. Perhaps this bore out the reports of European travellers who visited Borneo in the seventeenth and nineteenth centuries, during South East Asia's age of European mercantilism, when the sultanate was invariably found to be in decay. Nevertheless today's Sarawak was a part of Brunei's sultanate until James Brooke became its overlord. Sabah, as British North Borneo, was also Brunei territory until it was commandeered by the Baron Overbeck, together with Alfred Dent and a consortium of London businessmen who formed the North Borneo Chartered Company in 1881 and ruled until the arrival of the Japanese in the Second World War.

I was dragged back to the present by a shout from Bacal who had found a crab making its way across the rocks. We were high above sea level and a long hike from the coast. How had the crab got there? We toyed with the idea that it had been dropped by a bird – the displaced arthropod baby of a passing stork. Later we learnt that it was a true Land crab, living well away from marine waters, but 'cheating' in its existence by retreating to puddles whenever possible. In the lowland forests of Borneo these crabs are very numerous and play an important role in the invertebrate community. Much later, when a new species of Bornean Land crab was named after Mark, we mused on whether destiny might have been trying to thrust the new species under his unwelcoming nose on this first encounter. Could this have been his preview of *Isolopotamon collinsi?* Probably not.

There are several types of Land crab. One of them, the large and savage Robber crab, or Birgus, of the Pacific Islands is especially interesting. It is not a true crab but a sort of Hermit crab (crabs which generally wear other shells, although as it happens the Birgus does not). They have massive pincers which, combined with their habit of climbing coconut palms, led to the belief that they could crack open coconuts. In fact they do eat coconuts that have already been opened by rats (although what they did before the rats arrived is a conundrum). These large crabs have a nasty habit of grabbing other species of Land crabs by the pincers. The victim sheds his limb in an effort to escape and the Birgus promptly cracks it open and feasts on the amputated flesh.

We descended from the summit and must have been two-thirds of the way back to the kampong when Yahyah, who had come to meet us, pointed fearfully towards a dark cave in the side of the hill. 'Lobang mati,' Yahyah said – 'the cave of the dead'. We moved towards the cave but Yahyah was wary of 'hantu' – ghosts. In retrospect it was thoughtless but at the time we did not fully understand Yahyah's complex explanation and so the three of us entered the cave, leaving a fearful Yahyah outside. There we found little piles of ashes. We were apprehensive lest we had offended Yahyah through unwittingly desecrating the site of a human cremation, but we could never grasp his flustered explanation about the cave.

When we reached the kampong we found Yahyah waiting for us,

deeply depressed. His depression worsened that night as Mark developed a headache and teetered on the verge of vomiting. Convinced that the hantu were working their evil on Mark, Yahyah refused to stray far from him. Nevertheless, the hantu were merciful and Mark soon recovered, although Yahyah told how the last two men to tamper with that cave had died.

Our evenings began to take on a strange dual schedule: first we ate at our home, ministered to our mosquito bites and prepared a warm drink in anticipation of Yahyah's arrival. Once he had come and the drink was finished we would all adjourn to his house. There we stretched out and lazily talked away the night, Yahyah along the back wall, Mark in the left corner, me in the middle and Andrew against the other wall. It is odd how inescapable such unconscious conventions can become. The Isteri sat in the kitchen or nursed Ruslan next to Yahyah. The stark interior of the house was disquieting in comparison with ours – our home was built of rough corners, of the natural ruggedness of banana leaves and worn bark, bamboo knuckle wedged against rough-hewn spar, and from every notch there hung a canvas bag, a pair of binoculars, elements of a collection of bones, feathers, notebooks and toiletry, all arranged to avoid crushing the mud wasps' nests. Yahyah's new home was a desert by comparison: sawn beams of wall and floor met in angular hostility and every smooth surface defied the desire to hang a treasure. I could not imagine how he could have so few belongings. The austerity was neutralized by two friendly objects, the half-made fishing net hanging in the window and a temperamental Tilley lamp. But whatever these surroundings lacked was balanced by the extravagance of the plans hatched in our conversations.

One night, as we lay awake in the dark in Yahyah's house, he suggested that we go shark fishing the next day. Our departure for this adventure was delayed because of the difficulty of catching eels as bait. According to Abdullah, Yahyah was extremely 'pandai' (clever) as an eel-catcher. While the tide was out Yahyah, Abdullah and Mark walked for miles up and down the edge of the swamp marking with sticks the position of burrows inside which the eels lived. Later, as the next tide went out, we all set out in the boat. Each time we passed a small marker stick that indicated the position of an eel's hole Yahyah or Abdullah clambered into the water and felt around for the mouth of the hole. They then eased a pliable stem of reed, about half a metre long, into the hole. A hook and line were attached to one end of the reed. They fed the grass slowly along the contours of the burrow like a sweep's broom in a chimney. The hook, baited with pieces of shrimp, advanced towards the resting eel which would snap at it and be caught. This, at least, was the theory of the exercise, but two or three hours later we had managed to catch only one eel. Nevertheless, Yahyah and Abdullah decided this would be sufficient and, as dusk drew in, we slowly made our way out to sea.

These eels, incidentally, figure largely in the legends of one of the longhouse peoples of Borneo, the Kenyah. They tell of a time when the fish decided that one among their number must be elected to undertake the job of rainmaker. Many refused, but finally the ancestor of the eels accepted, on condition that each of the other fish would give him a bone. It seems that the job of rainmaker was an unattractive one, for all the other fish readily accepted the bargain, each contributing a bone, which is how the eel of today came to have so many.

We were in Abdullah's big boat, about five metres long and rather like a punt, and it bucked ferociously at the slightest wave. We were well out to sea when Yahyah announced that we had reached a place famed for its sharks. The eel was cut into small portions and impaled on hooks tied at regular intervals to a long line, which was let out to sea. We waited for an hour or more while Abdullah ribbed Yahyah for choosing such a bad place. As always, the sea was alive with luminous creatures. As I peered into the rippling waves small fishes darted past, their heads haloed in a glow of light which seemed to come from below their eyes. I thought they were Lantern-eyed fish, for these have glands below each eye which contain luminescent bacteria. Some Lantern-eyed fish have a 'blind' which can be drawn across the light to switch it on and off, so to speak, as they swim. Others can rotate the entire gland so that it casts light inwardly – a window into their souls! The function of these lanterns is unknown. Eventually all the hooks were pulled aboard and we travelled on, further and further out to sea, before casting out again for another hour, but again with disappointing results.

It was now well into the night and as we chugged on towards the moonlit horizon I dimly saw the outline of palm trees in the far distance. Yahyah and Abdullah jumped into the water which, to my surprise, only reached their knees, and began to walk towards land. I took an oar and paddled the boat after them as they held aloft their torches of paraffin-soaked rags and paranged edible crabs on the sand below. We amassed quite a number of crabs which were loaded into the boat before we set off again. This time we headed for a place where Abdullah said we had a better chance of catching shark. The lines went out and the night rocked by as we waited for a bite. We fell in and out of sleep, huddled among mutilated crabs in the damp, smelly corners of Abdullah's boat. At 3 am the boat lurched, Abdullah and Yahyah sprang to the engine, paid out line to reduce the strain and, after a brief battle, landed well over a metre of shark. The splashings and commotions which ensued left us all drenched. By now it was cold and, as the lines went out again, our soaking clothes ensured that the remainder of the night was passed even less comfortably.

Dawn found us out of sight of all land and still with only one shark to our credit. However, the rising sun mercifully dried our clothes and quelled our shivers, and we lit a fire on the floor of the boat and cooked a delicious breakfast of roasted crab. By midday we had worked around in a big crescent, still failing to catch more shark, but coming in sight of land. Reaching a bay we beached the boat, disembarked and watched as, in the distance, a line of men waded along the shoreline raising long flattened clubs above their heads with which they beat the water's surface in unison. They shouted as they drummed the water to drive fish into nets positioned further down the coast. Our legs stretched, we set sail for home.

We had not gone far when a strand of seaweed beside the boat sprang to life and coiled hurriedly away – a serpent. I told the others what I had seen, but their only response was that they had seen a brace of mermaids! My point was taken, however, when we spotted two more of these creatures. To come across a snake basking on the surface of the sea might seem surprising, but there is an entire family of snakes which is adapted exclusively to marine living. Sea snakes, known to science as the *Hydrophiidae,* are most common in shallow seas or in the mouths of estuaries although some can be found far out in the Pacific. Of the 280 species of poisonous snakes in the world, about fifty belong to the *Hydrophiidae,* and their poison is known to be particularly potent; they can paralyse their prey – mainly eels – within seconds. A close look at a sleeping sea snake revealed that its tail was flattened from side to side and paddle-shaped in order to propel it through the water. It seems that basking on the surface in the sun is a common habit of sea snakes: some travellers have reported seeing them in quite large aggregations, drifting like serpentine spaghetti in the sunshine.

Leaving the sea snakes behind we cruised back home. Two hours after our arrival we were drowsily watching a troop of monkeys, having gorged ourselves on delicious shark meat. In Borneo, where everything was so new to us, each minute was certainly filled with its sixty seconds worth of distance run.

7

Gentle Nomads

Borneo is peopled by an intriguing diversity of tribes and races, whose origins and relationships have for the most part remained buried in the mists of legend, in spite of the efforts of anthropologists. We were to meet representatives of only a fraction of these peoples. The Punan and Penan are nomads of the interior, gentle, shy people often oppressed by the more settled and sometimes warlike riverside communities. By the river, villagers live in single longhouses; these groups include the Kenyah people, divided into many sects such as the Berawan of the Tutoh river, and the Iban or Sea Dayaks, most famed of Borneo's headhunters. There are dozens of other tribes too, the Kadazan or Dusun of the north, the Murut, and the peoples isolated far up in the Kelabit highlands around Bario. Then there are the coastal Malays, intermingled with Chinese and other settlers. We felt sure that among these people there must be individuals who would lead us to the tarsier.

By great good fortune we met an officer at the Royal Brunei Malay army camp at Berakas who shared our enthusiasm for Brunei's interior. Major Chris Browne had visited several remote villages already and among these were the homes of the Punan, a people living a nomadic hunter-gatherer existence in the deepest jungle. They of all people would surely know the tarsier. After much scheming, Chris arranged that we should be dropped by helicopter into a distant zone he had explored once before, in an attempt to find these shy people.

We arrived at Chris's house the night before our scheduled departure, to be warned in severe tones that a punctual start was vital: the helicopter would leave at 7.40 the next morning. By the time we had finished breakfast Chris had still not appeared. At 7.25 he shot through the room swathed in a towel, heading for the bathroom. At 7.30 he moved fast in the opposite direction. Five minutes from the projected take-off time Chris emerged. We piled into the car, which rocked under Chris's furious onslaught on the locked boot. Eventually conceding that the key was necessary, he sped again to the house. Minutes ticked by. As we screeched to a halt on the landing strip the helicopter blades were already revolving. We signed crushed indemnity forms as the machine rose from the ground. Seconds later we were in the air and flying over jungle; below us a misty cloud formation appeared woven around the crowns of the highest trees.

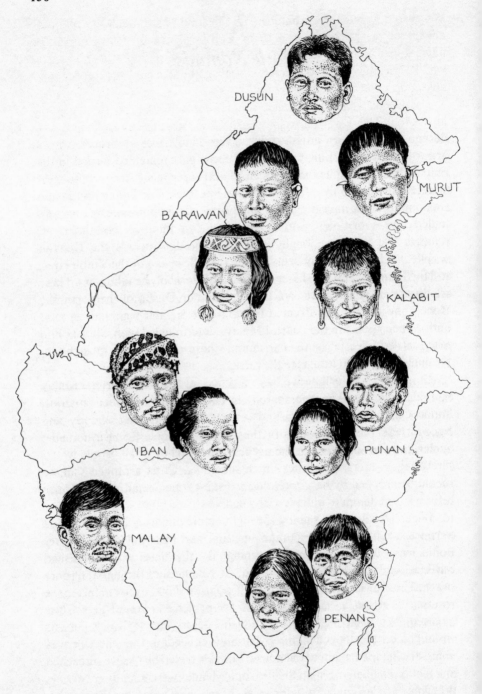

We peered through thick patches of this cloud to see unusually tall trees ahead, then leap-frogged over them. The lack of visibility was giving the navigator trouble – we overheard him telling the pilot that our direction was 107 degrees out – so we circled until he found a river with a recognizable course and our bearings could be reset.

Large burnt patches of jungle could occasionally be seen through gaps in the fog. These were areas of slash and burn agriculture, some now deserted and overgrown with scrub and seedling jungle, others with paddy growing. The mist cleared once, and a hornbill flapped frantically away only metres from us. I glimpsed a large red animal in the treetops for an instant, but it slipped from view, and we sped on. It could have been a Maroon langur, a fair-sized reddish Leaf monkey, but it seemed too heavily built, too cumbersome. I so much wanted to see an orang-utan, the great red ape, that I feared my eyes were deceiving me into believing that this was what it was. Whether or not the lumbering form was really an orang I will never know, but this glimpse reminded me of the excitement with which A.R. Wallace wrote in 1883 of his first contact with orang-utans in Borneo. Wallace spent almost two years in Borneo, from 1854 to 1856 and, like many travellers after him, he was preoccupied with finding orang-utans or 'mias', as they are called locally. Within a week of moving his camp to Simunjan in Sarawak, Wallace had his first sighting of the 'great man-like ape of Borneo'. He was understandably excited when, as he travelled the forest collecting insects, he heard a rustle in a tree nearby and saw above him a large red-headed animal meandering slowly along, hanging from the branches by its arms. But the mias was soon lost to view and swampy ground prevented him from following it.

Within a few days, however, Wallace was lucky enough to find a second orang-utan but the excitement I shared with him on reading his text jarred sickeningly as he continued: 'As soon as I approached, it tried to conceal itself among the foliage; but I got a shot at it, and the second barrel caused it to fall down almost dead, two balls having entered its body.' In the very next sentence of his account Wallace again finds himself out shooting with two of his guides when he spotted another well-grown orang. This one fell at the first shot but on hitting the ground immediately rose and climbed the nearest tree prompting Wallace to fire once more, again bringing his victim to the ground, this time with a broken arm and a wound in its body. His two Dayaks ran up to it and each seized hold of the animal by its hands, but although, as he continued, 'one arm was broken and it was a half grown animal, it was too strong for these young savages, drawing them up towards its mouth notwithstanding all their efforts, so that they were again obliged to leave go'. The wounded ape began to climb the tree again and, as Wallace says, 'to avoid trouble' he shot it through the heart. Another big male put up an even more serious resistance, fleeing from tree to tree on his smashed and crumpled limbs before a final shot brought him to the ground, still alive, but mortally wounded. This 4 feet 2 inch giant had an outstretched arm span of 7 feet 3 inches. His capacity for survival prompted comment from his assassin, who had killed seventeen orangs by the time he left Sarawak. The big male had both his legs broken by shot, one hip joint and the root of his spine completely shattered, and two bullets were found flattened in his neck and jaws. He is preserved today in the museum at Derby.

On several occasions Wallace had to cut down trees in order to extract orangs that had died near the crown and were wedged in position. However, his men were not faced with this tiresome task on the occasion when he shot and killed a juvenile animal which was wedged in the fork of a tree. As he said, 'As young animals are of comparatively little interest, I did not have the tree cut down to get it.' It would be unjust to lift quotations from an old text if the aim were simply to criticize or mock. Neither are my intention – far from it, for Wallace was a superb naturalist – but it is important to realize that the actions of an honourable man in the past may seem deplorable in the present. One may wonder what aspects of our own attitudes in Borneo will weather poorly with time?

Strain my eyes though I did, I saw no further hint of either monkey or ape in the treetops. Eventually we put down at the remote landing zone of Long Sukang. Chris had been to Sukang before and led us down a path and into the trees. We wound on down the track in the sweltering heat, coming to a huge area of freshly burnt land where the breeze still picked up little whirlwinds of ashes and where charred stumps of trees smouldered mournfully. In the distance, working among the embers, were two women clad in sarongs once colourful, now grey with soot. They were not Punan, but when we came to them they gave us rough directions to the area where they thought that Punan could be found. Twenty minutes later we came to an old bark house, in general style much like our own, standing on stilts amid two metre tall dry-paddy. It was here that the day, which had always had promise, started to take on a dreamlike quality. A man came out of the house to greet us. He was small, I would guess no more than five feet tall, and wore only a loin cloth. In appearance he was quite unlike anybody I had ever met. His features were different from those of the Malay people to whom we were accustomed: his cheeks were high, his skin light, and his heavy eyebrows were topped by a fringe that covered his ears and formed a long swathe reaching to the middle of his back. The man recognized Chris and strode forward to greet him warmly.

Once inside the house, my eyes leapt from object to object, from face to face, terrified lest I miss anything of this wondrous place. Above our heads on the struts of the roof lay blowpipes – two metre long poles, each the girth of a broomstick, with a tiny bore through their length and tipped with a spear head. Following my gaze, the Punan produced some cocktail-stick darts from the bamboo quiver that hung from his waist. I turned one in my hand, feeling the tip with my finger, noting how sharp it was. The end was coated with a black residue – through Chris's interpretation the Punan explained that this was a poison extracted from tree bark, which would kill a pig in three minutes but took five minutes to kill a man (although these are such peaceful people that they probably only know of the effect on humans from being at the receiving end of attacks from their warrior-like Iban neighbours). Below, through the slatted floorboards, we could see wild-looking swine that chomped and snorted. Outside, on the verandah, piles of rice were stacked in flat wicker trays drying in the sun.

There were quite a number of people in the house, mostly Punan, but some Kadazan – a related people that traditionally have friendly contacts with the Punan. Three women sat either suckling or gently rocking babies in cradles suspended from chest-expander springs which, as far as I could see, were the outside world's only remotely useful contribution to the furnishings of the house. The babies were swathed in shawls slung from the chest expanders to which a cluster of watersnail shells was attached. When the rocking motion of the spring stopped, the shells stopped rattling and the mothers knew that it was time to come and give the spring another push to set it in motion once again. The Punan's wife sat beside her baby as he bounced on the springs. The suckling infant oscillated gently, all the while maintaining a firm grip on his mother's breast.

We stayed for an hour in the house. We were all given hot milk; it tasted sweet and thin but from what beast it came I do not know. Mark, the only smoker of our number, was given a native cigarette; Chris warned him that it would be strong. The thick black fumes compelled him to pass it on to his neighbour almost immediately to the gentle amusement of the Punan who watched his every expression. As I grew accustomed to the dark room, I began to assimilate more detail. Hanging from the Punan's waist, beside his quiver, was a hollowed-out gourd. He explained that it contained plants and, seeing my puzzled expression, he tipped out a store of dried leaves, and some betelnut bark. When hunting is bad for these roaming people, chewing certain plants suppresses the hunger gnawing at their empty stomachs.

Conversation was difficult because neither the Punan nor ourselves were fluent in the lingua franca of Malay. I tentatively mentioned my interest in tampolili but the inquiry provoked no response. The conversation drifted over many topics. One of the Punan's relatives had been sick. I could not understand whether the patient was one of the people in the room, nor how he had been cured, but the thought of lonely sickness in the jungle tempered my romantic illusions about these peoples' lifestyle.

There are some wonderful accounts of their medicine. In 1966, for example, the Reverend Baartmans described in gripping detail the way a Punan shamaness (priestess), from a longhouse named Rumah Eilong, cured a sick woman. In a dark hut filled with concerned, breathless spectators, the wizardry of Punan physic began with the shamaness performing a violent dance around the patient, blowing repeatedly as if by so doing she would banish the spirit of the sickness from the room. The end of a jungle knife was then held to the patient's stomach while a lighted candle was moved about over her abdomen in an attempt to 'see' the site of the sickness. This done, the shamaness sucked at the crucial spot on the patient's stomach, but her attempt to suck out the sickness failed. After more attempts and more dances a blossom was cut from a palm tree. It was a very special blossom selected from those on the side of the tree which faced the rising sun when it has not yet reached its zenith. The blossom was sliced open and the fibres therein were long and slender, which indicated that there was hope of a cure, and so the dancing and sucking recommenced. Then, as excitement mounted and the impassioned shamaness sucked yet more fervently at her patient's stomach, the crowd gasped in unison as she began to spit out black debris, the core of which was formed by some sort of black stone. A cure had been effected. Nevertheless the patient was cautiously brushed with a hornbill's feather to ward off the danger of madness following the cure.

Plans were made in a rapid tongue which I could not understand. Eventually we were led from the house by a Punan man who took us out across the open expanse of the slashed rice garden, through another regenerating garden and back to the thick vegetation beyond. Here we entered another new world. The trees towered tall above us, cutting out almost all light, and from them hung lianas and creepers. The hot air felt humid and damp as we moved at a fast pace in single file. We were careful not to brush our bare arms and legs against any vegetation on which leeches lurked, ready to launch themselves on to a new victim. The first man in the line was less afflicted but by the time he had passed the leeches had been alerted to the approaching feasts and were rearing on their suckers, scenting us out.

There is something almost hypnotic about the wifflings of leeches as they detect a man's presence nearby. The jungles of Borneo's interior might almost be defined as a place in which one is never more than a pace away from the nearest leech. Just as within our scientific mythology we believe that leeches have evolved from ancestral worms, so the peoples of Borneo have their own no less wonderful explanation for the origin of these animals. It seems that in the early days of mankind a man once returned home after a hunting trip to find that his wife had been seized by an evil spirit, who had carried her off into the jungle. This malignant elf had fastened the unfortunate woman to a large flat rock by means of some magical adhesive. It was there that her husband eventually found her ensnared. The husband built a jerat trap (a form of leg snare), setting the noose just where he hoped the spirit would step. He was lucky and had soon snared his wife's captor whom he then grabbed by something above his shoulders (the spirit had no head since he had already lost it to head-hunters during his first mortal life). Keen not to die again, the spirit traded his life for a solvent which would free the woman, but once she had been freed the enraged husband sought revenge and killed the spirit anyway. His troubles were far from over, however, since his wife soon bore a child sired by the ghost. This child was somehow associated with the awful adhesive material, and clamped onto his wife's breast, milking, as it were, the very life from her. Days passed and the woman began to wither away. Then the husband, in a last bid to save his wife's life, asked the infant the name of a tree: the name contained a combination of syllables which, if they were enunciated properly, would necessitate the child opening its mouth. This the unwary brat did. The man speedily slashed it with his sword into many tiny chunks, each of which was immediately transformed into a leech, whose descendants have henceforth lain in wait to seize and suck upon humanity. Still, the leeches were painless in their attack, and so we continued on our way.

At one point Chris was a few metres in front of me; I ducked my head to avoid an overhanging liana that had ensnared my hat and I had to pause to disentangle it; a moment later I looked up and Chris had disappeared from view. I hurried on but he remained hidden from sight until I had rounded three or four more bends of the tightly winding trail. I realized then how deceptive was the apparent safety with which we were moving in the jungle. The heat was overpowering: tiny dry islands of light khaki material survived on dark, sweat-stained shirts. It is important to keep moving. Stop for long and the muscles stiffen, leeches gather and the eyelids grow heavy in the heat. We were in good condition, but a man exerting himself in the jungle can lose pints of sweat in an hour, and with it goes precious salt. After a while when you lick neat salt, you cannot taste it! On we strode through this moist world until we began to climb; the ground grew slightly firmer underfoot, the mire dried and suddenly we were in a clearing of which every detail is blazened into my memory with such clarity that I still catch my breath thinking of it.

A small platform of saplings with a roof of leaves stood a few centimetres clear of the ground. A charred rice pot steamed over a fire of twigs, and a young Punan woman was suckling her baby girl sitting under this 'Dulap' shelter – a woman whose face was so incomparably tranquil that as I moved into the clearing towards her, I scarcely dared to breathe lest the spell be broken. From I know not where a second girl appeared and sat down quietly beside the first. She shared the same light skin and demure expression. The mother was quite lovely, her light tawny skin smeared in places with earth and dappled by sunlight that sneaked through the thick canopy and leaf shelter of her roof.

Some minutes passed. The woman appeared to hear something in the jungle, although no unusual sound had reached my ears. The nursing mother turned, listening intently, and made a hooting call out into the trees. Almost at once a Punan hunter was in our midst, having material- ized only twenty metres to my side. Facially he was like the first Punan we had met but younger and with a graceful power that matched the young woman's beauty. He wore only a loin cloth, fashioned from bark. As he held his blowpipe-cum-spear, his pectoral muscles stood out from his chest as smooth mounds. My first impression was of a giant, but as he moved towards us and stood beside Mark, I saw that in reality he was tiny.

This Punan seemed pleased to see us. Chris had some photographs he had taken of other Punan in Sarawak and he showed some of these to the hunter. He was enthralled. They seemed oblivious of our cameras and ap- peared not to appreciate the connection between them and the photo- graphs. As I watched, entranced, a strange bleating cry kept emerging from the direction of the two women. I could not believe that it was the baby. Then the mother produced a small bag in which a baby gibbon was cradled. Cream fur, black face and hands, it was no more than twenty centimetres high and shrieked pitifully when she stopped cuddling it. Mark held it for some minutes but it was obviously terrified away from its 'mother'. With the appearance of this tiny ape, orphaned by the hunter's blowpipe and whose mother had been eaten by the woman who now suckled him, my rapt excitement was hardly bearable.

Photographing the gibbon I was sweating so profusely that I could barely see through the viewfinder for the perspiration which showered from my forehead. Nursing baby gibbons and piglets is not uncommon among the Punan. Indeed gibbons play an important role in the folklore of many of Borneo's tribes. It is said that, before there were hunting dogs, people used gibbons as guides to locate the whereabouts of game. There is an elaborate legend which explains why this custom ceased.

A particular chief among the Kelabit people of the Bornean highlands had an especially able hunting gibbon. One day the chief, whose name was Saluyah, sent his brother hunting in the company of the gibbon. Now it is said that there was one tremendous drawback to hunting with gibbons, namely that when the gibbon discovers some prey, such as a pig, in screaming and shouting to attract attention it can equally attract the attention of any enemy. This is exactly what happened on the day that Saluyah's brother was hunting. First he followed the gibbon and successfully tracked a wild pig which he killed. The gibbon moved on and was soon chattering again, so the hunter stealthily continued through the undergrowth. But he was not stealthy enough and found himself surrounded by a group of his enemies. They challenged him to fight, one against many; he was a superb combatant and, in a great and majestic struggle, he killed each and every one of his adversaries. This herculean task was more than the hunter's heart could withstand and, standing back from his slain enemies, he died of exhaustion. In time the gibbon returned home and soon Saluyah realized what had happened to his brother. He blamed the gibbon for leading his brother into the arms of his enemies. The vengeful chief was about to slay the animal when several of his people grabbed the unfortunate ape in an attempt to save it, as they believed it was too great an asset to destroy. An agony of disarticulation followed this squabble, during which the gibbon's arms were stretched and his tail (which in those days all gibbons had) was pulled from his body. In the tussle the ape escaped and fled to the forest where his descendants have been – tailless and with disproportionately long arms – ever since.

The man led us on from this small encampment, a monument to the way all Punan lived before the influence of different civilizations began to penetrate the jungle. The path was indistinct. As I was crossing a small stream spanned by a makeshift bridge of an old bough, the branch broke to send me down into the muddy water below. Thinking of leeches I struggled out quickly as Chris, following behind, laughed at my fate. He stepped out onto the remaining branch which promptly broke and plunged him into the same mud.

Walking through tropical jungle you do not actually see very much wildlife: in comparison with temperate forests there is not a lot there, and what there is moves out of your way. Nevertheless, on this walk we did see one marvellous creature – a Flying lizard. In fact we had been seeing a lot of them, but to begin with I had merely thought they were falling leaves, catching my eye as they flitted momentarily through strong beams of sunlight. Then I saw the silhouette of a small lizard leaning out from the trunk of a tree. As I paused to watch, it cast itself into the air, swooped just like the 'leaves' I had been glimpsing and landed on a neighbouring trunk. These lizards have a membrane of skin spanning the distal ends of elongated ribs. As they leap they spreadeagle themselves and so glide rather than fly. They were really quite numerous once I became adept at spotting them.

Just below the point where the lizard had landed I spotted what looked like a bunch of ripe grapes hanging from a low shrub. The 'grapes' were white and plum sized. They were the fruits of a member of the family *Euphorbiaciae* and make excellent ingredients for broth. Jungle people regularly 'harvest' them and it is easy to imagine how a casual harvest could, through tradition and elementary husbandry, turn such a food plant into a crop, such as with the rambutan and durian.

We walked for a long time before we came to another clearing of burnt ground. The Punan stopped. The transformation was eerie – one minute struggling through thick jungle and the next in a devastated clearing. Even the air had a different consistency. The hunter cupped his hands to his face and hooted out across the hillside. The air smelt strongly of fire and charred wood and I felt witness to a grave sacrilege. Far below us I heard a hoot in reply. Strain my eyes as I might, I could see no one. I had been deluded by the perspective, for the clearing was far larger than I had thought. What I had mistaken at first for a small animal in the valley bottom was actually a man, and the white object that had caught my attention was his hat. An old man gradually came towards us, wending his way between the smouldering stumps. As he came closer, Chris excitedly recognized him as the Penghulu whom he had met before. To the Punan, the Penghulu is the chief, the man to whom all the roaming groups of a given sept owe allegiance.

It took a further ten minutes before the Penghulu neared us. He was old, but not in the least bald. He wore a loin cloth and a tattered vest and his long silvery hair was tied in a tight bun behind his neck. Shaking hands with each of us in turn, each time he took his own hand (and with it our friendship) back to press against his chest. The Penghulu was obviously pleased to see Chris again and I felt how fortunate we were to have a guide with such a gift for befriending these people.

The Penghulu suggested that we go back with him to the longhouse in the centre of his people's territory. On the way we visited a ramshackle house on stilts where Chris had stayed with his soldiers on the first occasion he had come to the area, during a training exercise. It was then that he had first encountered the incredible hospitality of the Punan, who had guided him and his troops to this house to sleep. Moreover, the Punan had stayed awake all night to keep the dogs and pigs, which normally lived under the house, well away from the Malay troops who, as Moslems, regarded them as 'unclean'.

I doubt if it was much more than two kilometres to the longhouse, but it was a hot hard trek. The Penghulu insisted that we walk ahead of him, claiming that an old man would slow us down. We worried lest the heat and the pace we were setting would overtire this old gentleman. However, at the end of the path he was still only a pace behind us and seemed to have shed not a bead of sweat, whereas we were in a very dilapidated state. The path led to a river's edge and we clambered into a narrow longboat which leaked badly as we paddled across to the opposite bank, nervous lest our cameras were in for a dunking. Pulling the boat ashore we walked on down the sandy shore for some fifty metres before climbing a steep bank to a path which rounded a corner and brought us in full view of the longhouse. Innumerable pariah dogs immediately set up the most incredible rumpus but thankfully scattered from our heels as we walked to the house.

The longhouse was indeed a strange hybrid. The traditional design consisted of a long verandah, communal to the whole village, which backed onto a number of rooms, seven in this particular case, each the home of a family group. However, the roof here was made of corrugated iron, flown out by helicopter when the government had decided it was unacceptable to have people living as hunter-gatherers. The Punan, resisting the encroachment of these new and unsuitable materials into their lives, had built a series of bedrooms onto the back of the longhouse, extending each of the seven individual rooms (bileks) backwards. The bileks were floored with widely placed slats of bamboo, roofed by leaves and closely mimicked the little leaf shelter we had seen in the jungle.

The Penghulu's wife appeared shortly after our arrival, an old woman with a cheery face which had obviously once been lovely. She wore only a sarong around her waist. Heads appeared out of each of the doors to view the strangers. A rather odd old man walked towards me. He wore a loin cloth and carried his blowpipe. His hair was long but not grey, although he seemed to be older than the Penghulu, and his eyes were strangely vacant. He slipped quickly past me. Later I edged to the back of the verandah to see what he was doing. I found him just as he was aiming his blowpipe; he fired, but I could not see what he had shot at. He looked displeased and fired another dart into the air. Perhaps he was testing a freshly made pipe. Anyway, he climbed back inside and disappeared into his bilek. Chris explained that he had seen this man before, that he was deaf and mute but he still hunted pigs, largely by smell, as his sight too was failing.

We were told of a technique for manufacturing blowpipes, but I do not know if it is true. A small cavity is cut in the centre of the cut end of the pole which is to be bored. A pebble is then lodged in this cavity and the pole is carefully positioned in a river at a place where the current runs fast and straight. The pole is fixed so that it lies exactly along the line of the current, with its cut cross-section perpendicular to the flow. The pebble is jostled and turned in its cavity, like a pea in a penny whistle, and eventually is driven straight through the pole. If this technique really is used then it would provide an answer to how these pipes were bored prior to the Punan learning to be smiths.

Behind the longhouse a monotonous thumping took up a harmony with the jungle birds. I wandered around to investigate and found two girls in a small clearing, husking rice. On the ground lay an old dry tree trunk, roughly planed to lie flat. In the centre of the log was a flat-bottomed hole,

the size of a large jam jar. A handful of rice was thrown into this chamber. Then the two girls each took a grip on solid poles, just narrower in diameter than the rice chamber itself. Standing one at each end of the flat log, they began to pound the imprisoned husks from their grains. The handles of the poles were smooth and dull, once defiant splinters had been moistened by sweat and chafed into papery submission by unyielding skin. The two girls worked silently, methodically, their toes gripping, then releasing as they poised on the log, pounding and sweating their survival from the land.

The deaf man's wife came on to the verandah with him. She was old and shrivelled but had jet black hair, and her legs were so thin that when she sat down to smoke her ulu cigarette, her legs bent double, her thigh and calf were almost parallel. She, like several others, seemed strangely oblivious of our presence. As we sat on the verandah talking with the Penghulu and his people, the dogs set up a terrible fracas again. Down the path came the people from the leaf shelter. It was awesome to see them weaving through the forest fringes, the powerful man, striding with springing pace, followed by the two women, one carrying her child and the gibbon in a wicker selabit on her back. I cannot exaggerate the unity between these people and their surroundings: they seemed to feel every vibration of the jungle, to respond to every sound, not with the jerky movement of a trained eye but with fluid instinct. They strode onto the verandah, and the hunter came up with unhesitating warmth and shook our hands. The two women disappeared into a room but reappeared moments later with water jars which they carried down to the river. When they returned, carrying the jars on their shoulders, they were dripping wet, sarongs clinging tightly around their bodies, sturdy but not fat and radiating health and beauty.

As we talked with the people about tampolili it became apparent that they did know much about the animal, which to them was called 'kat'. If we were to stay for a week or so then they would surely catch some for us, teach us how to use blowpipes, how to stalk wild pig, how to build jungle shelters. The Penghulu's excitement and my own mounted, only to crash as I remembered the helicopter that was to call for us that night, and that our time in Borneo was rapidly drawing to a close. So we talked on and on, gleaning as much as we could from these people about their way of life, their beliefs, their hopes and fears. They used to be animists, but quite recently a new faith, Bungan, had spread among them, and among other people of Borneo's interior.

It seems that in 1948 a Kenyah tribesman from Indonesia known as Jok Apoi had a particularly poor harvest. One night he dreamt fitfully about his misfortunes, and in his dream a goddess named Bungan appeared to him. With sound good sense she proposed that his bad harvest could be attributed directly to the number of overbearing prohibitions that beset his working time. Like all other animists Jok Apoi frequently had to down tools when a certain bird called or a deer cried. During the past season these awkward auguries had so outnumbered good omens that Jok Apoi had been almost hamstrung in his efforts to produce a crop. No sooner would he pick up his hoe than a deer would bark and compel him to rest again. The goddess said that were he to worship her instead of heeding the voices of the jungle, then it would suffice to put a hen's egg in the palm of his hand and point it in the direction in which he proposed to go towards his garden each day. This done, he would be required to impale the egg, still pointing in the appropriate direction, on the end of a stick wedged in the ground outside his house. If he did these simple things she assured him that he could safely discount all the cries of the various birds and beasts which would have previously prohibited him from working. Jok put this into practice and, while it must have required a steely nerve on his part to ignore the cry of the deer, his crops flourished. Naturally other people envied his success and soon the religion of Bungan was acquiring converts. In 1952 Jok travelled from Indonesia to his cousin in Sarawak where, quite understandably, the faith has also spread.

It would be easy to imagine that the birth and rebirth of such beliefs could follow a cyclical pattern: once too cumbersome to be workable, a religion can be neatly jettisoned and replaced by a simpler one; but as time passes the new deity could, through advancing folklore, in turn require more and more cumbersome displays of faith by its disciples.

We were brought hot tea and durian as we sat on the verandah of the longhouse. Durian fruit may euphemistically be called an acquired taste. A large yellowish fruit, it smells of rotting flesh or onions, depending on your mood. Nevertheless, an idiosyncratic quirk of almost everyone who has spent time in South East Asia is an addiction to this fruit. Historically the durian had its own role to play in eroding man's egocentric view of the world. Nineteenth-century poets and moralists had been seduced into the comforting belief (based on observations of trees in the English countryside) that small fruits always grew on taller trees in order that their fall should be harmless to men who moved below, and that large fruits always developed near the ground. It was in an account of the addictive durian that A.R. Wallace attempted to debunk this theory by pointing out that the durian not only grew high aloft and to a large size, but was also armed with exceedingly unpleasant spikes and so really was dangerous to humans lingering below. Nowadays the durian is also cultivated, but apparently the crop is under some threat. The durian flower is pollinated by a fruit bat, and the numbers of this species of bat are dwindling because reclamation of mangrove swamps is reducing their staple food supply. If the bats go, then so too may the cultivated durian.

That evening the helicopter returned for us. The longhouse was in full view as we hovered above the landing zone. Everyone was in sight. All our new-found friends were clambering up onto the roof of the longhouse, waving and shouting to us in the air. My heart full, I promised myself that one day I would return and learn how to build shelters, to use a blowpipe and to find the tarsier.

In fact I did return to Borneo in 1978, to the Mulu National Park. That expedition, led by Robin Hanbury Tenison, is described in his book *Mulu – The Rain Forest*, so I will only mention it briefly here. In Mulu I met the Penan people, whom initially I thought were synonymous with the Punan, differing only in the idiosyncratic use of a vowel. However, I learnt later that they were a different people, with a different language, although a similar forest-dwelling, hunter-gatherer lifestyle. But I spent more time in contact with another Bornean people – the Berawan of Long Terawan – in Mulu. The Berawan occupy the riverside longhouses up the Tutoh and Baram rivers; their people live in only five settlements but are a cultural offshoot of a more populous group, the Kenyah. The men of Long Terawan worked with the expedition members, and a man named Jacob Melai was of particular assistance to me.

Jacob was the son of an important elder in Long Terawan and was a tremendous source of information. At the time I was conducting a pilot study of civets, with Margaret Wise, another biologist. We fitted a civet with a radio-transmitter attached to a neck-collar and thereafter, by following the signal, monitored its movements by night in the jungle. Jacob learnt how to use the radio-tracking equipment and was soon helping with the tracking. As we got to know each other better and became friends, we talked more and more about the history of his people; we talked of the headhunting days, of the Japanese occupation, of the spirits that required propitiation in the jungle around us. One day Jacob said that, if I wished, one of his uncles would take us to a special place of the spirits. Several days after my enthusiastic response, his uncle arrived and the three of us set out by river.

Not far downstream we moored the boat and cut through the forest. After a while we came to the place. Jacob's uncle, Tama Lang, clambered into a muddy gully through which trickled a rather putrid-looking creek. Tama Lang was old and fat. He moved ponderously, his long silver hair tied in a bun and his pierced ear lobes stretched down towards his shoulders. He stood knee deep in the water and, leaning forward, he began to scrape up bundles of rotting leaves in order to dam the stream. This done, Tama Lang stared at the rising water till a telltale bubble slithered to the surface. At that spot he began to excavate more and more leaves from the detrital depths of the stream bed. Bubbles rose in rapid succession and the air hung with sulphur. Tama Lang placed the dredged leaves across the stream further up, damming it again to make a pool. Soon the hot water bubbling up from below filled the pool till he was standing in water up to his waist. Steam began to rise into the humid air above. The old man climbed out of the water and announced that all was ready. He took an egg from his bundle and placed it at the edge of the pool, murmuring a greeting to the spirit as he did so. Jacob asked what gift I had brought for

the spirit, and told me I must repeat the words that Tama Lang said and tell the spirit my name and where I came from. I said the words after Tama Lang and, as I did so, cast a two pence piece into the bubbling water. The sulphurous stench might have indicated otherwise, but Tama Lang concluded that the spirit seemed well satisfied, so the three of us slithered into the pool and sat in the water, immersed to our chins and surrounded by the foul breath of the earth's core. At the point where the bubbles of sulphur crept through the leaves you could feel the warm current seeping up between your toes, so hot it was only just bearable. We had bathed for a quarter of an hour or more when Tama Lang decided our bodies were healthy again. We climbed out and sat on a rotting log, talking of the spirits and of the past, and lazily drying ourselves while watching the occasional leech humping enthusiastically towards our bare flesh.

In Berawan language Tama Lang told of the time of the Japanese confrontation, and Jacob translated into a hybrid of Malay and English. The Japanese occupied Borneo and other East Indian islands during the Second World War (in New Guinea they were greeted as Ancestors, hopefully arriving with the so-called secret of Cargo – namely, how to make ships arrive filled with free supplies of cargo for the tribesmen, as they apparently did for the white colonists). The Japanese had treated the Berawan people harshly and Tama Lang's voice took on the quiet weight of one who remembers with hatred. He told of how the Japanese soldiers had burnt the longhouse and how they had destroyed almost every item of the Berawan's precious heirlooms. The villagers fled to the jungles and, cloaked in the safety of silent footsteps and poisoned darts, had conducted a war of attrition on the occupying troops. When the war ended in 1945 some Japanese survived but, according to Tama Lang, the Berawan were not interested in the surrender of a people who had so defiled their treasures. So over the months, one by one, each Japanese head was severed from its unwary owner and took its place in the sacred cave. Jacob also told me of how the spirits had protected the Berawan of Long Terawan in their war; on one occasion the men had been rowing a long war-boat up the Melinau river, many warriors paddling in unison. The Japanese lay in ambush on the river banks, so the warriors rowed straight past them – the perfect broadside target. The soldiers opened fire, strafing the boat with round after round of automatic fire. The warriors called upon a god (a god of the eagle, if I understood correctly) and rowed mightily. Once out of range they paused to count their losses, but not a man was wounded and not one of the hail of bullets had struck the boat.

Tama Lang paused in his story telling. Through the canopy the sun was bright, but a heavy cloud had gathered. Tama Lang stood up. We must leave for fear of Hujan panas – hot rain. Whan it rains while the sun is shining brightly – the gloriously refreshing rain where each drop of water carries a rainbow – than it augurs ill. The spirit, Hujan panas, strikes and kills. During such rain the Berawan wear crosses of charcoal daubed on their foreheads for protection. So we returned to base-camp.

The civet we studied was fascinating. Jacob helped me catch it after being advised on the best technique by the unrivalled hunter Lang. (Tama Lang, incidentally, means father of Lang; many people in Borneo's interior change their names quite often, depending on the birth of a son, the death of a relative or, perhaps, whim or omens in a dream.) The trap we used was a form of leg snare, called jerat in Malay. We built a two hundred metre long line of jerat across a strip of forest in the alluvial plain of the Melinau river, in a place where Lang had advised that civets would travel. First we built a hedge of vegetation, and at every twenty to thirty metres we left a gap. Next a footplate woven of creepers was placed in the gaps and held in a cocked position by a small wooden peg. A sapling was then bent over and tied to the peg. The whole arrangement was so constructed that any animal standing on the footplate would jolt the peg and release the taut sapling. Also attached to the end of the sapling was a noose, and as the tree sprang up so it would draw the noose around the captive's foot. Jacob and Lang assured me that civets were frequently caught in this way for the cooking pot and that they were invariably unharmed by capture. In fact, when we caught the civet it narrowly escaped damage to its leg, which would certainly have resulted if it had remained for longer in the snare; trapping with an unmodified jerat is a risky business. Nevertheless, once the civet was radio-collared and released we could follow it wherever it went. By day it slept in one of a number of rocky outcrops in the alluvial forest. By night it foraged on the forest floor, or in bat-inhabited caves. It covered an area of fifty to sixty hectares in its nightly travels. By night, Margaret, Jacob or myself would stalk after it, pinpointing its position with the radio and then searching with a spotlight shrouded in red celluloid until we spotted the animal.

One night, soon after collaring the civet, it turned up at our camp. I was sitting on the steps leading up to the expedition's longhouse as the radio signal blasting through my headphones reached maximum volume. I must be pretty well sitting on the animal. Suddenly I realized that was almost exactly what I was doing, for a rustling noise beneath the steps was followed by the emergence of the civet's ungainly tubular body into the clearing. In the light of the red torch I could see every detail of its body. It paused, its nose apparently leading a twitching existence of its own, then it quickly scuttled forward and a crispy morsel succumbed. A glow from the bileks revealed that Robin and Nigel, the expedition's chief organizers, were still awake in the longhouse. I edged inside and caught their attention. For the next quarter of an hour the three of us perched on the verandah and were treated to the most relaxed glimpses imaginable of the civet's night life. The pleasure of seeing the animal was almost equalled by the pleasure of seeing my companions' delight as we watched the civet slither like a shadow through the moonlight. As the small hours drew on we could watch it catching frogs and crickets around the camp clearing, as it had doubtless done, undetected, on many nights before.

On subsequent nights the civet sometimes arrived quite early. Once Margaret and I had already stalked it for the best part of an hour when Jacob emerged from the house where the Berawan working for the expedition slept. The men were having a party and we were invited in. Inside, a narrow corridor stretched the length of the longhouse and each side was bordered by a slightly raised shelf where people slept. The house was full— some slept, others, heads propped up on elbows, watched the proceedings, volubly commenting on anything and everything. Two shy Penan were there, diffidently shouldering a succession of Berawan jibes. Our arrival caused the boisterous conversation to come to a standstill but Jacob, as always the perfect master of ceremonies, persuaded one of his cousins to begin playing a guitar-like instrument with high twanging notes. The youth ran his fingers up and down the wooden neck of the instrument, rapidly plucking individual strings in a complicated melody while shyly murmuring the words of a traditional ballad. Meanwhile a glass filled with yellowish beer was passed towards me down the line of lazing men. It was a noxious brew. I sipped and nodded in polite approval, but muttered to Jacob that the liquid had been collected from the civet. To my horror he quickly translated my remark – shyness vanished in a volley of thigh slapping and the party became, to my relief, riotous once more. A man got up and, crossing to a space on the sleeping shelf opposite where I sat, began to dance, coiling in strangely disembodied pantomime. His concentration lapsed and, laughing, he retreated to the dark shadows again. The men chanted for Sabang, the best dancer of all, while the musician played on and more drink was poured. At last Sabang consented; he would perform a warrior dance. He stood in the space cleared for dancing, holding a parang. A goatskin was brought forward and cloaked his shoulders. Suddenly he shuddered as every muscle in his body snapped into readiness and his knees slowly bent till he was poised, as if to spring.

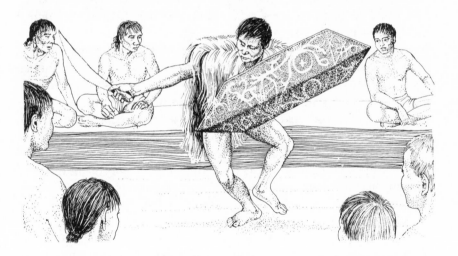

Slowly one foot was lifted while he began to turn on the other, still crouched low; the angled knees somehow encircled each other and Sabang pirouetted around so slowly that each degree ached as he revolved through it. And as he turned his right hand slowly drew the parang up to the level of his face and then sliced the smoke-laden air with a ghostly slow stroke. Twisting and turning in parry and in lunge he danced, poised for hanging seconds on the ball of one foot while crouching and rising again to

peer into the distance at an approaching enemy. Only power and balance
born of a lifetime in the jungle could bestow the control these agonizingly
slow movements demanded.

The dance finished amid deserved applause. Now the men shouted to
me to dance. There was no way to say no. An embarrassing pause
followed as I struggled to untie the knotted laces of my jungle boots in preparation for this definitely barefoot activity. Once on the dance floor my
antics were a pitiful disaster. First I discovered how difficult it was simply
to stand up on the springing bamboo floor, far less to stand on one leg. My
simplest attempts to hold Sabang's crouched position caused red hot
pains to shear up the tendons of my calves within seconds, and a carefully
conceived pirouette ended as I toppled to an ungainly heap on the floor.
Nevertheless, it seemed to make good comedy if nothing else!

Jacob and I travelled the neighbourhood in search of civet signs. We
concentrated our efforts around fruiting trees, since much of the forest
wildlife swarmed on such trees during the brief period for which they fruit.
Individuals of some species of tree fruit simultaneously, but perhaps only
once every six or seven years. Other species fruit asynchronously. Either
way, the fruiting strategies may be geared to 'outwit' herbivorous insects
that would gorge on the trees' prospective offspring. Many trees fruiting
simultaneously may swamp the herbivores (where numbers of herbivores
in the district may anyway be low through food shortage, if none of that
species of fruit has been available for five years). Alternatively, by fruiting
asynchronously, trees may, so to speak, throw their predators off the trail.
The fig is a species which lives isolated from its fellows, and individual
trees flower and fruit at irregular times. At a given moment somewhere in
the jungle there is a fig in fruit, but you may have a long walk to find it.
Fruiting figs are enveloped in a congregation of insects, monkeys, birds –
all busily making the most of the fruit while it lasts. We sought out figs,
thinking that their fruits would attract civets, although as it turned out our
radio civet did not use them. Some species of fig tree are themselves
extraordinarily barbarous plants. They begin life as seedlings growing in a
mud-puddle at the crown of a mature forest tree. Slowly the parasitic
seedling grows, dropping its roots towards the ground, winding them
around the apparently defenceless host. When two roots meet on their
twining journey they anastamose, fusing their flesh to build a ramifying
net around the bough of the victim. By the time the fig tree's roots have
reached the soil and gained firm purchase there, they will have encircled
and overwhelmed the original host in a union of spliced wooden sinew that
quite literally strangles it to death. In time the dead tree within the fig's
heart will rot away leaving an intricate tubular pattern of roots etched
upwards through the jungle air as a hollow memorial.

Fig trees enter a wonderful relationship with *Blastophaga* wasps. The wasps have special pouches on their legs in which they carry pollen from one fig tree to the next. Once the wasp has pollinated a flower it lays its eggs in special ovaries in the flower designed to harbour their eggs. The hatching wasps then pick up another generation of pollen as they emerge from their cradles. The young wasp must then seek out a different fig tree to pollinate since all the buds on its own tree will have flowered synchronously, so a newly emerged wasp will find only ripe fruit on its own tree.

As we walked along muddy trails, peering into the jungle on either side of us as we searched for fruiting trees, we quite often saw signs of the Penan. Their broad squat feet left deep prints in the trail as their toes worked the mud. The Penan tracks were intermingled with those of their hunting dogs – unattractive pariahs, thin-coated and black-tongued. Beside the jungle trails, sharp eyes could pick out saang – fronded message sticks. These sticks were knotted and bedecked with rattan in ways which informed the reader of who had passed by, how many were in the party, how long they intended to travel for, and I think much else besides. Apparently the number of slivers pared in the fresh bark indicated the number in the party; the number of knots in a length of rattan foretold how many days it would be before the group passed that place again; a rolled leaf at the bottom of the stock indicated that the journey was a long one. One of the expedition members, Philip Leworthy, once went hunting for pig with a Penan. They had not gone far before the hunter stopped and 'read' a message stick. He abandoned the trip, saying that his friend had killed the particular pig he had been hoping to hunt.

In a similar vein the Penan spoke of hunting monkeys in a most sophisticated manner. They seemed to know the size and membership of each group of Leaf monkeys and claimed to select their victims carefully. They killed young males in preference to females, for example, and had cropping programmes which would meet with the approval of any modern wildlife manager. This is not only exciting because it highlights the intimacy with which the Penan thrive within their environment and their sensitivity to ecological principles, but it is also interesting because this image contrasts strongly with some other reports of their hunting in the same area twenty years ago. In those days the image of the Penan hunter was of a rather indiscriminate, although not wanton, killer. Food seemed to be in abundance. Today, in contrast, the Penan spoke of a shortage of monkeys, of a danger of having to kill too many of the breeding stock, problems out of which their concern for thoughtful harvesting grew. It is fascinating to speculate that this apparent change in hunting philosophy over the past two decades is real (not just a misunderstanding of language) and attributable to the increasing population pressure of Penan in smaller areas of forest preserves like Mulu where food may start to become limiting, so affecting the Penans' behaviour, just as a changing relationship with its environment changes the behaviour of any other species.

One of the Penan men inhabiting the forests of Mulu was named Nyapun. During one conversation with him he mentioned Tua Nidem. I knew that Tua was a polite form of address for a superior, but I could not understand the word Nidem – at the time this was just another of the many words which I did not understand. It was only later that I recalled that the professor of social anthropology at Oxford is called Rodney Needham. On return I dropped him a note and we met in the serenely ornate surroundings of All Souls College. Sure enough, Needham had done the fieldwork for his doctoral thesis on the same community of Penan in 1952. He could not be sure exactly who Nyapun was because, as he explained, Penan frequently change their names. As we sat in academically worn armchairs, Needham in a dark suit and polished black slippers, I listened spellbound to his tales of near-starvation during a year with the Penan, of how his eyebrows were plucked to comply with their dislike for body hair, of how he had been a Penan. Surely no one man could live in more exhilarating and contrasting societies than those in the shade of Oxford gargoyle and Bornean blowpipe.

8

The Blowpipe and the Shear-pin

As I have mentioned before, Brunei is bisected by the strip of Sarawak named Limbang. The more northern section of the sultanate is called Temburong, and there it is still possible to find the traditional longhouses of the Iban people. Admittedly the homes of the Brunei Iban are less spectacular than those of their cousins in Sarawak whose longhouses may be forty doors long as opposed to a mere ten to fifteen doors, but they are, nevertheless, fascinating. The Iban are the traditional longhouse people, and it is only recently that previously nomadic peoples, like the Punan, have copied them. The longhouse, although on dry land, is built on stilts and is the communal property of the village. In fact, it really is the village! An arbitrary measure of length may be the number of 'doors', but many of the longhouses I visited had no partitions inside and in reality had only one door at either end. Some had a common area running the length of the house at the front, but at the rear were divided by partitions into bileks. Whether or not there are many doors or partitions, the entire village lives in the one house which may be divided within on the basis of family groups.

Mark, Andrew and I arrived at Temburong, to stay at the army head-quarters. We were to travel by Land Rover from there, attempting to visit every one of fourteen longhouses marked on the map. As with the Punan, we hoped that these traditional hunters would be good people to guide us to the elusive tarsier. When we had spoken of tampolili with the Punan, we had met a blank reception, and it was only after protracted linguistic contortions that we had discovered that in their language it was called 'kat'. Thus when we stopped the Land Rover at the edge of the track and dismounted to walk the kilometre to the first longhouse in Temburong we fully expected to have difficulty in explaining our problem.

As we climbed the ladder leading up to the longhouse, it was the realization of a dream for me to meet the unfairly named 'wild men of Borneo', for it was the Iban that were the notorious headhunters of Victorian novels. Stepping into the dingily lit longhouse it seemed like the loft of an old farm barn; chickens pecked here and there, the floor felt well worn and friendly and from every beam and rafter hung mysterious and entrancing objects – bits of cloth, rope, baskets and sacks were strewn everywhere. I could not see most of these pieces of bric-à-brac clearly in the dim light, but even those I could see left me no wiser as to their function. It seemed strange that only a few very old men and women and some young children were in the village. The explanation was that the others were away in the paddy fields, harvesting rice or hunting. The old men were covered in tattoos, the skin of their torsos, arms and necks lost in a swarm of intricate patterns symbolizing the history and folklore of their people.

Among anthropologists, the Iban, or Sea Dayaks, are believed to be descended from Malay stock (known as proto-Malays) and typically they live by shifting agriculture based on dry rice grown on the hillsides in jungle clearings. The Iban almost invariably built their houses near river banks and, apart from the other advantages afforded by the river as a method of transport, this is at least partially to do with their warlike history. We met old men who remembered their youth when the Iban were famed for their headhunting, and among the men of these people virility and bravery still earn the highest esteem. As one might expect from a people living in such intimate contact with the natural world around them they are animists, like the Punan had been before their conversion to Bungan, and attached god-like qualities to many of the trees and animals of their surroundings. They also worship a pantheon of named gods and goddesses believed to have the same appearance as men and including Christian and Bungan gods.

At each longhouse we visited, the elders would shake their heads gravely as we described the animal we were in search of. They had never heard of the tarsier, they knew nothing of tampolili or of kat. Invariably they would repeatedly induce us to settle for 'kukang', the Slow loris, almost imploring us to do so, offering us help if we would change our quarry. Cup after cup of sickly sweet tea was drunk, and I began to doubt that the Iban really had a word in their language to describe the tarsier.

It was in Sembilang that we met a gaunt elder, his body so heavily tattooed that he was bluish-purple in colour. He shot a piercing gaze at me as I mentioned the Punan word 'kat'. He nodded gravely, almost fiercely at us, and whispered the word 'ingkat'. He was displeased at my enthusiasm for this. Then, speaking quickly in hushed tones, the old man unfolded a remarkable tale. All his people knew ingkat, he claimed; the difficulty we had encountered in getting them to talk about it was because they did not want to admit to having seen these animals. Certainly ingkat was rare though it was still seen, but the little creature had a terrible aspect for the Iban seeing it, the huge, round, forwardly projected eyes, the human-like hand and, worst of all, the ingkat's ability to turn its head through 180 degrees and look straight backwards – the old man told us that some people believed that a hunter who encountered an ingkat would find no food on that excursion. But others, he continued, believed its malevolent powers far surpassed merely thwarting a hunting trip. A man who saw an ingkat when his wife was pregnant ran the risk that the woman would lose her child. Others held that those at whom a tarsier stared over its shoulder would die. With this combination of abortive and fatal properties I now understood the difficulties we had encountered in getting reports of tarsier. Such dire consequences certainly put a premium on turning a blind eye to 'ingkat', 'kat' or 'tampolili'. So, paradoxically, we had found the people best equipped to lead us to the tarsier, but least likely to do so.

The very name of the tarsier developed into quite a mystery. There was no doubt that Yahyah called them tampolili, not only to us but when he was speaking to other Malays. However, when we returned to Britain I could find no reference to this word in books on Bornean wildlife. At last the trail led to a Dutch text by J. Hendrich van Balen who gives the name tempiling from a source in west Borneo (and the name rengseng from certain Dayak peoples). I guess that tempiling and Yahyah's tampolili were dialectic variations of the same name for the tarsier.

The old Iban also related a fabulous account of midwifery among tarsiers. He described how, when a pregnant female tarsier approached full term, she is attended by other tarsiers. As the birth approaches these midwives all press on the expectant mother's abdomen, helping her push out the infant. While it sounds incredible, such stories often have a kernel of truth; following them up is frequently rewarding. I do not know of any scientific accounts of other primates assisting with birth, but I have seen a female cat collaborating in the most intimate way with one of her sisters as she gave birth. The helper licked her sister's kittens dry and severed their umbilical cords. It would be foolish to dismiss the old Iban's tale without wondering what observations originally lay behind it.

To cajole the Iban into contravening their beliefs would have been of dubious morality, even if it were possible, and so we abandoned the idea of enlisting their help. Furthermore, it would also have been injudicious for us to set out to look for an animal they so feared when we would have to depend on their hospitality on such a trip. We therefore decided to cut our losses and return to Kampong Menunggol, where we would continue to watch Proboscis monkeys. First, however, we visited the remainder of the longhouses.

On the way to one longhouse we came across a different style of architecture – a hybrid between a longhouse and a simple kampong house, it was L-shaped. There we met a small group of Murut people who wore wonderful tattoos. In their folklore there is a sound reason for doing so. There was a time, apparently, when the Murut had every reason to be frightened of crocodiles who occasionally killed and ate them. Then, the legend claims, there came a day when one crocodile mourned greatly as his wife was in terrible labour, unable to deliver her eggs. The male crocodile wandered forlornly around in search of help for his wife and eventually came to a large Murut kampong. There he found a woman who, after she had recovered from her initial terror at the sight of this reptilian visitor, was persuaded by his eloquence to accompany him in order to assist his ailing wife. When the crocodile and the woman reached the river he told her to grip hold of his tail, whereupon he dived deep, plunging into the nest where his stricken wife lay. The Murut woman and the crocodile discussed the problems of producing the eggs and somehow reached a solution which enabled the eggs to be speedily delivered. The crocodiles were understandably grateful and rewarded the woman by telling her that if she and all her people wore a particular pattern of tattoo from that day forth, then they would never again be hurt by a crocodile.

By night we wandered along the outskirts of the forest with a dimmed torch, casting here and there for animals' eyes reflecting in the darkness. We hoped to catch sight of a tarsier. For the most part we heard rustles and saw nothing. Then, as we peered along our beam, we realized that what had initially seemed like another oddly shaped shadow was a creature staring myopically at us. The shadow was a white animal, the size of a rat, with a thick naked tail and an extraordinary long thin snout. Its white colour seemed to blend to nothingness in the weak torchlight, but while the animal might otherwise have been easily dismissed as an illusion, its strong smell gave compelling substance to its ghostly body. We had already crossed its path several times as clearly evidenced by the clinging smell. This was a Moonrat, an insectivore closely related to hedgehogs, whose most remarkable feature was its nose. Not only was this extraordinarily long, but it terminated in finely embellished pink 'petals' which formed a rosette around the nostrils. Why these ornate sculptures of tissue are that particular shape I do not know, but I presume that the overall structure increases the nose's effectiveness to detect odours.

There are myths in which the Moonrat features as a king in the animal world. In those days the king Moonrat told his subjects that he must travel to other lands and that they must serve him by making a boat for his journey. This they did, but the king complained that the boat they built was too big. The subjects set to work to pare away slivers of wood to diminish the size of the vessel. Again the king said the finished boat was too large. Eventually the subjects had whittled the boat away until it was nothing more than a splinter. A lifetime of labour and craftsmanship seemed to have been wasted and the boat builders were aghast to see the Moonrat pick up the remaining splinter and use it to pick his teeth. They harangued him as to why he had treated them so shabbily, whereupon the

Machiavellian Moonrat replied that if there was to be no revolution in his kingdom then he must keep his subjects busy. The other animals were furious. They rubbed and jostled against the king in their frenzy and in so doing they daubed him with each of their individual odours. The result was an unwholesome stench which has lingered with Moonrats to this day, and which still banishes them from the court of the kingdom where they once reigned and which they now shun, moving only at night by the light of the moon.

The next day we set out before dawn. Soon we had left the Land Rover far behind and, as dawn rose, we were walking through the jungle towards the remotest of the Temburong longhouses. The air resonated with the cries of gibbons.

The bubbling whoops we heard were the so-called Great Calls of the females, and are probably less enchanting to the ears of a gibbon audience than they were to us, since they are part of the declaration of territorial rights. Each gibbon family maintains an exclusive territory, and each morning neighbours hoot at each other to confirm their tenancy. The

classification of gibbons has posed something of a problem, because individuals vary greatly in colour. Even within a single pair there may be dark and light individuals, at least on the Malayan mainland. Among Bornean gibbons this confusion has been partly resolved by the characteristics of the Great Call. The female of the Agile gibbon gives a long shriek, in comparison with the Bornean gibbons to which we were listening. The two species are very similar in other respects too, but their distributions throughout Borneo do not overlap, presumably because they would be in severe competition by virtue of their similarity. On mainland Malaya a Cambridge zoologist, David Chivers, has studied three species of gibbon and found that the two very similar species – the White-handed and the Black-handed – never live in the same area, whereas the larger Siamang can coexist with the White-handed gibbon. The Siamang eats more foliage than fruits, in comparison with the smaller species and thus, in spite of its larger size, requires a smaller home range (leaves are more abundant than fruit). Siamang gibbons are also unusual in having inflatable throat sacs which are distended during territorial calling, presumably acting as resonating chambers and are visually impressive to adversaries.

The gibbons around us seemed, from their voices, to be quite numerous. They swing through the branches on their long arms at high speed, moving in pairs with associated offspring. Their thumbs are especially modified, linked to the wrist with a ball-and-socket joint, for greater flexibility. Seeing them move, the origin of the similarity between the Iban words for gibbon (empliau) and for spider (emplawa) becomes obvious.

The reason for the dichromatism among Bornean gibbons (i.e. two colour phases, one dark, one light) is unknown, but it seems very likely that when an explanation is eventually unearthed it will relate to ecological factors. In a very different part of the world, by comparison, two colour phases of the Arctic fox sometimes intermingle. One is pure white in winter, the other slatey blue. A clue to the *raison d'être* of these two phases lies in the discovery that populations with a higher proportion of the blue phase are found on smaller islands. One possibility is that the blue phase is better adapted to survival through camouflage on unfrozen beaches than on interior frozen wastes, and, because larger islands have relatively more interior compared to coastline, they have correspondingly more white foxes. However, not even a tentative explanation of this sort is yet available for gibbons.

The dawn calls of gibbons are as much a hallmark of the Bornean jungle as are leeches and this mystical hooting must also have been a wonderful sound to the ears of Iba, and Iban headhunter of old. Iba, so his descendants tell, was once too impetuous during a headhunting expedition with the unfortunate consequence that securing a head cost him a severe spear wound in the thigh. He narrowly escaped death at the hands of the vengeful family of his victim, only just managing to scramble out of sight, still clasping the severed head, into the safety of a bush. As the jungle night wore on he weakened and seemed certain to die but at first light a gibbon called out to him that were he to follow its call he would be led to safety. This he did and after an arduous journey reached his people's longhouse. Years later, when Iba died, his relatives saw his spirit transformed into a white gibbon which sprang from his deathbed and bounded away into the nearby jungle. From that day hence Iba's descendants have never eaten gibbon.

I do not know if the people at the next longhouse on our way observed Iba's taboo. I think it was called Sebut, but I cannot be certain. When we arrived there the sun was still rising. There were more people in evidence than at the other longhouse, mainly women with young children who had stayed to look after them rather than going off to the fields. Facially they were quite like the Punan, with similarly light coloured skin and strongly sculptured cheeks and eyebrow ridges (and like the Punan, the Iban plucked their eyebrows). Several of the women in the longhouse had black hair that, in the sunshine, was tinged with deep red lights. The features, customs and beliefs of the various people of Borneo provide an almost endless source of speculation about their ancestry. There are few parts of the world where an ethnologist could revel in a more varied collection of people of different shapes and colours.

Of course the people themselves have their own ideas about how this came about. The villagers of the Mekong river in Laos, for instance, tell the story of a vine which sprouted from the nostrils of a dead buffalo and which, as it grew, bore three large fruits. As the fruits ripened a chieftain noticed some movement from within them and, piercing them with a hot iron, he found to his surprise that streams of people poured forth through the charred holes made by the hot poker. In an effort to aid their escape he took his knife and cut further holes, and it was the people who came from these knife cuts that formed the lighter skinned Mongoloid people, while those who escaped through the dark charred holes were the ancestors of the darker skinned Malays. How the chieftain originated is not mentioned, but then the explanation of the origin of God is beyond the scope of most religions.

Today the bulk of the population of the islands of the South China Sea is 'Malay'. These people probably arrived in southerly migrations from the Asian continent around four or five millennia ago. Of course, the land bridges and fluctuations in the sea level in the last Ice Age which so affected the distribution of various animal species among the islands of the Pacific Ocean also affected the movements of ancestral man. However, the conventional wisdom seems to be that migrations of peoples throughout this region have consisted largely of southerly treks from the continental land mass, with one race after another heading southwards to inject their own culture into those that were already established. Chinese and Indian traders, Europeans and Arabs have all made their mark with the introduction of their own ideologies and religions.

Inside the longhouse a beautiful game cock strutted authoritatively.

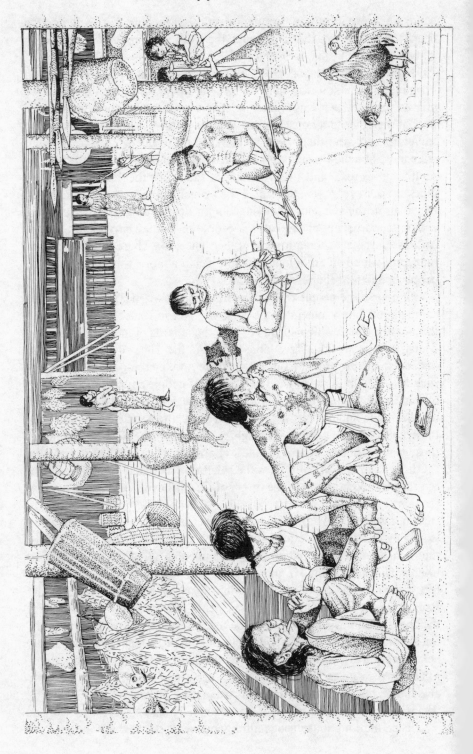

Cockfighting is a national sport for the Iban – it used to be popular in Britain too until it was banned in 1849; Henry VIII, for example, had a cockpit in his palace at Whitehall. A large part of the floor area of this longhouse was completely communal, and stretching along its length were wooden bunks around each of which were a few personal possessions, blowpipes and gongs.

Large brass gongs nestled in the corner of the longhouse. They have tremendous ceremonial and traditional value, and are also the unit of currency for legal recompense. A culprit judged guilty of abusing the law may be fined in gongs if the offence is a major one. Beside one gong there hung a bundle of peculiar skins, each a mosaic of scales. They were the skins of pangolins, extraordinary mammals with habits like anteaters and a skin covering more like a crocodile's scales than a mammal's fur. Large vats of fermenting rice wine – tuak – stood against the wall. Tuak is dangerous stuff in small doses, but Iban courtesy demands that guests never have small doses. Your cup should never be drained and you cannot say no, and in these quantities, it is deadly. I once drank a similar brew, rice beer, called borak, with a botanist friend in a Berawan longhouse. I think we drank a pint each with the hospitable Temonggong (headman). Afterwards, the only way to descend the long muddy plank that led down the steep bank to our boat was to fall down it, slithering into the water below.

In the darker corners of these Iban longhouses we saw dusty human skulls, reminders of the day not long past when these people were famed and feared as headhunters. The taking of a head was an important part of a man's growing up. There are vivid accounts of reputedly lurid dances performed by the headhunters' women, the motive force behind the hunting forays according to anthropologists. These women sang special head songs, dancing with the severed head and stuffing its mouth with food in hideous intimacy. Among the highland Kelabit these songs might last for days, recounting past tales of heroic warriors. One such dirge told the story of a woman called Burong Siwang who sang joyously when her warrior son returned after an epic foray to claim the head of a previously acclaimed rival named Tokud Udan. Part of the song shows the special role of women in heaping accolades on their hunters: 'Now spoke Burong Siwang, "I said my son was the very best. No one under the clouds, no one in all the villages can compare with him. Before, others tried to fight him but were always defeated. You have his head! I am so happy my child." They gave out the head-cries, gathering at the fence, declaring Tokud Udan's head the finest: "His face red like a fire glow, he is the very finest." '

The Iban revelled in headhunting and, by all accounts, they completely dissociated the act of killing or the gory smoking and preparation of enemies' heads from any unpleasant or reprehensible emotion. On the contrary, Sir Charles Brooke, the Rajah, once described the requests he received from his Iban workers for permission to go on a headhunting foray as being childishly enthusiastic: 'Their urgent entreaties often bore resemblance to children crying after sugar-plums.' The white rajahs tried to dissuade these people from their tradition. They confiscated heads and imposed fines to this end, and led one longhouse against another in retributive raids when the law was flaunted. Brooke describes his efforts to impose the ideals of one culture on another as the 'unflinching work of years, but before many months were over my stock of heads became numerous and the fines considerable'.

Nowadays headhunting seems to be confined to the reminiscences of old men. Some of the longhouse people still regard Penan as something akin to slaves, talking of 'my Penan', and this attitude may have its roots in the readiness with which they apparently once took Penan heads, days when it seems that the Iban women were as much as any other the motive force behind the tradition, spurring their menfolk to ever finer triumphs of decapitation.

At Long Sebut we again sought out an old man to talk to. Conversation drifted to the way that the jungle and its fauna were changing. The old man harkened back to the 'good old days'. Now the rhinos were gone, and much else besides. His father had remembered the time when there were rhinos, and knew a man from a nearby longhouse who had killed one at a mud wallow. The man knew many yarns about rhinos; fanciful stories abound in direct proportion to a species' rarity. In the case of the Sumatran rhinoceros the former curator of the Sarawak Museum, E. Banks, quotes a lovely story in his 1931 book of how rhinoceros are supposed to excrete into streams and thereafter to eat all the fish that float stunned (either morally or chemically) to the surface. Just as the rhino plays a large role in Chinese sexual mythology (through the supposed aphrodisiac qualities of its horn) so some of the Iban people believe that a woman's infertility can be cured by pouring water through a rhinoceros's penis onto her head! This organ has clearly captured the imagination of adventurous thinkers among the Bornean people: the rhino's genitals bear an embellishment reminiscent of a 'T piece' at the tip; some tribesmen fashion a similar structure from bamboo or hardwood with which they embellish the end of their own genitals. This operation involves piercing a hole through the glans, which is kept open by a peg of wood or bone through which appropriate titillators can be threaded, such as hairs and bristles. The device is known as a palang. Tom Harrisson, the late Curator of the Sarawak Museum, reports that this practice, which is especially prevalent among the Kenyah in Indonesia, is supposed to add to the stimulation of the inner walls of the woman's vagina. In his paper on this topic he notes wryly that, 'It is, in this, in my experience, decidedly successful!' The Berawan of Long Terawan went in for these devices too, and the bearer of one indicated this by a fish-hook shaped tattoo. They used shear-pins from outboard engines, and local folklore jokingly maintained that the beginner sporting a one-and-a-half horsepower Seagull outboard pin palang would graduate with the years to a mature forty horsepower by middle age, with the variation of an upper class stainless steel version versus lower class brass. The story is bizarre enough to be credible!

As the old Iban talked about rhinos he also mentioned another creature. To start with, he seemed to be describing tapirs but so far as we knew the last evidence of these creatures in Borneo was remains found in caves and dating from 6000 BC. The old man remembered stories of a large black and white beast. Perhaps he was referring to banteng cattle. In the context of so many stories of extinctions caused by man, Lord Medway has suggested an ironical twist to the tapir tale. Tapirs eat shrubs which border the tracks along the forest edge, so for these animals to flourish the original forest must be disturbed to generate succulent shoots for food. This is in contrast to the rhino which is so bulky that it can disturb the forest for itself, breaking down the vegetation and thereafter cropping the fresh shoots. During the last Ice Age the weather changes resulted in a patchwork of forest and open spaces. This would have been ideal for the tapir but as the weather became more clement, the evergreen rain forests grew as a more uniform carpet over Borneo. The only hope then for the tapir was that some other agency, like man, would disturb the forest in such a way as to create ample secondary vegetation to browse upon. In Malaya this seems to have happened, for tapirs still flourish. But people living in immediately post-glacial Borneo had no cause to clear the forest, so agrarian societies arrived too late for the tapir, while arriving too soon for the jungle and its inhabitants of today.

We had just sufficient time in Temburong to visit all the longhouses before the scheduled date arrived for the helicopter to come for us. The visit had been both interesting and exciting, although in some ways sad, since the Iban were well advanced along the road leading from their old world to a new one, and I could not help feeling that the journey would leave them weary.

We arrived back in Bandar Seri Begawan on the day we had been invited to a musical soirée by Peter Gautrey, the British High Commissioner. So instead of heading straight back to Kampong Menunggol, we spent an afternoon in town, feasting on coffee and parathas in our favourite café. Later, while Mark and Andrew were buying supplies, I went to the post office where the afternoon's business was brought to a temporary halt when a cashier recognized me as one of the notorious Monkey Men. The entire staff and the customers were soon gathered to hear the most recent instalments of our adventures. The evening at the British Residence was quite a change for us, but I must confess I felt somewhat apart from the conversation; among the guests I only recall that there was a kitten, aptly called Kuching, that sat on my knee, and a young man called Willy who had something to do with building an airstrip or a navigation system for Harrison and Crosfields. The Gautreys were kindly and hospitable; we had gula melaka at dinner and they seemed to appreciate the contrasting worlds we were spanning when we described the setting in which we had last eaten this Nipa sugar. The Residence offered a blissful view of Kampong Ayer at night. Wayfarer's palms grew on the hillside and as dusk settled the distant reflection of lamps on the water glistened between their fronds. We spent the night there. Clean white sheets felt quite extraordinary.

We returned to Kampong Menunggol next day, and Andrew and I then set off in the boat to photograph some of our other neighbours on the mud flats, the crabs. At low tide, when large areas of mud were exposed, the ground appeared to move with hundreds of thousands of tiny crabs feeding on the fresh supply of plankton and delectable detritus washed up by the previous tide. Most of these crabs were no more than a centimetre

across and almost all were vividly coloured. Little patches of sapphire, red, yellow and green scurried hither and thither along the tide line. Among them were the Fiddler crabs. The males of the Fiddler crab share something in common with the Proboscis monkey in that, through the process of sexual selection, one organ has reached gigantic proportions: for the Proboscis monkey – the nose, for the Fiddler crab – a front claw. The evolutionary process that gives rise to these male adornments stems from the female's inclination to select a mate which has something bigger or better than those of his fellows. If such a process continues over generations and as a consequence males with this feature have a better chance of reproducing, then the characteristic will spread. The result of this tournament will be bigger, brighter and hence better ornaments. This is probably how, over thousands of generations, one of the Fiddler crabs' front claws became so enlarged that it is almost as heavy as the whole body. The claw is vividly coloured and is differently coloured in different species; some are yellow, some red, some blue.

Thronging the mud flats, the male Fiddler crabs wave their gauntlet up and down in a semaphore language that broadcasts a challenge to neighbouring males or perhaps an invitation to females. As with all good things, the male Fiddler has a penalty to pay for this enormously enlarged claw – he can only eat with the smaller claw – and thus to gain his daily sustenance the male crab has to do twice as much work with the smaller claw as the female does with her two more moderately proportioned appendages.

Moving along the shoreline the variety of species of crabs quite suddenly alters dramatically (perhaps because of differences in salinity) and the colourful carpet that throngs the mud changes hue. These crabs are so finely adjusted to the conditions of mud, water and food type in the swamp that even minor changes can cause one species to be replaced by another and so give rise to this crustacean rainbow.

Another interesting inhabitant of the mud flats is the Soldier crab. As high tide approaches and the Soldier crab runs the risk of being exposed to the action of waves or attack from predators, so it scrapes a little crater in the mud. It then builds a pill-box, made of little pellets of mud, around the crater until it is encased within a mud igloo. As the water continues to rise, the Soldier crab digs down, pushing more and more mud on top of it. The resulting cavity is sufficiently deep to resist the action of the waves and to protect the crab, encased within a bubble of oxygen, until the tide passes.

One day when Yahyah was fishing he caught another hard-shelled animal, a crab only in name, the King crab or Horseshoe crab. In fact King crabs are ancient Arachnids, members of the same class of animals as today's spiders and scorpions. About three hundred million years ago, in the Triassic period, Arachnids were much more numerous than they are today and the fossil record shows that King crabs were in existence then. Most of these ancient forms became extinct millions of years ago but the King crab has continued to scuttle about on the swamp water like an upturned saucer. As the specimen Yahyah had caught swam unhappily around the inside of my billy can it seemed extraordinary that not only had its forebears inhabited a world with a very different fauna from that which we know today, but the land masses, islands and seas of that world were also completely different in their size and position.

On close inspection the bodies of these antique animals looked more like automata for an outer-space cartoon. The King crab has a hinge crossing its body and by flexing at this hinge and levering with its 'front edge' (it definitely had an edge rather than a head) and the long spine that serves as a tail, it soon began to burrow into the soft mud. Its robot-like mannerisms were enhanced by the presence of four eyes! In fact, two were simple eyes (the two in the middle) and two were compound eyes, like those of insects, made up of hundreds of separate facets. The scientific name of the species which swam dolefully around in our billy can was a majestic compromise – *Carcinoscorpius rotundicauda,* or approximately, round-tailed crab-scorpion.

It was during a late night sortie with a dim torch that we found one of the smaller Bornean primates behind the kampong. We had spotted a Slow loris: its eyes stood out like floodlights in the torch-beam as it methodically made its way, hand over fist, down a slender branch. The loris was grey and rounded, kitten sized, with strangely thin legs and a body that looked awkwardly tailless. This was the animal named 'kukang', which Yahyah had mistakenly thought we were looking for when we had first described the tarsier to him. After a pause in the shadows of our spotlight's beam, the loris ambled along its branch as if in melancholy resignation that each branch could only lead to another the same. Suddenly, with uncharacteristic determination, it snatched at the branch ahead and caught a fluttering cricket. A moment's munching and the loris paced on, and out of view.

As our days in Borneo drew to a close, we determined to have one last attempt at finding the tarsier and to combine this with a visit to the Niah caves. These caves, situated in the north of Sarawak, have become famous in the anthropological world through the discoveries made in their vaults by Tom and Barbara Harrisson. It was our good fortune that Barbara Harrisson was actually visiting Brunei on one of the occasions when we made a trip to Bandar Seri Begawan to collect supplies. We met her at the Government Rest House and were enthralled by her exciting tales of the excavations she and her late husband had made at Niah. We had less than a week left in Borneo when we returned from this meeting to prepare for our departure from Kampong Menunggol. As we started to pack up we accumulated an audience of mournful onlookers whose long faces did little to improve our own falling spirits. Yahyah seemed to accept our departure with grim resignation, but his two younger brothers would periodically break their staring silence by asking unanswerable questions of why we had to go. Yahyah wandered off to fish for a while and returned with a large sting ray which he had skilfully landed without injury to himself. I asked him if I could have the tail and he promptly cut his hand while trying to cut if off for me!

That night we arranged with Yahyah that he would take us around the kampong for our friends to say 'balek' to us. We thought it meant 'au revoir' but in fact it means 'come back' so our farewell must have translated oddly! It was dark when Yahyah arrived for us and he led us down a muddy path by the glow of his bamboo torch. Arriving at the junction which led to Abdullah's house we were surprised when he turned sharply down the hill along the other trail. We protested that we wanted to say goodbye to Abdullah, but Yahyah insisted that we follow him. The path led down a steep hill, slipping over a natural stepladder of exposed roots. At the bottom we came to an old house, built of bamboo and bark like ours, but much larger. The house was crowded with people, including an old woman. She was Yahyah's mother and this was her home. We had never met her before but she knew all about us, recognizing each of us and putting names to our faces. Almost everyone we had met in the kampong was present. Abdullah was there with his wife, and Ahmad, Ramli, Bacal and Yahyah's Isteri. Yahyah's cousin Chiply and his wife had prepared a splendid meal for us. The pretty spinster, Ahmina, was there, leading her blind father by the hand. He played all evening on a type of guitar, chewing and spitting an areca nut, losing himself in a different world and taking the rest of us part way there with him. Late that night we said 'balek', and went to sleep fitfully among our filled rucksacs. At dawn Yahyah was waiting for us as we loaded the boat at the jetty. We handed him a collection of photographs of his family and gave him our primus stove. 'Jangan lupa kawan,' he said – 'don't forget your friend'. I'm sure we never will.

The next day, armed with a crumpled foolscap sheet of instructions, supplied by Barbara Harrisson, of how to find and approach her most trusted Iban guides, we set out for Niah by Land Rover. I still have that sheet of paper. It is covered with good advice and precise instructions: 'Follow the plank walk for about 40 minutes'; 'Bats leave from 5.45 – 7.30 pm'; 'Water in Camp Cave is *good*'. With us came Clint, an Englishman working for a bank in Brunei. Clint had visited Niah once before and had been so impressed that he was determined to make the trip again; he had procured the Land Rover for us. Niah would be the furthest south we were to travel in Borneo, only three degrees north of the equator. The caves are famed for their population of swiftlets and bats, but there are indications that the swiftlets' numbers are declining (perhaps by 60 per cent since

1939) and one Lesser Bent-winged bat was recently found to be carrying ominously heavy loads of DDT residues.

On the first leg of the trip we were accompanied by Clint's Chinese wife. After we had entered Sarawak and driven for perhaps another two hours, we made a slight detour to visit a friend of hers. Yau was a timber merchant, originally from Hong Kong and now enormously rich and of correspondingly enormous girth (he claimed to weigh eighteen stone). This generous giant loaded the Land Rover with food and drink to sustain us on the long dust road to Niah. He also insisted that we must take firearms, believing that there was a real danger from guerillas. Yau had two wives. As a young man he had fallen in love with a girl from Hong Kong, but force of circumstance had separated them. As the years passed and he had made his fortune, he married another girl in Sarawak and lived contentedly with her. Often, however, he dreamed of his youthful love and eventually he traced her and married her too. The three of them could not have been more cordial in their welcome to us.

Leaving Clint's wife with Yau, we continued down the road towards Niah. We had made plans for our return: we would meet Yau and Clint's wife for a large banquet before our departure from Sarawak. As it happened it was a little difficult to keep this appointment. On the return trip along the dirt road from Niah, Clint, in a fit of injudicious exuberance, drove the Land Rover into the dust cloud thrown up by the United Nations car he was trying to pass. The Land Rover executed a neat pirouette and rolled through a complete revolution as we bounced down a slope into the jungle below, to the detriment of its wing and Clint's ribcage. That, however, is another story.

We eventually arrived at the settlement at Batu Niah and, following Barbara's instructions, engaged a boatman to take us downriver to the caves. Several Iban were loafing around on the jetty where the boatman left us, so we asked for the people Barbara Harrisson had recommended to us. The mention of her name prompted great excitement. She had obviously been very popular. Eventually it was decided that a man by the name of Sa'adi would guide us to the caves. We set out straight away, walking in convoy along the narrow raised plank walks which had been built at the time of the excavations. We started to climb and, after twisting around the mountainside, began to rise above the tops of the trees. A path had been etched into the side of the hill and as we moved up it I was introduced to yet another exciting face of Borneo. The air that drifted from the jungle hung with moisture; in places surface water seeped through sodden leaves. Everywhere I looked there were butterflies, bedecked in beautiful colours. A butterfly cloaked in sophisticated black and iridescent greens settled on the path not a metre in front of me. I could hardly believe my good fortune, for the butterfly was a Rajah Brooke's Bird-wing. This butterfly, perhaps one of the most striking in the world, is a famous member of the fauna of Borneo. That its beauty has attracted such attention is understandable, but its biology is no less enthralling. These large velvet black butterflies have a band of emerald green serrations spanning their wings from tip to tip. For years their reproduction puzzled naturalists, for a huge proportion of individuals captured in the wild were males – in fact of the order of a thousand males to every one female fell victim to lepidopterists' nets. This peculiar state of affairs was explained by the discovery that although the sex ratio is actually almost equal, the females spend all their time in the upper storey of the jungle, never descending to the floor below where the males are normally captured.

We continued to climb up the path and then, turning a corner, came to the caves. The first was the Traders' Cave, and I was astonished to find the extent of settlement within the cave even today. A scaffolding of poles runs along the walls and supports a series of planks connecting one area to another and joining one room to the next. By now the sun was sinking. Sa'adi led us on through the scaffolding to a small hut, looked after by an ancient Iban. Here, the old man proudly told us, Barbara Harrisson had stayed during her excavations. When Lord Medway worked at Niah he had also used the same bed. The old man asked us to sleep in the hut. We were out of our league in the company of these pioneers of Borneo's natural history, but we gladly accepted.

That night we clustered into the little room which overflowed with the history of exploration and talked with the men whose lives were interwoven with the caves. In the warm glow of a rusty Tilley lamp we learnt that the settled Penan at Niah have an unusual account of their own origins. One of them, Tabilan, son of Pungut, has recorded the story of how the first Penan of Niah stemmed from a brother and sister who lived there together in perfect naïveté. But one day the brother, while out hunting, saw a pair of squirrels mating and, being attracted by the concept, immediately went home to put his observations into practice. The children of this incestuous match grew into adults and were advised by their parents to mate as well and in turn their children did likewise, and the fruits of that union included a boy who was the great-grandfather of Tabilan himself. This story is especially interesting since incest is decried throughout so many human societies.

At dawn next morning we set off into the main chamber of Lobang Besar – the Great Hole. It was an extraordinary place, a huge cave with the ceiling towering a hundred metres or more above us. The air was moist and dripping as we slipped and slithered up the red substrata, climbing the hill within the cave, known as Bukit Terayeng. Everywhere the soil was pitted where water had dripped erosively from above. In some areas large holes had been excavated, providing a clue to one of the strange industries for which the Niah caves are famed. The caves are inhabited by hundreds of thousands of bats of seven different species and by three species of swiftlet. There are probably about 450,000 bats and 200,000 swiftlets in the caves and their dung accumulates on the floor in huge quantities. It is quarried as guano by the Iban farmers and by Malays who sell it as a fertilizer rich in ammonium phosphates and sulphur. In fact, guano is one of the richest of all known natural fertilizers. Peering into one hole we saw a tragedy of over-exploitation: the spade had cut through the fresh red deposits of dung and bitten deep down through orange-coloured layers to the rocks below, to the creamy deposits of fossilized guano. These contain the wonderfully important archaeological remains of Niah's past inhabitants. Removing the fossil deposits is strictly illegal, but was clearly widely practised. In fact the guano collectors are not supposed to dig at all but only to sweep up each day. There is a long and documented history of the quota being exceeded. G.E. Wilford first drew attention to it when he pointed out that the 1951 yield (65,900 kilograms) was treble that of five years before. When Bob Stebbings visited the cave two years after us he estimated that the annual yield had much more than doubled again since Wilford's day. If so, the daily extraction rate was probably exceeding the Museum's guidelines by twentyfold! The guano produced each day weighs the equivalent of a small family car, and thus required a lot of food consumption. It is estimated that the swiftlets, which mainly eat ants, consume some 12,000 kilos of insects each day, while the bats consume about 7400 kilos more each night, or a total insect harvest of about the weight of six female elephants every twenty-four hours! This gives some measure of the productivity of the jungle.

Alfred Russel Wallace mentioned in his book *The Malay Archipelago – The Land of the Orang-Utan and the Bird of Paradise* how impressed he was by the way rotting jungle vegetation concentrated insect numbers. During four months of collecting in the virgin jungle, Wallace had amassed 320 different kinds of beetle. On 14 March 1855 he moved to an area where there was an abundance of rotting trees and stumps as a consequence of a coal mine being established in the forest. There, in less than a fortnight, he doubled the numbers of his collection. He averaged twenty-four new species every day, collecting seventy-six different species on one record-breaking excursion, of which almost half were new. There seemed to be quite a lot of tree felling associated with the cultivation around Niah, so perhaps rotting wood was boosting insect numbers there too. Nevertheless, to return to the elephant-equivalents of insects eaten by the community, the annual harvest might be almost 2430 elephants in these caves alone. Bob Stebbings followed swiftlets by helicopter as they emerged from their caves, and some foraged over quite long distances, perhaps embracing up to 3500 square kilometres of jungle. The bats may also travel widely. This would mean that the cave community harvested just under one elephant-equivalent in weight of insects from each square kilometre every year.

Continuing towards the back of the cave, we climbed and the path began to wend its slippery way between treacherously jagged rocks. Beneath us, in the centre of the cave, sitting in a pool of light cast by the sun, we could see a small structure built like a table on which there were several bottles and fronds of palm leaves. This structure was an altar to placate the spirits in the hope of saving the lives of some of the men working at the other main industry of the caves. From the floor of the cave stretching incredibly to the high ceiling were thin scaffolding poles of belian, about the thickness of the average domestic broom handle, laced together with fibre. They not only spanned from the floor to the ceiling, but also ran in spider's web fashion around the ceiling above us. By grasping a bamboo pole at ground level, it easily swayed between the furthest extent of one's arms. I shudder to contemplate how much the sway would be if one was halfway up such a pole, but to climb them to the ceiling was the profession of the men who earned their living collecting swiftlets' nests. One of the three species of swiftlets which inhabit the cave builds its nest solely out of its own black feathers and saliva which solidifies to form a cup-like structure in which the eggs are laid. It is from the nest of these Black-nest swiftlets (and from the even more prized White-nest species, which do not occur in Niah) that the famous Chinese birds' nest soup is made.

The story of how the birds' nests are collected is just as frightening as one would imagine from seeing the bamboo scaffolding. The birds' nesters work in teams of two, one to collect the fallen birds' nests and the other armed with a long hoe-like tool to scrape them from the shadowy roof of the cave. The tool, called a penyulok, has a beeswax candle attached beside the blade of the hoe so that the operator can see what he is doing. The precision required is mind-boggling. Perched aloft the swaying wooden scaffolding the birds' nester probes around nests with his penyulok, poised seventy metres above cavernous slippery darkness. Each part of the accessible roof is owned like a farm plot, and for the two months of the swiftlets' breeding season is busily harvested.

As we clambered up the steep slope of Bukit Terayeng, the hill within a mountain, I was transfixed by the appalling danger these birds' nesters face. At the top we were greeted by a noisy multitude of hairless bats roosting above, and then we began to drop down towards the darkness in the depths of the cave. The path grew slippery. The steep descent was punctuated by rocks and slime moulds. The torch became an insignificant glimmer in a cosmic darkness which engulfed us as our laboured breathing ricocheted around the walls. At the bottom of the slope there was a hollow filled with a pool of guano, slippery as a pigstye and hung with the stench of bats. Sliding forwards I gripped at rocks for handholds. How strange it is that unfamiliarity is such an enemy of courage; only a few hours later, more tired and bruised, we struggled back along the same route on our homeward journey. The same path, differing only in that it had been travelled before, was familiar then and, far from being frightening, it seemed to welcome us.

The cave ecosystem is self-contained, a black box into which rainwater seeps and out of which it flows again. Within, amid the hollows of darkness, an intricate world thrives – a world whose denizens seem to care nothing for opinions of their appearances, for no one can see them in the darkness. Where there is no light there is need for neither sight nor colour, for neither splendour nor display. Fish exist which never leave the confines of lakes in the darkest abyss of the cave: they are blind and white, cadaverous images of their cousins in the outside world. Delicate though the relationships may be among the animal communities which inhabit these murky fortresses, caves seem to me to be harsh places; nowhere is this harshness more poignant than in the victims of the birds' nesting trade. As the dislodged nest plummets down from the cave roof, swiftlet chicks grasp the rims of their tumbling home firmly. The picker-up below prises open their feet and throws them to the ground where they are left to die, a fate which is speeded by a hungry assemblage of rats, snakes and a multitude of predators from the outside world such as civets and cats, which scour the cave bottom by night for victims. Following one day of birds' nesting activity, Lord Medway once counted ninety-seven discarded swiftlet chicks. He returned to the site four days later when all he could find was, as he described luridly, 'one backbone resting palely on a pile of a black stickiness that moved slowly with white maggots'.

Even without the interference of the nest gatherers, swiftlet chicks face natural hazards. This was dramatically apparent when, during the Mulu expedition to Sarawak, Margaret Wise and I watched a breeding colony of White-bellied swiftlets (*Collocalia esculenta*) in one of the small caves of the Mulu National Park. The cave, in a limestone outcrop named Bukit Pala, was about three metres high, and in the roof there were ten hollow domes or cupolas. These domes looked just as if somebody had taken cores out of the roof, and were up to seventy centimetres deep and fifteen centimetres in diameter. We found sixteen swiftlet nests in the ten cupolas nearest the cave's entrance; presumably the cupolas deeper in the cave were not colonized because they were too dark. (The White-bellied swiftlet is unable, like some other swiftlets, to find its way in darkness by echo location.) Every two days Margaret and I weighed the nestlings, from one gram at hatching to about eight grams at eighteen days old. It was on the eighteenth day that disaster struck. The cave was invaded by a swarm of ants, a species of a genus called *Pheidologeton,* which are known to inflict a painful bite and sting. The ants climbed the cave walls and swarmed into the cupolas where the fledglings lay in their nests. The swiftlet fledglings fell or leapt from their nests and, as they lay on the dark cave floor below, they were eaten alive by other ants. The ants moved on after two days in the cave, during which only three nestlings had escaped their pillaging. Margaret continued to weigh two of these survivors, who both lost weight dramatically over the next nine days, before starting to grow again faster than before. Sadly even these nestlings were doomed, as before they could fledge the salivary glue which held their mossy nests to the vertical walls of the cupolas gave way. In Niah Lord Medway witnessed just this sort of nest collapse, apparently due to the activity of a larval moth *(Pyralis)* eating the glue. We suspected that the deterioration of the nests which led to their collapse was exacerbated by the habit of both parent birds and other, non-breeding individuals, of roosting on the outer rim of the nest by night.

Following Sa'adi we came through an outlet at the back of Lobang Besar into sunlight and walked some distance through the jungle before reaching a second cave. This cave, known as Lobang Kain Hitam, the Cave of the Black Cloth, was an area in which many of the Harrisson's discoveries were made.

At the back of the cave Sa'adi showed us a series of red drawings, painted in haematite. These pinkish sketches were mostly of spindly creatures which may have represented the centipedes or millipedes that abound in the caves. Nearby were excavated graves of people who had inhabited the caves over 4000 years before. Some of the oldest remains date to a period which began 20,000 years ago. The corpses lay on wooden 'burial boats' and, to judge by their size, the people had been very small in life, perhaps little over four feet tall. Barbara Harrisson had told us that she had excavated 166 Stone Age burials in Niah. Thirty-eight of these were of Mesolithic age (dating from between 4000 and 20,000 years ago) while the rest were Neolithic (2025-3200 years old). One of the Neolithic skeletons was dated to 500 BC. The pose of the dead showed that considerable thought had gone into their burials. Of the older graves, eighteen contained people in a carefully placed 'knees-up', flexed position, while four were seated. The position of their arms was correlated with their sex: women had their right arm tightly flexed and their left arm covering their groin. Most intriguingly, seventeen remains were found where the dead had been mutilated in some way or another. Some had been dismembered. Some bones were charred from fire, other bodies were contorted or had been beheaded. Did this indicate sacrificial victims, perhaps even cannibalism? The interpretation of such mutilated remains in Stone Age sites the world over leads to unbridled speculation. In some cultures the most respectful thing to do with the dead may be to eat them. Among the Yanomamo of Amazonia the cremated remains of a relative are carefully kept and served little by little in hot drinks at future important occasions. Certainly the presence of charred human bones in the Niah caves does not necessarily mean the flesh had been cannibalized in a predatory way; if it was eaten at all it could have been with sombre respect.

Another insight into the scene that might have greeted a visitor to the community's fireside all those thousands of years ago came from a few fragments of domestic dog teeth. At least some of these indicate that the dog was really quite tiny, and very different from the pariah dogs which are frequently associated with ancient communities. The skull and dentition of a pariah dog is very similar to that of a wild type of dog such as a wolf or jackal but in the case of some of the teeth from Niah there could be no such confusion. The role that these little dogs may have played in the lives of the cave people is quite unknown. Perhaps it is only a coincidence that in similar prehistoric sites in Japan common remains of domestic dogs are also of a rather small animal.

Looking across the wooden boat-graves, a small 'window' opened in the cave wall, into a cliff face. A beam of dust-laden sunlight burst through the window and shone above the line of graves. We left quietly.

We returned to Lobang Besar from Lobang Kain Hitam, slipping over the guano-covered rocks, until at last, ahead of us, came the circle of light which indicated the top of the rise at the crest of Bukit Terayeng, before the descent down to the open mouth of the cave. Above us the bats twittered and scraped their claws on the rock. Sa'adi told us that part of the famed colony of naked bats was directly overhead. Looking up at them in the dim shadows of the cave roof I was for once thankful to be wearing my spectacles, as a mist of guano rained down upon us. Peering at the ground I could see that in addition to dung, much else of great interest was showering down. Seemingly deformed insects stumbled hither and thither on monstrously powerful legs. These were parasitic wingless earwigs, known by the ponderous name of *Arixenia* and said to feed on skin scales and secretions of the bats. These earwigs that we saw on the floor were doomed, for once lost from their bat host their winglessness becomes hopelessness. Their fate carries with them a chain of disasters for each earwig carries fleas and these too are specific to the naked bats – a vivid example of the old allegory that bigger fleas have smaller fleas upon their backs to bite them, and so on, *ad infinitum*.

Hot and filthy, we reached the mouth of Lobang Besar. There, near the site where we could still see the graves and bones of some of the former inhabitants of the cave, we took time to sit and look. The cave where we sat had been a centre for groups of Punan who were among the longest settled of their people. The strange hill within the cave behind us saw the early seeds of their community – in an all too dramatic way, according to Mohamed Bin Husain, a man of Punan stock who lived in the vicinity of the Niah caves. He once related to Lord Medway a story which his grandfather had told him of the origin of the caves. The story revolved around the hill within the mountain. Nowadays it is called Bukit Terayeng but in days gone by, according to Mohamed Bin Husain's grandfather, it was just another nameless hill out in the open. On this hill lived a man named Terayeng, the headman of a small village sited on the hill. It is necessary to know two things to understand the story: first, in those days people were reputed to be able to become invisible at will, and second, whenever one wanted to extend one's house or build a fresh one it was necessary first to make a sacrifice and then to plant the victim in the ground beneath the new upright of the building. It was apparently the custom that the sacrifice should be a human child. The story relates how Terayeng and his followers stole the grandchild of an old woman named Piera for this purpose. Soon Piera noticed that the child was missing and, as she searched for him, she passed near the place where men were building an extension to Terayeng's longhouse. There she spied blood seeping from the ground beside one of the new uprights. Piera's mourning was obviously in vain and, after days of weeping, she determined to commit some sorcery against the villains who had stolen her only grandchild. First she caught a frog and, having dressed it in human clothes (a simple feat for people who could readily become invisible), she began to beat gongs and to create music. Soon all Terayeng's men gathered around. Then Piera released the frog which, in its terror at the crowd, jumped hither and thither and appeared to dance, so making the men laugh and attracting more and more of them. At this point her sorcery began to work and in the end, in spite of attempts at counter-wizardry by Terayeng's brother, all the men were turned into rocks and their houses into the caves which now envelop Bukit Terayeng.

So legend has it that the rocks in the caves are graves and it is thus appropriate that among the bats overhead was one species with a morbid reputation. The Tomb bat has white (and so presumably ghost-like) fur, and its head is tinted with chocolate brown. These bats often reside in tombs, which are presumably just as cosy as any other 'cave'. Nevertheless the habit has, not surprisingly, caught the imagination of many people. A chilling story followed Lord Carnaervon's discovery of Tutankhamen's tomb in 1922, which was well populated with these bats. Soon after opening the tomb Carnaervon and members of his party died mysteriously. An alternative explanation to the activities of vengeful spirits might be that the explorers contracted histoplasmosis, a fungal disease carried by bats.

The day was almost over and as I lay back and looked at the ceiling the bats were becoming agitated. Soon hundreds of thousands of them were flying towards the mouth of the cave and out into the dusk, following their own routes across the roof. The exodus bore no resemblance to the disorganized jumble of bats that I had somehow expected. Thick black lines stretched across the roof of the cave, each vein drawn by a mass of bats' bodies. There are at least seven species of bat living in the Niah cave complex and each species follows its own particular flight path from the cave each night.

The bats paused as they left the cave, milling within a perfectly traced sphere. Then, as if at a signal, the sphere spawned an upward spiralling ribbon of bats, weaving a path off across the treetops. The contours of the ribbon seemed fixed in space; bends and twists in it hung immobile in the air as thousands upon thousands of bats steered within the same invisible guidelines. The spherical cauldron of bats was momentarily emptied and the ribbon thinned and trailed away. Another surge of bats started to leave the cave, refilling the sphere, and beginning another left-handed spiral upwards. A large bird swooped across the cave entrance and hung in the air above us. It was a Bat hawk. At that moment the now bursting ball of bats began to empty into another ribbon and the hawk swooped straight for the leading bats. It smashed into a bat, braked hard and fumbled. The crippled bat dropped like a stone. The hawk overshot and swooped back to move like lightning towards the falling bat, but was just too slow and the broken body fell into the jungle, as the bird swerved across the treetops.

I lay back, resting on the red guano. It was much darker now and I was almost falling asleep, covered in mud and sweat and aching from the day's walking. I knew by then that we were not going to find the tarsier, but as I lay in the company of the spirits of men whose bones were within metres of me, men who, thousands of years before, must have lain in the same spot watching black lines of bats drifting across the roof above them, I felt a deep gratitude to the elusive creature whose trail had led me to these places.